FOUNDATIONS
of DIGITAL ART
DESIGN *with*
ADOBE CREATIVE CLOUD

AND

SECOND EDITION

XTINE BURROUGH

FOUNDATIONS OF DIGITAL ART AND DESIGN WITH ADOBE® CREATIVE CLOUD, 2nd Edition
xtine burrough

New Riders
www.peachpit.com

To report errors, please send a note to errata@peachpit.com

New Riders is an imprint of Peachpit, a division of Pearson Education.

Executive Editor: Laura Norman
Development Editor: Victor Gavenda
Senior Production Editor: Tracey Croom
Copyeditor: Linda Laflamme
Indexer: James Minkin
Proofreader: Becky Winter
Cover Designers: Crystal Adams with xtine burrough and Chuti Prasertsith
Cover Illustrations: Elena Rudyk & Paladin12 from Shutterstock
Back Cover Author Photo: Chad Phillips
Interior Designer: Mimi Heft
Compositor: Kim Scott, Bumpy Design

ISBN 13: 978-0-13-573235-9
ISBN 10: 0-13-573235-2

1 2019

For Parker and Martin, and art and design students

ACKNOWLEDGEMENTS

It has been an absolute pleasure to work with Laura Norman and her team at Peachpit. Victor Gavenda read this manuscript more times than I did. Thank you to Victor, Linda Laflamme, Ben Ferrini, Tracey Croom, and Cindy Teeters.

I am grateful for my colleagues in the School of Arts, Technology, and Emerging Communication (ATEC) at UT Dallas, and the support of our dean, Anne Balsamo. A special thank you must be expressed to those students who used this book in draft format as we worked the kinks out of exercises that appear in each chapter. Savannah Leigh Steele reviewed nearly all of the exercises for the first edition of this book and was a lifesaver during the writing process.

Thank you, always, to Christopher James at Lesley University College of Art and Design for showing me how to live a life full of passion for photography and visual communication during my undergraduate career. Steve Kurtz, Claire Pentecost, and Humberto Ramirez showed me how to be an artist/scholar and continued to demonstrate the critique process I learned from James in my time at Vermont College of Fine Arts. My gratitude for such holistic teachers is lived out in my daily "professor" performance. I can only hope to pay forward the love for life, creativity, and reflection I have learned by being in the presence of these artist educators.

This book includes a lot of images of art works that could have resulted in a great amount of permissions expenses. Nearly all of the images in the text were donated. Dear artist and designer contributors, I am forever grateful for your willingness to have your works included here. Thank you, thank you.

Finally, I have much gratitude for the ongoing support that my friends and family provide: Laurie Cella, Emily Erickson, Sam Martin and Paco Aragon—and Tate and Niles, Lucy HG Solomon and Matt Solomon—and Birdie and Rosie, Sabrina Starnaman, and my mom and dad. Paul Lester, Martin Lester, and Parker Lester, you continue to teach me in the UU tradition, with open minds, loving hearts, and helping hands. Thank you.

CONTENTS

CODA: REVISION PRACTICES ▸ 309

**BONUS CHAPTERS AVAILABLE IN DIGITAL BOOKS AND ONLINE FROM
WWW.DIGITALART-DESIGN.COM OR PEACHPIT.COM**

SECTION 5:
EFFECTIVE WORK HABITS

CHAPTER 13: AUTOMATION

CHAPTER 14: PAGINATION AND PRINTING

INTRODUCTION

WHAT ARE THE FOUNDATIONS OF DIGITAL ART AND DESIGN?

In the School of Arts, Technology, and Emerging Communication (ATEC) at UT Dallas, where I am teaching now, students encounter this book during their first year of coursework. However, knowing the origin story of this book is useful for understanding how I came to think about foundations materials for digital art and design students who might be completing coursework in various types of schools or programs, such as art, communication, design, digital humanities, media studies, and so on.

I originally designed this book before arriving at UT Dallas, when most of my students had little time in their schedules for classes that would heighten their understanding of visual communication: foundations of two-dimensional design, typography, drawing, and so on. Instead, they enrolled in a large historical survey course and some took an elective "skills" course, in which they learned some Adobe applications. Mastery doesn't happen in a mere sixteen weeks. At best, the skills course created awareness of the concepts and techniques that someone entering the creative professional industries should master.

First developed to serve these students, this book is now used by readers and educators in two-year and four-year fine arts and applied arts programs, college-level communications and media departments, and in some U.S. high schools. Knowing the breadth of my audience, the aim of this book is to offer the most information at the confluence of design (principles, histories, and theories), Adobe software, and examples of digital art for readers, educators, and practitioners with varied interests. My goal is to be thorough enough for university students and clear enough for high school students.

The majority of my students are interested in practicing the exercises and mastering the software, because they're anxious to jump in and create. Educators are interested in teaching art and design, because they're passionate not about software, but about media art, graphic design, animation, games, digital video, emerging forms of digital expression, and so on.

My approach to mediating this clash of interests is to write about and show as many ideas and examples of art and design history and principles as I can while demonstrating the use of the tools. For example, instead of showing students how to remove red-eye from a photograph (there are loads of videos on YouTube for such a specific endeavor), I demonstrate making a conscious design choice in regard to scale, proximity, the rule of thirds, or other principles while using Adobe's tools. I've tried to keep the exercises short, while also showing the fundamental tools in many of the Adobe programs. Most of the tools have changed very little since the first time I used Photoshop in 1992 (with the major exception of the development of layers in 1994, but I digress).

In ATEC, students attend a lecture, traditional studio, and computer lab. So this course (and this book) merges a traditional course in two-dimensional design with foundations of digital art and design practices. I start in Section 1, *Bits, Pixels, Vectors, and Design,* with material that's been presented by the authors and artists on whose shoulders I'm crouching: Donis A. Dondis (*A Primer of Visual Literacy*), Johannes Itten (*Design and Form: The Basic Course at the Bauhaus and Later*), David A. Lauer and Stephen Pentak (*Design Basics*), Wucius Wong (*Principles of Form and Design*), and others. It is this understanding of the language of design that I consider foundational. I also include examples of each principle or basic element drawn from contemporary works of digital art. Although this book may be assigned in a graphic design program, it's often read within the broader context of digital art. I have had many roles as an educator, from an education advisor on the AIGA Orange County board to a co-author of a trilogy of collections on remix studies—my personal identity as a digital artist is also part of this equation.

Two-dimensional design is followed by Section 2, *Digital Photography.* In the classroom, I find it easier to present basic vector graphics before introducing the pixel-loaded arena of digital imaging—Adobe Illustrator is often a much more forgiving application than Adobe Photoshop due to the insignificance of file resolution at such a basic level. In this text, photography is primarily considered to be another vehicle through which the basic elements of design can be understood. In our program, students use this portion of the text to learn to organize files, compose in a photographic frame, and understand color relationships.

Because photo manipulation is nearly as old as the medium itself, the natural follow-up to photography is Section 3, *Digital Manipulation and ~~Free~~ Fair Use*—where better to talk about contrast through juxtaposition? Collage and photomontage are historical legacies of the digital operations: cut, copy, and paste. While discussing these, I also bring forth contemporary strategies for sampling and licensing with copy-left or Creative Commons licenses in this section.

Section 4, *Typography*, teaches students to honor and manipulate type. This is essential, as most visual communication comprises type and image, and occasionally time. I studied photography in my undergraduate days at the Art

Institute of Boston; typography is an art that I learned during my professional life as a web designer in the 1990s and since then as a professor. It helped that I lived with one of the best typographic educators in Southern California in the early 2000s. I've talked with many educators who are strong in one area—photography, typography, web design, or something else—but feel a deficit in another. As such, I provide resources for additional materials throughout the book, both for students and educators who might be using this text in a classroom.

The *Coda*, at the end of the book, explains the important concept of revision. A student may assume that she has an experiential understanding of design principles after simply following the steps in a software application. Students and readers must remember, however, that reading a book on learning to play the guitar or manipulate imagery, is not the same as mastering the instrument or software. Practice, and of course revision, is the best way to learn the craft and become more efficient. I've included revision stories from artists and design professionals alike.

In addition, you'll find one bonus section online or in the electronic version of this book:

Automation is key to working efficiently, so one chapter in Section 5, *Effective Work Habits, (*available online or in the eBook) is dedicated to it. The other chapter addresses the question, "How do you suggest I make a portfolio I can send someone?" There's no one perfect answer, as each student has different talents and different needs. But learning pagination in Adobe InDesign can help students who want to create their own books—a handy skill for soon-to-be graduates or those applying for internships.

Lastly, I would like to offer an update of Dondis's scale that registers the differences (or similarities) among specific artistic media on a continuum of "fine" and "applied" art in FIGURE I.1. To demonstrate that the Bauhaus "would group any and all of the fine and applied arts on one central point in the continuum" [1], Dondis placed the media of the time grouped around a central point on the horizontal axis (FIGURE I.1).

REFERENCE [1] Donis A. Dondis, *Primer of Visual Literacy* (Cambridge, MA: MIT Press, 1973). 4.

All forms of visual message-making are influenced and analyzed by an understanding of the basic elements of design, on the screen, in print, as a hologram, or however else they may come to us on future platforms. Whether you intend to be a web designer, a social media entrepreneur, a digital installation artist, or a game developer, the design foundations offered in this book, coupled with the exercises in each of the software applications, will help you achieve your goals.

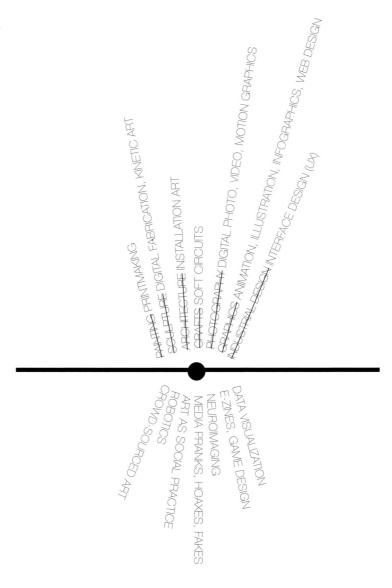

FIGURE I.1 Donis A. Dondis developed the original illustration in reference to the perceived intellectual divide between the two purposes, outcomes, or beliefs about art making. (The image is essentially the same, where the labels would have been the text appears here with a strike through it.)

Because all students or readers will have different hardware, software, and needs, you'll learn to use this book in the most fitting way for your setup in the following exercises.

EXERCISE 1 OPERATING SYSTEMS

When the Mac was released in 1984, it included a graphical user interface and a mouse, two visual user-oriented components that were missing from other personal computers (FIGURE I.2). Artists and designers developed a strong loyalty to Apple over time as their needs and concerns were often met first on the Apple platform. For a while, there was no question about which platform was best suited to making art on the computer: Mac. Universities now have Mac and Windows labs dedicated to art and design programs. In some creative industries, such as graphic design or digital photography, Mac (now rebranded macOS) is still the standard platform. However, web designers, game developers, and animators often work on the Windows platform.

FIGURE I.2 The first Mac computer sold commercially in 1984. It included a mouse and a graphical user interface instead of the ever-intimidating command line.

It does not matter if you use a macOS or Windows. Your files will transfer easily from one operating system to the other. (Be sure to include the file extensions in the name of your file—something you'll learn more about in Chapter 1, *The Dot, the Path, and the Pixel*). If you're creating multimedia art or designs, you'll want to view the work on both platforms. However, this should not dictate where you conceive and develop the project.

I've written this book using macOS. The screenshots were made on my Mac-Book Pro. However, every keyboard shortcut is provided in both macOS and Windows versions. For instance, the File > Copy command shortcut is listed throughout the book as **Command-C/Ctrl-C.**

That's it. The rest is more or less the same.

EXERCISE 2 DOWNLOADING WORK FILES, BONUS CHAPTERS, AND VIEWING SCREENCASTS

Some of the exercises in this book will require you to download a work file or a set of files before you begin. Readers who buy the print edition of the book will also want to download the bonus section on *Effective Work Habits*. All of the files are on the companion websites for the book at www.digitalart-design. com (FIGURE I.3) and at peachpit.com for registered users (see "Accessing the online content at peachpit.com" later in this chapter). I've also posted a link to the work files on my personal website (www.missconceptions.net), and there's a Facebook page for *Foundations of Digital Art and Design* where I post updates and answer reader questions [2].

REFERENCE [2]
facebook.com/
FoundationsOfDigital
ArtAndDesign

FIGURE I.3 A screenshot of the companion website, www.digitalart-design. com. You can download any necessary work files from this site before beginning to work on the exercises in the chapters.

REFERENCE [3]
bit.ly/video-demos or bit.ly/foundations-demos

REFERENCE [4]
bit.ly/youtube-demos

Most chapters include a screencast in which I have demonstrated my process for some part of the chapter's exercises. These offer me an opportunity to show a portion of the exercise that is better demonstrated in a live presentation than captured in images and text. They are also an archive of tutorial files that my students and I rely on for use outside of the classroom. These are accessible from the companion website. The screencasts for this second edition of the book are published on Vimeo [3]. The screencasts for the first edition of the book are preserved on YouTube [4].

ACCESSING THE ONLINE CONTENT AT PEACHPIT.COM

1. Go to www.peachpit.com/register.

2. Sign in or create a new account.

3. Enter the ISBN: **9780135732359,** and click Submit.

   The lesson files can be accessed through the Registered Products tab on your Account page. Click the Access Bonus Content link below the title of your product to proceed to the download page. Click the lesson file links to download them to your computer.

EXERCISE 3 THIRD-PARTY IMAGES

Many of the images in this book were donated by artists and designers. Some were available for me to use in a commercial publication because the copyright had expired or because the work was part of a government archive, which usually puts it into the public domain. To those who donated: *Thank you!*

You'll learn more about public domain, the copyleft movement and creative licensing techniques in the introduction to Section 3, *Digital Manipulation and Free Fair Use.*

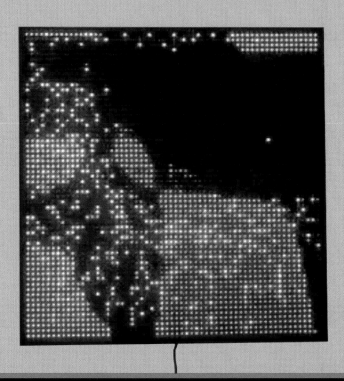

FIGURE S1.1 Documentation of Leo Villareal's light installation *Multiverse*, 2008. You can watch Villareal talk about the programming for this piece at https://youtu.be/ygIKBc9gaUQ.

BITS, PIXELS, VECTORS, AND DESIGN

IN 1995, Nicholas Negroponte wrote *Being Digital*, a book that would become a classic among digital art, media, and lifestyle enthusiasts. While resurrecting a text as seemingly outdated as Negroponte's digital hit may seem like the equivalent of starting this book with pictures of cave drawings, reflecting on the work from a vantage point of more than 20 years reveals Negroponte to be a true visionary. He wrote the manuscript long before streaming entertainment, social media, mobile technologies, and other common digital phenomena. Yet his predictions included developments similar to Apple's virtual assistant Siri, holographic imaging like that found in augmented reality, "high touch computing" in which touch-pad interfaces were once considered the "dark horse in graphic input" [1], videocassette rental stores going out of business by 2010, streaming video on the web (YouTube, Vimeo, Netflix, Hulu, and others), the end of getting lost thanks to what we commonly refer to as GPS (global positioning systems), and more.

REFERENCE [1] Nicholas Negroponte, *Being Digital* (New York: Vintage, 1996), 131.

REFERENCE [2] Negroponte, 229.

Being digital, Negroponte wrote, "has four very powerful qualities that will result in its ultimate triumph: decentralizing, globalizing, harmonizing, and empowering" [2]. These qualities are present in many of the works of art and design presented in this book. We'll investigate the decentralized nature of the Internet in Section 5, *The Web*, and the globalized economy and automated processes inherent to digital applications in Section 6, *Effective Work Habits*. You'll learn about harmony as a design strategy, but see it applied in many examples that utilize social media or require participation. Completing the exercises in this book will give you the knowledge of digital tools necessary to communicate effectively in a networked mediascape.

Digital technologies let us participate in realities beyond the physical world: virtual reality, augmented reality, screen spaces such as video games and the Internet, and so on. However, our understanding of these digital spaces is predicated on human perception, which is, in turn, guided by visual cues. While a digital artist might create media to develop an augmented reality educational game such as *Oyster City* (FIGURES S1.2 AND S1.3), a graphic designer might create media to communicate a concept in the physical world. Both artists and designers rely on their knowledge of human perception to develop effective visual messages.

REFERENCE [3] Negroponte, 105.

Visual images created on a computer are developed either as a sampled set of pixels or as vector coordinates. The pixel, developed at Xerox's PARC in the mid-1960s, was initially "a shape-oriented approach to computer graphics in which amorphous areas were handled and textured by storing and displaying images as a massive collection of dots" [3].

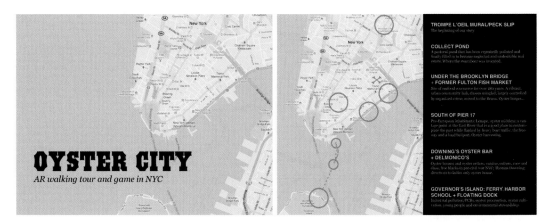

FIGURE S1.2 Title slide and overview of sites in *Oyster City*, an augmented reality game and walking tour by Meredith Drum, Rachel Stevens, and Phoenix Toews (oystercity.org).

FIGURE S1.3 Panoramic view (top), East River view (lower left), and user interaction (lower right) in *Oyster City*.

The dot is the most primary visual element. It is the simplest way to point to the existence of something. A dot is either present or not. Place a single black dot in a field of white, and you'll be quick to judge which is the figure (or the positive space) and which is the ground (or the negative space), as in Leo Villareal's light installations (see **FIGURE S1.1** at the beginning of this section). It's no wonder that the dot was the go-to method of image creation in the earliest computer graphics. In the Huffington Post, Villareal wrote, "I am interested in lowest common denominators such as pixels or the zeros and ones in binary code" [4].

Coincidentally, the dot has been used as a primary method of mark making throughout the history of art. Leo Villareal's digital work references pointillism seen in neoimpressionist paintings of the 1880s by Georges Seurat, Paul Signac, and others (**FIGURE S1.4**). The digital halftone also makes use of the illusory effects of placing small dots of color near enough to one another to express a photorealistic image.

REFERENCE [4] See www.huffingtonpost.com/leo-villareal/the-essence-of-light-thir_b_720351.html#141416

Listen to (or read) "One Dot at a Time, Lichtenstein Made Art Pop," Susan Stamberg's excellent review of Roy Lichtenstein's retrospective at the National Gallery of Art in Washington, DC, on NPR.org (www.npr.org/2012/10/15/162807890/one-dot-at-a-time-lichtenstein-made-art-pop).

REFERENCE [5] Sketchpad is discussed in Negroponte's book on page 103. To see a demonstration of Sketchpad, visit youtu.be/57wj8diYpgY

In 1963, before the invention of the pixel, Ivan Sutherland developed Sketchpad [5]. Users could draw lines with a "light pen," but the challenge of real-time computation and photorealistic rendering hindered Sutherland and other programmers from further developing his concept. The pixel (a term derived from the words *picture* and *element*) is to Sketchpad what the dot is to the line. Why compute an entire line when two dots could be used to establish its starting and ending points?

Of course, lines have visual qualities in addition to a beginning and an end. A line has a defined weight or thickness (also called a *stroke* in Adobe applications). It may be drawn tightly (a perfectly straight line, achieved in Adobe applications by holding the Shift key as you draw) or loosely and expressively to suggest a hand-drawn artifact.

In the exercises for Chapter 2, you'll learn to "see" the lines in a photograph. You'll trace the lines in the image to convert a detailed, photographic picture into a line drawing with a similar composition.

A basic unit of computing is a bit, or as Negroponte refers to it, "the smallest atomic element in the DNA of information. It is the state of being: on or off, true or false, up or down, in or out, black or white." Bits combine together to form a signal (visual, auditory, tactile, and so on). In the realm of design, lines are often viewed as contoured edges that surround shapes. An infinite number of forms can be made by combining any or all of the three basic shapes: the circle, the square, and the triangle. These shapes can be understood, to use Negroponte's metaphor, as the smallest element in the DNA of image construction [6].

REFERENCE [6]
Negroponte, 14.

DRAWING, LITERALLY, WITH A MOUSE

Joseph DeLappe's *The Artist's Mouse* (**FIGURE S1.5**) cleverly—and literally—traces mouse movements while "the artist" uses the contraption. DeLappe's project is an analog response to one of the earliest digital interface challenges: how to track the cursor's position on the screen.

By completing the exercises in Chapter 3, you'll learn to combine the basic shapes—the circle, the triangle, and the square—into complex icons. This activity provides a lesson in design and abstraction, as well as a way to understand computing processes. When simple elements are combined, the new combination can be exponentially more complex.

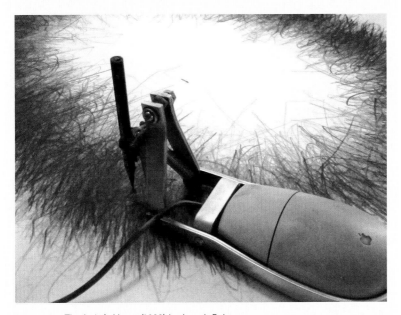

FIGURE S1.5 *The Artist's Mouse* (1998) by Joseph DeLappe.

In the first three chapters of this book, you'll work with the foundational elements of design—the dot, the line, and the three basic shapes—and you'll be encouraged to think about the relationship between these design elements and computing technologies. The dot is analogous to the bit, the vector line is created in Adobe Illustrator as a path between two dots, and basic shapes can be combined to form an infinite number of complex forms. Negroponte understood that "computing is not about computers anymore. It is about living" [7]. Artists and designers are essentially developers of the way we live—somewhere between the analog and virtual worlds—and the way we create meaning for such a visual landscape.

REFERENCE [7]
Negroponte, 6.

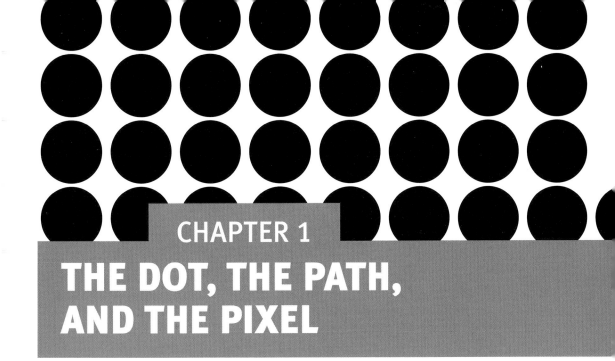

CHAPTER 1

THE DOT, THE PATH, AND THE PIXEL

THE EXERCISES IN this chapter show you how to create and manipulate dots and make meaning with basic design elements. Remember the observation we made in the introduction: When you place a single black dot in a field of white, you can quickly judge which is the figure (or the positive space) and which is the ground (or the negative space). A group of same-shaped circles creates a repeated pattern of dots. You read this pattern as one giant shape that dominates the composition. The pattern of black dots that you create becomes the foreground, while the white space is understood as the background (**FIGURE 1.1**).

The division between the foreground and background, or the *figure* and *ground*, is a visual tool that can be used to manipulate a viewer's perception. When it's difficult to distinguish between the figure and the ground, a viewer may have trouble deciphering the message. Messages may imply unintended meanings due to an unexpected shift of the figure and ground. Gestalt psychology, which studies human perception, has provided artists and designers with a set of laws and properties that are incredibly useful for predicting how a viewer

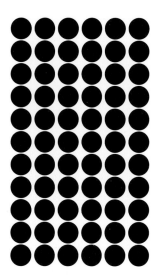

FIGURE 1.1 (LEFT) A pattern created by repetitive black dots is read as the foreground on a white background in this composition.

FIGURE 1.2 (RIGHT) Rubin's vase was developed in 1915 by Danish psychologist Edgar Rubin to demonstrate the instability of a figure and ground relationship. Images such as this are often used as examples of the property of instability in Gestalt psychology. pio3/ Shutterstock.

will interact with or perceive a visual work. *Multistability* is a Gestalt property that accounts for the shifting nature of figure and ground elements. Rubin's vase, developed by psychologist Edgar Rubin in 1915, is a visual demonstration of this phenomenon (**FIGURE 1.2**), whereby viewers can possibly see two dominant images at once because they are able to mentally invert the relationship between the figure and ground.

Once a pattern of dots is placed on a contrasting background, a new focal point can be made within the pattern by deleting a selection of dots. Those that are dismissed reveal the ground, which becomes dominant—if its shape is recognizable. Although the following exercises may seem abstract and elementary, you'll begin to notice that these basic techniques are commonly in play in digital art and design. For instance, Leo Villareal's light installations (see the introduction to this section) are visually translated as a series of repetitions of the activity: "create the dot pattern, then remove some dots." Roe Seafood, a fish marketplace and restaurant in Long Beach, California, sports a simple logo featuring the letter "r" missing from a pattern of various sized dots (in orange, representing the hard roe you might see atop an order of sushi) set in a circular pattern (**FIGURE 1.3**). In *Gyre II* (2011), Chris Jordan re-creates Vincent van Gogh's *The Starry Night* (1889) using 50,000 cigarette lighters, equal to the estimated number of pieces of floating plastic found in every square mile in the world's oceans (**FIGURE 1.4**).

The exercises in this chapter will show you how to use the Ellipse tool in Adobe Illustrator to create a series of dots that form a pattern. Then you'll experiment with removing dots to invert the figure/ground relationship. Before we begin, it's important to understand how the software interprets your commands.

PATHS AND VECTOR GRAPHICS

Adobe Illustrator is primarily a vector graphic application. When you draw a circle with the Ellipse tool, you're instructing Illustrator to create an anchor point on each of the four "sides" of the circle: think of a circle as the face of a clock, with anchor points at the hours of 12, 3, 6, and 9. These anchor points hold mathematical coordinates that have a relationship to one another (FIGURE 1.5). When you scale the circle, you're simply multiplying the coordinates by a common factor. Vector graphics are smooth, scalable, and plotted by anchor points.

PIXELS AND BITMAP GRAPHICS

In contrast, Adobe Photoshop is primarily a bitmap application. When you draw a circle or even paint a dot with the Brush tool, you're instructing Photoshop to create pixels. Each pixel contains one unit of color. If you zoom in close enough, you can actually see the pixels that make up a bitmap image (FIGURE 1.6). Pixels are finite. They can't be scaled by a common factor, so file size and resolution are extremely important. (You'll learn more about these topics in Chapter 5, *Resolution and Value*.)

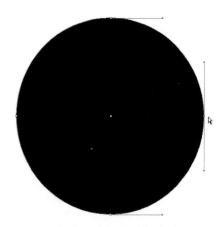

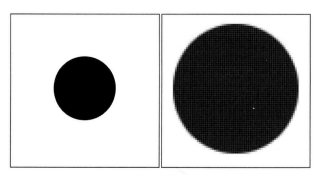

FIGURE 1.5 Anchor points are visible in the edges, or contours, of this circle. The blue square at 3 o'clock (where the mouse is pointing) is a selected anchor, while the white squares at the 12, 6, and 9 o'clock positions are unselected.

FIGURE 1.6 In Photoshop, you can make a circle by filling an elliptical selection with black color. Zoom in, and you'll see each black, square pixel that makes up the image. On the left is a view of a filled circle in Photoshop at 100% view. On the right is the same circle magnified to twice its size.

WHAT YOU'LL NEED

You don't need to download files to complete the exercises in this chapter. You'll simply use your ability to see, think, and perceive in Adobe Illustrator.

WHAT YOU'LL MAKE

In the exercises for Chapter 1, you'll develop a figure/ground study with black dots on a white background (FIGURE 1.7). Your digital composition will reference late nineteenth-century pointillist paintings (look back to the section introduction, FIGURE S1.4) and the expression of digital technologies in code as "on" or "off" (ones or zeroes, true or false, present or missing, and so on).

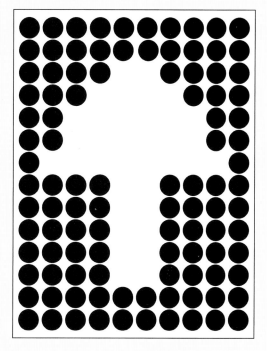

FIGURE 1.7 You'll choose which black dots to remove to make your final composition. Here, the selection of missing dots might represent an arrow.

FILE PRESETS IN ILLUSTRATOR

1. Open Adobe Illustrator. Choose the Window menu > Workspace > Essentials Classic. You can set or reset the current workspace (that is, return it to its default arrangement) at any time by choosing Window > Workspace > Reset [whichever workspace is active]. You'll want your workspace to look like mine so the screenshots reflect more closely what is in front of you so choose Window > Workspace > Reset Essentials Classic now.

2. Choose the File menu > New or press **Command-N/Ctrl-N** to create a new document.

3. The New Document dialog box offers a variety of document presets (or templates) in several formats grouped under tabs by category. You can change the format, depending on how you want to display the work. The categories include Mobile, Web, Print, Film & Video, and Art & Illustration. Additional preset document choices and output settings regarding file resolution, pixel area (width and height), color mode, and more will change for each of the environments suggested by those common tabs. Click the

Throughout this book, you'll see a note regarding the workspace used at the start of the first exercise in each chapter.

In this book, we'll list the macOS version of a keyboard shortcut first, followed by the equivalent shortcut in Windows.

Print tab to make a file that will print sharply when you're finished. Select the first template (Letter 612 x 792 pt) to create a letter-sized document (8.5 by 11 inches), and then click the Create button **(FIGURE 1.8)**.

The new document appears as a blank white page. In Illustrator, the page is called the *artboard*. Anything you place on the artboard—typography, graphics, or photographs—will print or be exported to a published file.

4. It's never too early to begin saving the file. Choose File > Save As and name the file **chapter01.ai**. Notice that "Adobe Illustrator (ai)" is the first option in the Format menu (in Windows, choose "Adobe Illustrator (*.AI)" from the Save As Type menu). For now, we'll save in this format. Click Save, then click OK in the Illustrator Options dialog box that appears next.

EXERCISE 2 SHAPES, FILLS, AND STROKES

1. The Ellipse tool is buried beneath the Rectangle tool on the Tools panel on the left side of the application window. Press and hold the mouse button on the Rectangle tool to display the tools grouped with it. Select the Ellipse tool from the group **(FIGURE 1.9)**.

FIGURE 1.9 Load the Ellipse tool from the Tools panel. Notice that this tool "hides" or is grouped behind the Rectangle tool.

2. Click from tool to tool and notice that whenever you choose a new tool, the Control panel displays options specific to that tool **(FIGURE 1.10)**. The Ellipse tool is one of several shape tools. It is used to draw a shape. As you'll see in the next step, shapes are made of a fill color and an outline, called a *stroke*. The Ellipse tool options include menus for fill and stroke colors, the weight of the stroke, and more.

FIGURE 1.10 Set the Stroke or other tool options in the Control panel at the top of the application window.

3. Drag with the Ellipse tool on the artboard. As you drag away from the starting point (where you clicked), the ellipse grows. As you drag back toward where you initially clicked, the ellipse shrinks. Do this a few times to master the movement of drawing an ellipse on the artboard. After you've practiced making several ellipses, you'll delete all of them. Choose the Selection tool—the first arrow in the Tools panel (FIGURE 1.11).

4. The Selection tool is used to choose objects for the purpose of copying, moving, rotating, scaling, deleting, applying effects, and so on. Click one of the ellipses to select it; then press the **Delete/Backspace** key on your keyboard. To select all the ellipses (so you can delete all of them at once), click anywhere outside one of the ellipses that's outside the group (FIGURE 1.12) and drag the Selection tool over all the shapes (FIGURE 1.13). This is called *marqueeing*. When you're finished, all the ellipses will be selected, made visible by a blue path around each shape and identifiable anchor points (FIGURE 1.14). If you didn't quite pick up every shape, click anywhere on the artboard to deselect and marquee over all the shapes again. While they are selected, press the **Delete/Backspace** key to remove all the shapes.

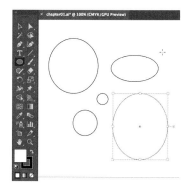

FIGURE 1.11 Five ellipses were drawn. The object remains selected when you let go of the mouse, until you take further action. Clicking anywhere outside of it on the artboard will deselect the shape.

WATCH OUT! The default stroke and fill values are black and white, but if you're working in a shared computer lab, you never know what those settings might include. If you made ellipses that have no assigned fill color, you'll be able to select the shapes only by clicking directly on their contours (or outlines).

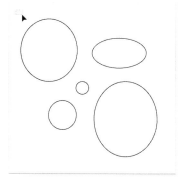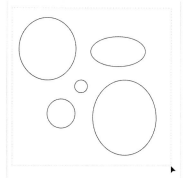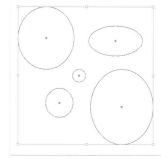

FIGURES 1.12, 1.13, AND 1.14 To *marquee* over a group of paths, first load the Selection tool. Drag from the empty artboard to make a box around all the items you intend to select. Release the mouse, and notice whether all elements are selected. If they're not, click on an empty area of the artboard to deselect and try it again.

5. Select the Ellipse tool again. This time hold the Shift key while you draw a new shape to constrain its proportions. Instead of drawing an ellipse, draw a circle (FIGURE 1.15).

6. Click back on the Selection tool. With the circle selected, you can now change its properties. The circle is defined in Illustrator as a *path*. The path is governed by a set of anchor points. These anchor points define the path's edge, which is the *stroke* surrounding the circumference of the circle. The area inside the shape is called the *fill*. The stroke and the fill each contain information such as transparency or opacity, hue, saturation and brightness, and weight (or the width of the stroke).

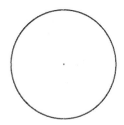

FIGURE 1.15 Draw a circle with the Ellipse tool by holding the Shift key while dragging the mouse. The Shift key will keep the proportions constrained— this key can be used with the Rectangle tool, for instance, to draw a square.

With the circle selected, look at the bottom of the Tools panel, and you'll see icons for the fill and stroke. In my document (FIGURE 1.16), the icon for stroke overlaps the fill icon.

7. Click either the Fill or Stroke icon to move it to the front. Don't click the curvy arrow above the two icons. (Doing this will swap the fill and stroke colors, which can be confusing when you're learning to master this area of the Tools panel.) With the stroke in front and the circle still selected, click the button with a red slash to set the stroke to none, to turn off the outline (FIGURE 1.17).

FIGURE 1.16 The Fill and Stroke icons are near the bottom of the Tools panel. In this screen capture, the Stroke icon lies on top of the Fill icon. You can click the Fill icon directly to make it overlap the Stroke icon.

FIGURE 1.17 Beneath the Fill and Stroke icons are three buttons directly related to fill and stroke. The first applies a color in a selected path's fill or stroke (whichever is on top in the Tools panel), the second applies a gradient, and the third sets the fill or stroke value to none. This essentially renders the fill or stroke invisible.

FIGURE 1.18 Open the Color panel from the set of icons in the panel bar on the right side of the application window.

FIGURE 1.19 Fill a path with black quickly using the black color chip in the Color panel.

8. While the circle is still selected, click the Fill icon to bring it to the front. The Color panel will probably expand on the right side of the application window if it isn't already showing. If you don't see it, you can click the Color panel button (FIGURE 1.18) or choose Window > Color. Click the black color chip in the Color panel to fill the circle with black (FIGURE 1.19).

 EXERCISE 3 FIGURE AND GROUND WITH REPEATED DOTS

There are various techniques for creating a pattern of black dots (or circles) on the artboard in Illustrator. For instance, you can copy, paste, and move a single dot repeatedly to create a line of dots and then copy that line and paste it repeatedly. Or, you can define a brush with the dot as a pattern and "paint" the line of dots. There are probably other methods as well. Your way of creating digital media will be different from anyone else's, which is one of the reasons the applications are so robust and can be overwhelming to learn. In this exercise, you'll copy, paste, and move a single dot, because it's essential that you feel comfortable performing this action. Copy, paste, and move are three common commands; they are performed similarly in most Adobe applications and are accessed with the same key commands.

1. Choose the Selection tool, and click the circle to select or activate it—press the mouse button (or trackpad) and keep it pressed until instructed to let go. With the button held down, press and hold the Option/Alt key (with your non-mouse hand) while you drag the circle to another position on the artboard. Let go of the button, and then release the key. This is the swiftest way to make a copy of a path, just be sure to release the button *before* you release the Option/Alt key. Delete the new circle, as you'll perform this activity again with an additional key. (See Step 4 in Exercise 2 for a refresher on selecting and deleting.)

2. Once again, press and hold the button down to begin the copy process for the circle. Then press and hold the Option/Alt key *and* press and hold the Shift key (that's two keys with your non-mouse hand); finally, drag the circle to a new position on the artboard **(FIGURE 1.20)**. You'll notice that your movement is constrained to lines at 0°, 45°, or 90° relative to the page. Release the mouse before you release the keys.

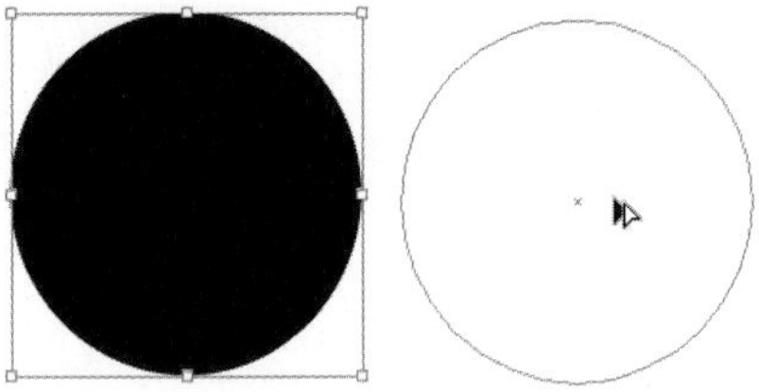

FIGURE 1.20 Hold the Option/Alt key while dragging a path with the Selection tool to create a copy of it. If you also hold the Shift key while Option/Alt-dragging with the Selection tool, the copy will move in a limited set of directions.

When you combine key commands with mouse actions, remember to release the mouse before you release the keys. For instance, when pressing the Shift key to constrict a mouse movement, you should always complete the task, release the mouse first, and then release the Shift key.

3. To make a straight line of dots, Shift-Option/Shift-Alt-drag the circle repeatedly across the top of the artboard **(FIGURE 1.21)**. Don't worry about the distance between the circles or at the margins. You'll adjust the spacing in the next steps.

4. How many dots did you make? Depending on the size of your original circle, you may have any number of repeated dots (figures) on the white space (ground) of the page. Consider the page of dots as a set of rows and columns. Your goal is to create a grid of 10 columns (the number of horizontal dots) and 14 rows (the number of vertical dots). You'll probably need to scale your dots in order to fit 10 across the top of the page. The work file documented here has six dots, if your file is like this one you'll need to decrease the scale of the dots to fit four more on the page. Whether you need to increase or decrease the size of your dots, follow these same directions: Marquee all the circles with the Selection tool (Step 4 in Exercise 2). You'll see a box with anchor points surrounding all the circles. Click one of the four anchors at the corner and hold down the Shift key while dragging toward the circles (to scale down) or away from the circles (to scale up) **(FIGURE 1.22)**. You'll have to judge visually how small the circles need to be to fit more or fewer of them on the page.

FIGURE 1.21 Multiple copies of the dot on the artboard.

FIGURE 1.22 Scale all the dots at once by selecting all of them and then scaling the group using the Selection tool.

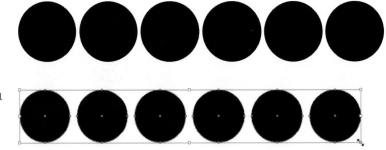

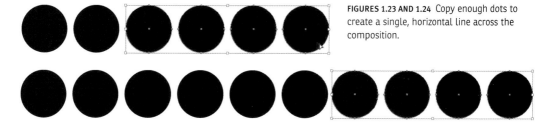

FIGURES 1.23 AND 1.24 Copy enough dots to create a single, horizontal line across the composition.

5. Use the Selection tool to deselect the group of circles by clicking on an empty part of the artboard. Select the number of circles you need to reach a count of 10 by marqueeing that number of circles.

    or

    Click one circle and hold the Shift key while clicking each of the others (this is called *Shift-clicking*) to select multiple circles. Press the Option/ Alt key and then the Shift key to begin dragging a copy **(FIGURE 1.23)** of the selected circles in a straight line. Move the circles to fill the space across the page in your first row **(FIGURE 1.24)**.

SCREENCAST 1-1 THE PATTERN BRUSH

See a video demonstrating how to define a pattern brush and apply it to the composition. This method is probably easier than what you labored through in Exercise 3, but it's a less essential skill. The repetition you did in Exercise 3 will help you to remember your new skills.

All screencasts are available on the companion website, www.digitalart-design.com, or on the Vimeo playlist, bit.ly/foundations-demos.

GROUPING AND ALIGNMENT

1. Press **Command-A/Ctrl-A** to select all the dots on the artboard.

2. The dots are probably aligned, because you used the Shift key while copying and moving them. If they're not, click the Vertical Align Top button in the alignment area of the Control panel **(FIGURE 1.25)**. Actually, because all the dots are the same size, you can use any of the vertical alignment buttons (Top, Center, or Bottom). If your circles are like those in Figure 1.25, no changes will take place on the artboard.

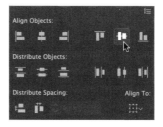

FIGURE 1.25 Align multiple paths (in this case, dots) by clicking the Vertical Align Top button in the Control panel.

TOOL TIPS The Align and Distribute button icons can be difficult to read when you're first learning Illustrator. Hover the cursor over each button to see the tool tip that displays its name. If tool tips are not enabled, check the Show Tool Tips box in General Preferences by choosing Illustrator > Preferences > General/ Edit > Preferences > General (**Command-K/ Ctrl-K**). This can be useful for any tools you don't recognize.

3. The distribution of the dots, that is, the spacing between each dot, is likely to be uneven. Choose Align To Selection from the Align To menu to align the dots as they relate to each other, rather than to the Artboard (**FIGURE 1.26**). While all the circles are still selected, click the Horizontal Distribute Center button in the Control panel to space them equally (**FIGURE 1.27**). (Use the tool tips to help you locate it.)

4. While the dots are selected, use the Left, Right, Up, and Down Arrow keys on your keypad to nudge the group of dots into a position on the page where the top, left, and right margins appear to be equally distant from the group of dots (**FIGURE 1.28**).

5. Select all again (**Command-A/Ctrl-A**), if all the dots aren't already selected, and choose Object > Group (**Command-G/Ctrl-G**) to group the row of dots. Now the Selection tool will treat all the dots as one unit.

FIGURE 1.26 You can align elements on the artboard to the dimensions of the artboard, to a key object, or in relation to elements that have been selected. In these exercises, we will be aligning the selected dots as they relate to each other in the selection.

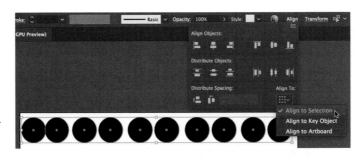

FIGURE 1.27 Notice the differences in the negative space between the selected dots before and after clicking the Horizontal Distribute Center button. The negative space is not distributed evenly in the top image, which would be easily noticed in repeated rows.

FIGURE 1.28 While all the dots are selected, use the arrow keys to nudge the group up, down, left, or right. Keep an eye on the margins of the page and aim to create equal negative space there.

6. Hold Shift and Option/Alt-drag to copy the first row of dots to create a second row (FIGURE 1.29).

7. Repeat Step 6 until you have 14 rows of dots on the artboard (FIGURE 1.30).

8. Do you need to adjust the alignment or distribution of your grouped rows? If the portion of the Control panel containing the alignment and distribution buttons doesn't appear, choose Window > Align to open the Align panel. If you do need to redistribute the rows of dots, you'll probably want to use the Vertical Distribute Center button.

FIGURE 1.29 Use the Selection tool with the Option/Alt and Shift keys to create a copy of the first row of dots.

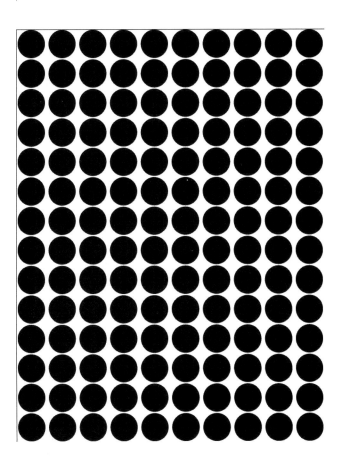

FIGURE 1.30 The artboard is full of rows of dots. Now a pattern of black dots has become the foreground of the compositional space. The background is white. You also might say that the black dots are the figure, and the white space is the ground.

WATCH OUT! The Align panel will organize single paths or grouped elements. If your circles are in a group, you may see a different result upon clicking the same Align button when selected circles are not grouped. Be mindful of what exactly you're aligning.

EXERCISE 5 · A FIGURE AND GROUND OR "ON" AND "OFF" STUDY

In this exercise, you'll delete some of the dots to make a recognizable form appear in the sea of black dots. The white space (what was the ground) will become the figure as the black dots move to the background (ground). You'll do this with the Selection tool, although in Chapter 3 you'll learn how to use the Direct Selection tool to modify parts of paths or just some paths within groups.

1. Press **Command-A/Ctrl-A** to select all.

2. Choose Object > Ungroup (**Shift-Command-G/Shift-Ctrl-G**) to ungroup all the rows, freeing every dot on the page.

3. Use the Selection tool to select and delete one dot at a time as you create a white form within the pattern of black dots by "turning off" the dots. Try making a letterform, arrow, smiley face (**FIGURE 1.31**), or something else.

FIGURE 1.31 Various figure/ground studies can be created by deleting black dots from the patterned composition. When the white space begins to look like a familiar graphic icon, the figure and ground relationship reverse: The white space becomes the figure, while the black dots are newly understood as the ground.

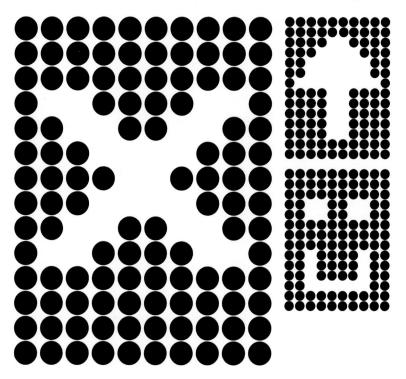

 **LAB CHALLENGE**

Express each letter in a word (using a typeface of your choice) with a repeated shape such as a circle, square, or image.

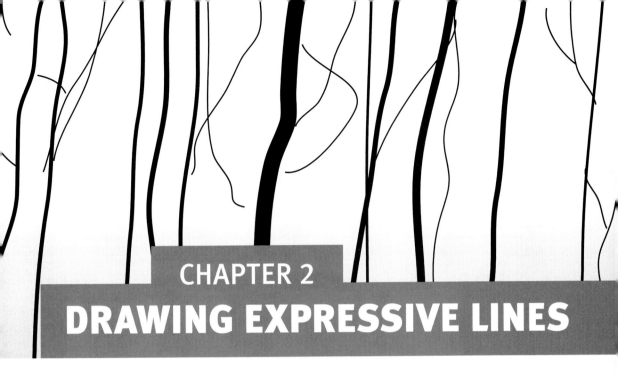

CHAPTER 2
DRAWING EXPRESSIVE LINES

THE EXERCISES IN this chapter encourage you to study lines as design elements. Specifically, you'll examine the lines found in a landscape photograph of trees. As you can see in FIGURE 2.1, the dark lines produced by the bark of the trees are read in stark contrast against a winter sky. You'll use the Pencil and Paintbrush tools and explore the Gradient and Layers panels in Adobe Illustrator.

A group of similar lines creates a repeated pattern that is easy to read and understand when the weight (or thickness) of the lines is contrasting. Thicker lines will seem to push to the front of the composition, while thinner lines recede into the background. The same is true for dark and light values, respectively. In Chapter 1, *The Dot, the Path, and the Pixel*, we focused on the separation between the foreground and background of the composition space. In this chapter, lines will express the individuality of each tree in the landscape. Although foreground and background are less likely to shift in this composition, you'll begin to see how the sizes and values of design elements affect human perception.

FIGURE 2.1 The original photograph used for the study in lines in Chapter 2's exercises was created by Aleš Jungmann. It is available on the Wikimedia Commons website.

FIGURE 2.2 In this March 2007 photograph by Staff Sgt. D. Myles Cullen, members of a Chinese military honor guard march during a welcome ceremony for Chairman of the Joint Chiefs of Staff Marine Gen. Peter Pace at the Ministry of Defense in Beijing, China. Notice how each red flag and its pole divides the rows of marching men. The poles themselves stretch in opposite directions, from the earth toward the sky. At the same time, each row of marching men can be read as a set of vertical and diagonal (their front legs) lines. PJF Military Collection/Alamy Stock Photo.

REFERENCE [1] Maggie Macnab, *Decoding Design* (Blue Ash, OH: HOW Books, 2008), 62.

Because a line connects two dots, it makes sense to follow a chapter study on dots with one on lines. In her book *Decoding Design*, Maggie Macnab articulates the complexity of the line by referring to the anchor points at each end of the line as a pole. "The poles, while repulsed in their division, are attracted back to one another—the paradox of this principle" [1]. A line can be used to join two elements or to separate parts of a whole (FIGURE 2.2).

A line can be *tight* or *loose*, meaning it can be straight and mechanical (tight) or flowing and organic (loose). The plans for an architectural space, for example, will be clean and organized. The "hands" of Alicia Eggert and Mike Fleming's *Eternity* clock form a composition of tight, black lines on a contrasting white background (FIGURE 2.3), while flowing water in Colleen Ludwig's *Cutaneous Habitats: Shiver* demonstrates free-form movement (FIGURE 2.4).

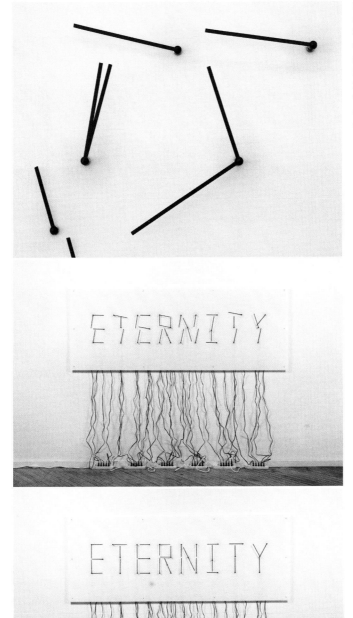

FIGURE 2.3 Alicia Eggert and Mike Fleming, *Eternity*, 78 x 96 x 3 inches, 2010. Electric clocks, acrylic, and power strips. *Eternity* uses the hour and minute hands of 30 electric clocks to spell the word "eternity" once every twelve hours. Photo credit: Mike Fleming.

FIGURE 2.4 Colleen Ludwig, *Shiver* from the series Cutaneous Habitats, interactive environment, 2012. *Shiver* integrates programming, electronics, and a recirculating water system into a prefabricated, architectural framework with water-resistant fabric walls. Images © Colleen Ludwig.

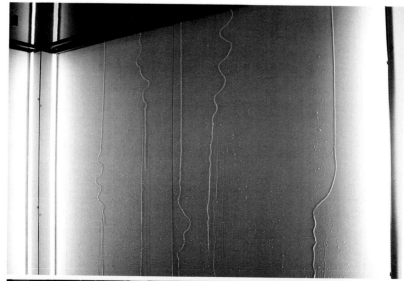

The exercises in this chapter will show you how to create a series of lines using the Pencil and Paintbrush tools in Adobe Illustrator. You'll experiment with various strokes (line weights) and values to alter the perception of depth between the foreground and background elements.

SAVING AND SHARING FILES

When you save a file, you have many choices to make. How will you name the file? Are you collaborating with others? If so, will you all adhere to the same naming conventions? What type of file do you want to save? What do you plan to do with the file once it's saved? If you are submitting files to a call for projects or an instructor, have you been given directions about the file name and its format? How you answer these questions will play a role in how you choose to name and save your files. What follows are a few general guidelines that will help you determine how to save and share your files.

File names should be concise, organized, and descriptive. If you're working on a series of files or collaborating with others (for instance, if you're a student submitting a file to an instructor who is in effect "collaborating" with you and all of your peers), you should consider naming all files for one project with a consistent naming convention. File names should not include spaces or foreign characters, and they should always include an extension (for example, .ai, .psd, .jpg, and so on). The file name "My BEST picture ever!!!!!!!" is sloppy—it includes spaces and exclamation points, mixes upper- and lower-case letters, lacks the file extension, and, worst of all, it doesn't describe the content of the image. In my classroom, I ask students to label all files with a description followed by their first initial dash last name dot file extension, all in lowercase, for example, chapter02-x-burrough.ai. I insist on file names with all lowercase letters, because many of my foundations-level students later enroll in interactive media design classes where lowercase letters are the norm. (It saves time troubleshooting code if you know that the file names don't utilize uppercase letters.)

FILE NAMING If an image is saved in two different formats, the files will have different file extensions. Therefore, you can keep the same file name in place, resulting in something like: x-burrough.ai and x-burrough.pdf so it's clear the two files refer to the same project.

In addition to how you name your files, you have to consider the saved format. Best practices include always saving the file in its master or native format (for instance, always save an Illustrator file in .ai format). The master file can be edited at any time in the application in which the file was originally developed. In addition, you may want to save a separate file for sharing. The file formats JPG and PDF are often used for sharing photographic images or type and image layouts. These formats compress the file (which means that some data is lost), resulting in a smaller file size. Most importantly, viewers don't need Adobe applications in order to open or print these formats, as all computers can display JPG and PDF files via basic previewing applications, the freely downloadable Adobe Reader application, or even a web browser. Although applications that can open a PDF can read recent versions of Adobe Illustrator files, commercial printers will likely request the file in PDF format. It's common to save two versions of the same file: one in the master format (which can be especially useful for later revision) and one in a format conducive to sharing a finished work.

WHAT YOU'LL NEED

Download the following source materials to complete the exercises in this chapter:

✔ The **chapter02-workfiles.zip** file, which contains Aleš Jungmann's original photograph (**trees.jpg**). It also contains samples of the finished illustration in Illustrator and PDF formats (**chapter02-results.ai** and **chapter02.pdf**).

WHAT YOU'LL MAKE

In the exercises in Chapter 2, you'll create a study of expressive lines in Adobe Illustrator by transforming a black-and-white photograph into an abstracted vector illustration (**FIGURE 2.5**). Your digital composition will consist of a set of loose, hand-drawn lines.

You'll also learn the ability to see lines in all aspects of the original image.

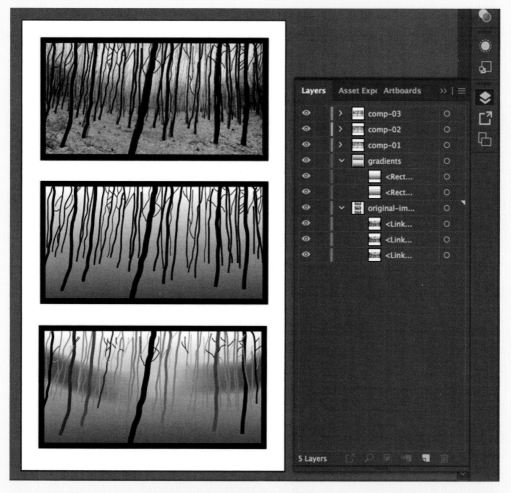

FIGURE 2.5 The final results file for exercises in Chapter 2 includes studies of lines in a black-and-white photograph. Aleš Jungmann's photograph appears courtesy of the artist. It can also be found on Wikimedia Commons, commons. wikimedia.org/wiki/File:Ales_jungmann_krajina_1994-1997_8.jpg.

PLACE AND LOCK AN IMAGE

EXERCISE 1

1. Copy the original photograph by Aleš Jungmann, **trees.jpg**, from the folder **chapter02-workfiles** and paste it into a folder named **chapter02**.

2. Open Adobe Illustrator. Choose File > New and adjust the following settings: Select the Print tab and set the paper size to Legal (612 by 1008 points or 8.5 by 14 inches). In the Preset Details (on the right side), name the new file **chapter02** and choose Inches from the Units menu **(FIGURE 2.6)**. Click Create.

3. Choose File > Place to add the photograph of trees to the artboard. In the dialog box that opens, browse to the file **trees.jpg** in the **chapter02** folder you created in Step 1 **(FIGURE 2.7)**. Your cursor icon will change to a *loaded graphics cursor*—click anywhere on the artboard to place the image **(FIGURE 2.8)**.

WORKSPACE > ESSENTIALS CLASSIC Set the workspace to Essentials Classic by choosing it from the menu in the Application bar or by choosing the Window menu > Workspace > Essentials Classic.

FIGURE 2.6 Start your new document by selecting and modifying a profile.

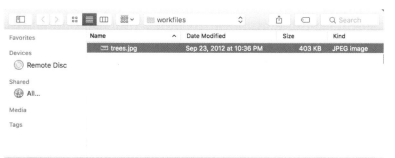

FIGURE 2.7 Browse for a file to add it to the artboard using File > Place.

 1/1

FIGURE 2.8 Click the loaded cursor to place the image onto the artboard.

FIGURE 2.9 When the image is in position on the artboard, you'll see equal margin spacing on the top, left, and right sides. There should be plenty of room for you to work toward the bottom of the page.

WORKSPACE You can set or reset the workspace anytime. Reset the workspace by choosing Window > Workspace > Reset [whichever workspace is active]. You'll want your workspace to look like mine so the screenshots are more likely to reflect what's in front of you.

4. The photograph will appear small on the page. Because you'll eventually create your own vector abstraction based on the image, don't worry about file resolution for printing purposes. (This topic is thoroughly investigated in Chapter 5, *Resolution and Value*.) In this situation, it's safe to enlarge the photographic image. Use the Selection tool to click the image, and then hold the Shift key while dragging any of the four corners outward from the image. Drag the image to the top of the artboard while keeping an eye on the margin spacing—aim for equal margins on the top, left, and right sides of the image (FIGURE 2.9).

LINKS AND TEMPLATES

Among the options at the bottom of the place dialog box are Link and Template. If you choose to link images to the Illustrator document, the size of the .ai file will remain small because Illustrator will reference the images where they are saved on your computer rather than embed them in the .ai file. However, if you want to view or print the .ai file from another computer, remember to transfer the image files together with the .ai file. (If the image files are not saved in the same relative position to the master .ai file, you may need to relink them, too.) I often encourage new students to leave the Link option unchecked and embed images within the file. The Template button automatically places the image on a locked layer at a reduced opacity. We will not use this feature in Chapter 2, but it can be helpful if you plan to use vector tools to trace a bitmap image on a separate layer.

5. You'll be drawing lines on top of the image in the next exercise. If you don't lock the image, you may unintentionally select and move it while you're trying to work. With that in mind, lock the image now in anticipation of the next steps. This is easily accomplished with the Layers panel. Click the Layers icon in the panel dock on the right side of the application window (FIGURE 2.10). The Layers panel will appear. Any paths you draw or images you place on the artboard appear in the Layers panel.

FIGURE 2.10 Click the Layers icon to access the Layers panel. (You can also choose Menu > Layers.) The Layers panel displays paths and images added to the artboard.

FIGURE 2.11 By default, all media is stored in **Layer 1**. You can expand and collapse a layer by clicking on the arrow to the left of its icon.

FIGURE 2.12 Click the unlabeled box to the left of a layer to lock it inside **Layer 1**.

6. Click the sideways arrow next to **Layer 1** to flip it into a downward pointing arrow, revealing content saved on this layer (**FIGURE 2.11**). The image appears in **Layer 1** as <Image>. Click the unlabeled box to the left of <Image> to lock it inside **Layer 1** (**FIGURE 2.12**).

FINDING PANELS If the Layers panel icon is not easily visible, you can always open it by choosing Window > Layers.

WHY NO LABEL?

The Toggle Lock area in the Layers panel, to me, has always been an interface design flaw. The lock appears when you click inside the otherwise unnoticeable "lock area." It would be better if there were an "unlock" icon there for Adobe newbies, but this is just one of those interface areas you'll have to remember. The concepts of locked and unlocked are polar opposites, just as the two points that create a line will inevitably be positioned in opposing directions.

UNDERSTAND LAYERS

The Layers panel is a standard feature in many Adobe applications. Illustrator and Photoshop treat layers slightly differently because of the difference between how art is created in vector and bitmap applications.

In Illustrator, you begin with one layer. Each time you add content to the artboard, it's added as an element that's part of **Layer 1**. You can lock individual elements. You can lock entire layers. You can create and delete layers. You can rearrange what's referred to as the *stacking order* of layers to make content appear more in the foreground (towards the top of the panel), or background (towards the bottom of the panel) of the document, in front of or behind other elements. When you click where there are multiple elements, the topmost unlocked element will be selected. Much of this is also true in Photoshop, although you'll see in later chapters that it's safer to work with each element (graphic or text) on its own layer in bitmap applications.

One of the primary roles of layers is to help you organize your document. In the following exercises, you'll create new layers to make the content of separate compositions easy to find.

EXERCISE 3 CREATE LINES WITH THE PENCIL TOOL

1. Click the Create New Layer button at the bottom of the Layers panel (FIGURE 2.13). **Layer 2** will appear on top of **Layer 1**.

2. Double-click the name **Layer 2** and type the new name **comp-01**; then press the **Return/Enter** key or click anywhere outside the text field to set the text (FIGURE 2.14). You'll draw all the new lines for the first composition on this layer.

3. Find the Shaper tool in the Tools panel on the left side of the application window. Notice that the Shaper tool, like many of the tools, has a small arrow in the bottom-right corner. Pressing and holding the mouse button on the arrow reveals several related tools that are bundled with the visible tool. Press and hold on the Shaper tool and select the Pencil tool (FIGURE 2.15).

4. The default fill and stroke values for the Pencil are no fill and a black stroke. Check the Fill and Stroke controls at the bottom of the Tools panel or on the Control panel and set them to no fill with a black stroke if the default settings have been modified (FIGURE 2.16).

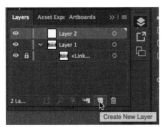

FIGURE 2.13 The Create New Layer icon appears at the bottom of the panel next to the Trash icon. (I always tell students that birth and death live next to each other.) The bottom of a panel is often the location for Create New and Trash icons in Adobe programs.

FIGURE 2.14 Double-click the name **Layer 2,** and simply type on top of its name to rename it.

FIGURE 2.15 Clicking the small arrow in the lower-right corner of a tool's icon reveals related tools that are bundled with the top tool.

FIGURE 2.16 Set the Pencil tool to a black stroke with no fill: Click the Stroke button at the bottom of the Tools panel (or the left end of the Control panel) and select the black swatch; then click the Fill button and select the [None] swatch.

5. Use the Pencil tool to draw a line along the contour of the tree that's most in the foreground (or the tree's outline—you can choose the side). When you finish drawing the line, it will remain selected. Modify the weight of the line by increasing its stroke value in the Control panel at the top of the application window (FIGURE 2.17). I set mine to 12 points, resulting in a line that's nearly the same width as the trunk of the tree.

6. Repeat Step 5 to trace enough trees to create a recognizable abstract line drawing of the photograph. Change the weight of each line (the stroke value) as you develop lines that appear in the background (FIGURE 2.18). Watch out for areas where two lines seem to connect (for instance, in those tiny sideways branches in the background). When you draw a line with the Pencil tool, it's constructed by a series of anchor points. The line remains selected after it's drawn. If you draw another line on a new area of the artboard, the first line becomes deselected, and the second line is selected. If you try to draw a line that connects with the first line, instead of creating a new line, you'll end up modifying the first (selected) line. Inevitably, you'll do this when you don't intend to. You'll have to manually deselect the first line—use the Selection tool to click in any white space on the artboard—then reselect the Pencil tool and draw the second line.

FIGURE 2.17 Modify the weight of a selected line by changing its stroke value in the Control panel.

KEYBOARD SHORTCUT While you're using the Pencil tool, you can easily access the Selection tool by pressing the Command key in macOS (or the Ctrl key in Windows). Holding this key while you're using the Pencil tool temporarily converts the tool into the Selection tool. When you release the key, the Pencil tool returns.

FIGURE 2.18 Continue to trace trees. Watch out for intersecting lines. You will need to deselect the path before drawing a new line that intersects with the previous drawn line.

7. Select the Rectangle tool, and draw a black border around the image, covering the film edges. Modify the stroke value to match the weight of the line shown at the edge of this photograph **(FIGURE 2.19)**.

FIGURE 2.19 Use the Rectangle tool to create a border.

 DUPLICATE THE COMPOSITION

1. Rename **Layer 1** so that it better describes the content on the layer. I named mine **original-image**.

2. Toggle off the eyeball (or visibility) icon next to the **comp-01** layer so you can see the original image layer set behind it **(FIGURE 2.20)**. The stacking order of the layers prevents you from seeing lower-level layers when top layers contain content that covers the same areas.

3. Expand the **original-image** layer if it is not already expanded and unlock the image **(FIGURE 2.21)**.

FIGURE 2.21 Expand the **original-image** layer and click the lock icon to unlock the image.

FIGURE 2.20 Toggle off the eyeball icon in the Layers panel to view the original layer.

FIGURE 2.22 Select the image within the Layers panel by clicking the blank area at the far right of the layer.

FIGURE 2.23 Choose the Selection tool and use **Option-Shift-drag/Shift-Alt-drag** to copy the image twice. New images appear in the **original-image** layer in the Layers panel.

4. Select the image within the Layers panel by clicking in the last column to its right (**FIGURE 2.22**), called the *selection column*. When you see a box (mine is blue, yours may be another color), you've selected a layer element. Look on your artboard to see that the image has been selected.

5. Choose the Selection tool. **Option-Shift-drag/Shift-Alt-drag** to create a copy of the image beneath the first original image. Repeat this process to make a second copy (**FIGURE 2.23**). Once they are placed, edit the spacing of the margins (the negative space) so they are even. You'll reference these images when you create the next two compositions.

ADD A GRADIENT BACKGROUND

EXERCISE 5

1. Click the eyeball icon to toggle visibility for the **comp-01** layer on. Don't expand the layer. Click in the selection column (**FIGURE 2.24**). This selects everything contained within the **comp-01** layer. Every pencil stroke you created is selected. Choose Edit > Copy, or press **Command-C/Ctrl-C**.

2. Before pasting all those paths, create a new layer and title it **comp-02**.

KEYBOARD SHORTCUT
Press the **Shift** key and the appropriate arrow key to move items faster—they travel by ten units rather than one unit at a time.

3. While the **comp-02** layer is active, press **Command-V/Ctrl-V** or choose Edit > Paste. If your document is like mine, you'll end up with a pasted set of lines that are not aligned with the second original photograph (**FIGURE 2.25**). While the lines are selected, use the arrow keys to move the composition of lines into position over the second photograph. I used **Shift-Left Arrow** to move my composition of lines to the left significantly faster than if I didn't use the Shift key.

FIGURE 2.24 Clicking in the selection column of the collapsed layer selects everything stored within it.

FIGURE 2.25 Pasted items land on a new layer.

4. Create a new layer to store gradient fills. Name the layer **gradients** and drag it to the stacking position just above the **original-image** layer (**FIGURE 2.26**).

5. Deselect the lines on the **comp-02** layer if they are selected. Click the **gradients** layer in the Layers panel to make it active. Draw a rectangle (use the Rectangle tool) on the **gradients** layer that's the same size as the compositional space of the middle photograph. Make sure the Fill icon is selected either at the bottom of the Tools panel or on the Control panel, and double-click the Gradient tool to open the Gradient panel on the right side of the document window. Click the tiny triangle to the right of the gradient swatch to open the gradient menu, and choose the first option to apply a two-point linear gradient from white to black (**FIGURE 2.27**).

6. Modify the angle of the gradient to –90 degrees. If you choose positive 90 degrees, the darker value will be on top, where the sky should appear white (**FIGURE 2.28**).

FIGURE 2.26 A layer can be moved to a new stacking order by dragging it into position in the Layers panel. The **gradients** layer is dragged into stacking position just above the **original-image** layer.

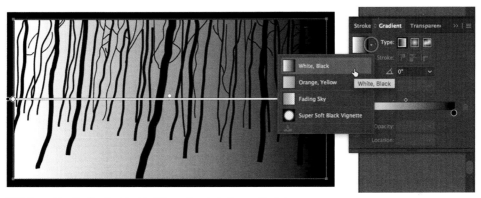

FIGURE 2.27 Use the Gradient tool to fill a rectangle in the **gradients** layer.

FIGURE 2.28 Choose Window > Gradient to modify the gradient settings. The Type setting determines how the gradient is distributed and the angle determines the direction of the gradient.

BE CAREFUL! If you followed the last few steps but didn't see a change on your artboard, you may have deselected the gradient fill before modifying the settings in the Gradient panel. Select the gradient fill on your artboard and then try those steps again.

7. You can modify the colors at the two ends of the gradient spectrum at any time. You can also add an additional "pit stop" of color or value by **Option/Alt-dragging** one of the color chip handles in the Gradient panel. Double-click the black color chip near the bottom of the Gradient panel. This will open a Color panel specific to the Gradient settings. Adjust the dark value so it's 80% black (dark gray) rather than true black: Change the 100% K (or black) value to 80% **(FIGURE 2.29)**.

FIGURE 2.29 Double-click the black chip in the Gradient panel to open a Color panel controlling the Gradient settings. Set the dark point to 80% black.

 ## CREATE DEPTH WITH CONTRASTING VALUES

EXERCISE 6

In this third composition, you'll modify the value of some of the lines to create greater compositional depth. Depth and space are alluded to in two-dimensional space by properties that appear in our three-dimensional reality. The size of the trees becomes smaller as the viewer perceives the depth of the forest (both in terms of their height and the line weight of their contours). The overlapping position of the trees also helps the viewer perceive depth. These two values (size and overlap) were translated from the original photograph in black and white. However, atmospheric perspective accounts for the depth that's perceived due to less visibility through contrast as items are farther from the viewer's plane of vision. In this case, you'll need to modify the values of the trees toward the background to allude to the atmospheric perspective.

You'll also add a final diffused line to the third composition to separate the horizon line from the ground. All aspects of the original image can be translated with one basic design element: the line.

1. Repeat Steps 1, 2, and 3 from Exercise 4 to create a third composition. This time copy **comp-02** and name the new layer **comp-03**. You'll also need to copy, paste, and position the gradient for the third composition on the **gradients** layer **(FIGURE 2.30)**.

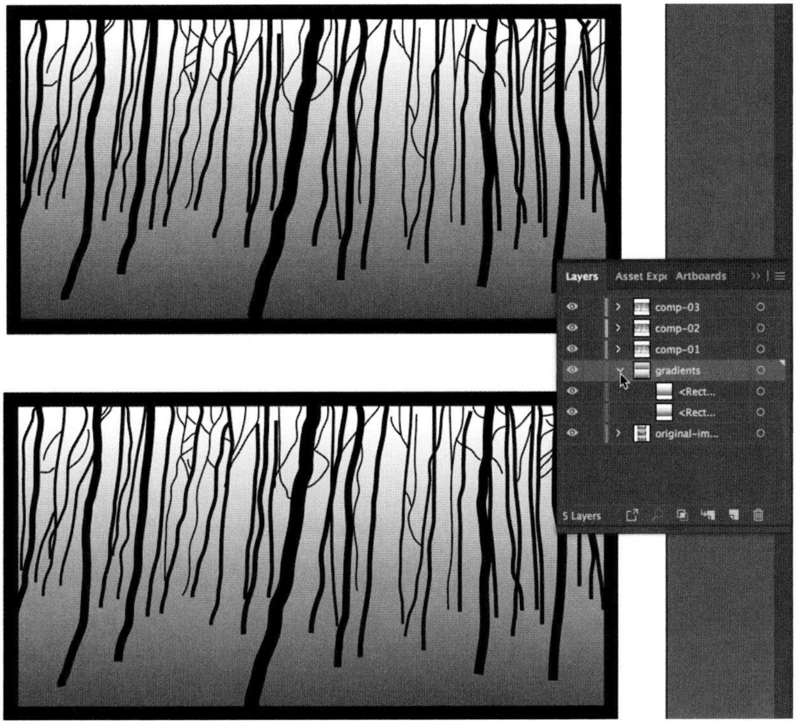

FIGURE 2.30 A view of the Layers panel with the new layer, **comp-03**.

SCREENCAST 2-1 ADD THE "SWOOSH" AT THE HORIZON

I added an extra line at the horizon using the Paintbrush tool with a gradient and the Feather effect **(FIGURE 2.31)**. View the online screencast to see my process.

FIGURE 2.31 The final results of Screencast 2-1.

All screencasts are available on the companion website, www.digitalart-design.com, or on the Vimeo playlist, bit.ly/foundations-demos.

2. Leave the tree you drew in the very front black (the one with the trunk that extends all the way to the bottom of the frame). Choose the Selection tool and click one of the trees/lines near the foreground. In the Color panel, open the panel menu (in the upper-right corner) and choose Show Options. Set the Stroke value to 90% black (**FIGURE 2.32**).

3. Select the next set of near-foreground trees together. You can select multiple lines by pressing the Shift key as you click each one. If you accidentally add a line to your multi-selection, Shift-click it again to remove it. Set the value to 80% black (**FIGURE 2.33**).

FIGURE 2.32 Use the Selection tool to select a line; then change its Stroke value using the Color panel.

FIGURE 2.33 Hold the Shift key and click to select multiple trees with the Selection tool. Use the Color panel to decrease the stroke values on all of the selected lines.

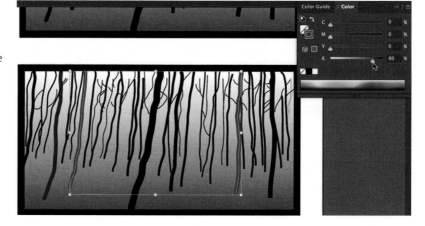

4. Repeat Step 3 as you set another group of lines to 70% black, then 60%, and so forth as you move backward in the compositional space. You may leave some of the smaller twigs black as they overlap other tree branches. This contrast between black and mid-gray will help the viewer see the details in the forest.

EXERCISE 7 USE MASTER FILES AND SHARED FILES

1. When the design is finished, save the master file—either press **Command-S/ Ctrl-S** or choose File > Save As to rename the file or to save a duplicate of the file in a different location on your hard drive. Save the file in master format, meaning .ai (Adobe Illustrator), the format that is specific to the Illustrator application. You can click OK through the Illustrator Options dialog box unless you'll need to open and edit the file in a prior version of Illustrator. (If so, see the following sidebar about backward compatibility.)

SAVING FILES FOR BACKWARD COMPATIBILITY

If you're using a different version of Adobe Illustrator at home than you used to create this drawing (in a public computer lab, for instance), save the file using a compatible version. Choose File > Save As, name the file, and save it in .ai format. The next dialog box allows you to save with backward compatibility. For instance, if you're using Adobe Illustrator CS6 at home, you can choose that format from the Version menu **(FIGURE 2.34)**.

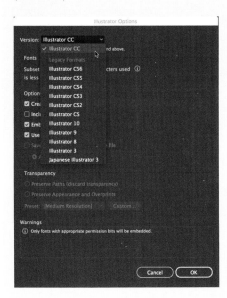

FIGURE 2.34 Choose File > Save As to save a native file. In the Illustrator Options dialog box, choose a version to save a master file compatible with your system settings.

FIGURE 2.35 File formats, such as PDF, are available in the Format menu (or in Windows, in the Save As Type menu) of the Save As dialog box.

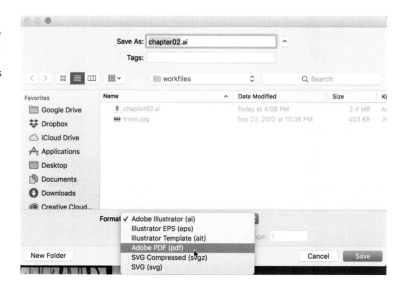

2. Use of the .ai format is imperative: If the file is in this format, you'll always be able to open and edit the file using Illustrator. However, you'll also want to save your work in a format optimized for sharing. For this purpose, vector graphics are most often saved in PDF, SVG, or PNG file formats. Save the file as a PDF now. Choose File > Save As (**Shift-Command-S/Shift-Ctrl-S**) and then choose Adobe PDF from the Format menu (or in Windows, from the Save As Type menu) **(FIGURE 2.35)**. The next dialog box contains a lot of information about how the PDF will save, which is more thoroughly covered in Chapter 11, *The Grid*. For now, click the Save PDF button and view the two files in your folder. As described earlier in this chapter, you can use the same name on both files because the file extensions (which are, officially, part of the name) are different.

 **LAB CHALLENGE**

Find or take a photograph of an athlete, and develop a "tight" pencil illustration of their action or movement using the Pencil tool (or by exploring the Paintbrush tool) in Illustrator.

CHAPTER 3
MODIFY BASIC SHAPES

THE EXERCISES IN this chapter build upon the introduction to Section 1 by leading you to create complex graphic icons from the three basic forms: the circle, square, and triangle. You will use the Pen, Add Anchor Point, Convert Anchor Point, Direct Selection, and Reflection tools, and you will explore the Pathfinder panel.

Combining simple shapes to develop complex forms is a visual strategy employed by every illustrator or logo designer. As such, the three basic forms should be well understood as psychological tools. Rudolf Arnheim, a master of perceptual psychology, clearly articulates the dynamic nature of visual experiences. Arnheim noted that shape and form is perceived in relation to every other lived experience and the simultaneous visual play within a composition. Compositions include "interplay(s) of directed tensions" which can be read as "psychological 'forces'" [1]. So, as Johannes Itten, one of the select Basic Course teachers at the Weimar Bauhaus school, describes, "the character of the square is horizontal and vertical, that of the triangle, diagonal,

REFERENCE [1] Rudolf Arnheim, *Art and Visual Perception: A Psychology of the Creative Eye* (Berkeley: University of California Press, 1974), 11.

REFERENCE [2] Johannes Itten, *Design and Form: The Basic Course at the Bauhaus and Later* (London: John Wiley & Sons, 1975), 62.

REFERENCE [3] Itten, 62.

REMINDER When you read about the contrast between something that "is present" and something that "is not," you should be able to connect this idea to binary digital relationships (off/on, yes/no, present/hidden) as well as to the formal design property of figure/ground or positive and negative space.

and that of the circle circular" [2]. Each of these shapes can be harmonized or distressed by the horizontal, diagonal, or circular shape of the other. In Chapter 2, you learned to see how repeated lines are understood on a visual plane through shifting values and contrasting weights. In this chapter, you will work with basic forms, while the lines will simply represent the perimeter of an object, or the difference between where a shape is present and where it is not. You will notice how perception is influenced by the dynamic nature of shape relationships as you build your composite icons.

Because a shape is the culmination of a line that either curves or is angled back onto itself, it's no stretch of the imagination to follow a chapter study on lines with one on shapes. "To produce a work of art," writes Itten, "creative imagination should have many possibilities to draw on. To find the simplest and clearest form, the thinking, in terms of variations and combinations, must be developed by means of exercises" [3]. Logo designers sketch hundreds of designs before arriving at their final compositions (**FIGURES 3.1 AND 3.2**). In this chapter, you will work on two compositions, on separate artboards, by creating and modifying three basic shapes. However, the lab challenge encourages you to continue this practice. The more relationships between these basic forms you can see and develop, the clearer you will be able to see and think visually.

All complex shapes are created from the three basic forms. 2pxBorder, a web design firm in New Zealand, created a virtual kaleidoscope to mesmerize viewers who visit their "Kaleideolism" web project. In their "watermelon," "colored pencils," and "toolbox" kaleidoscopes, you can dynamically change

FIGURE 3.1 Logo/icon sketches by Ron Romain for MyShinyMonkey.com.

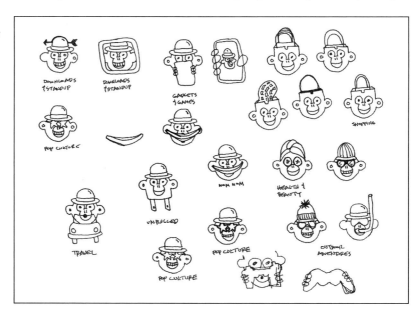

the relationship between the circles, squares, and triangles in a web browser (FIGURE 3.3).

The exercises in this chapter will result in your development of three complex shapes based on circle and rectangle relationships in Adobe Illustrator. You will then experiment with various modifications to the shapes that will result in the perception of recognizable graphic icons.

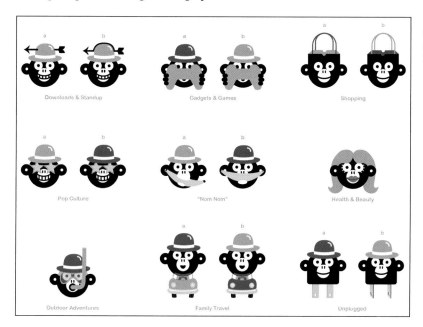

FIGURE 3.2 Final icons created by Ron Romain for MyShinyMonkey.com.

FIGURE 3.3 Screenshots from "Kaleideolism" by 2pxBorder. Dynamic relationships between circles, squares, and triangles are seen in this playful study of basic shapes. See kaleidolism.2pxborder.co.nz.

SIGNS AND LOGOS

Read more in Roland Barthes, *Elements of Semiology*, Trans. Annette Lavers and Colin Smith (NY: Hill and Wang, 1973) or *Mythologies*, Trans. Annette Lavers (NY: Farrar, Straus and Giroux, 1972).

When basic shapes are combined into simple forms they can create visual marks that are easy to remember. These forms act as visual signs to indicate a language-based idea. For instance, think about the graphic signs you might see while traveling, eating out, or attending a public event. Roland Barthes, a post-modern philosopher whose work in semiotics is applied to visual culture, posited that there are three types of signs: symbols, indexes, and icons. Symbolic signs stand in for an idea, indexical signs point to an idea, and icons are abstract forms that represent an idea. In the realm of graphic design, a successful logo might take any one of Barthes' formats. However, most logos are simple, abstract forms (more closely aligned with an iconic sign).

REFERENCE [4] David Airey, *Logo, Design, Love: A Guide to Creating Iconic Brand Identities* (Berkeley: New Riders, 2010), 22.

The first trademarked logo can be seen on the Bass Ale bottle: a red triangle in close proximity to the script-styled "Bass" (**FIGURE 3.4**). As David Airey writes in his book, *Logo Design Love*, "a truly enviable iconic design will also be simple, relevant, enduring, distinctive, memorable, and adaptable" [4]. Although this all may sound like a simple recipe, designing a logo to represent a company's brand that meets each of Airey's criteria is incredibly difficult. This chapter is a primer for artists who may seek further development on the study of logos, icons, mark-making, and graphic design.

FIGURE 3.4 The logo for Bass Ale (from the 1870s) was the first to achieve trademarked status. Denis Michaliov/ Alamy Stock Photo.

VECTOR CURVES

While you're modifying basic vector shapes in the following exercises, you'll notice that the straight paths are defined by anchor points and that curves are controlled by anchor points and Bezier handles. The handles allow you to control the Bezier curve, named for a French engineer who used them to design automobiles. You can move or reposition the anchor point at the midpoint of the curve with the Direct Selection tool and drag the end of the handle (there's one on each side of the midpoint) to lengthen or shorten it. The longer the handle, the softer (or smoother) the curve. Handles can also be repositioned with the Direct Selection tool to tweak the contour of a curve. If you're reading this without looking at a curve in Illustrator, it may seem abstract. You'll find Bezier handles a bit more intuitive after you modify some curves in Exercise 4.

WHAT YOU'LL NEED

Download the following source materials to complete the exercises in this chapter:

✔ The **chapter3-workfiles.zip** file contains one photograph in the **chapter3-start** folder (**icons.jpg**), showing icons on a pair of bathroom doors at a restaurant. It also contains the **chapter3-results** folder which holds samples of the composition that you'll create.

In these exercises, you will benefit from the ability to perceive simple shapes within complex forms.

FIGURE 3.5 These icons made for restroom doors combine basic shapes to represent the binary symbols for "Men" and "Women." Not a fan of binary representation? Me neither! The Lab Challenge is meant for you!

WHAT YOU'LL MAKE

As you work through the exercises in Chapter 3, you will practice seeing the relationship between forms in a photograph and derive iconic graphics from them using the Pathfinder panel (**FIGURE 3.5**). Your digital composition will contain two artboards showing the new shapes.

EXERCISE 1
CREATE A DOCUMENT WITH ONE ARTBOARD AND SET GUIDES

1. Create a new document in Adobe Illustrator as follows: Press **Command-N/ Ctrl-N**, or choose File > New Document. In the New Document dialog box, click to select the Print category. Choose Inches from the menu to the right of the Width value, then set the width and height to 8 by 3.5 inches (**FIGURE 3.6**). Click Create.

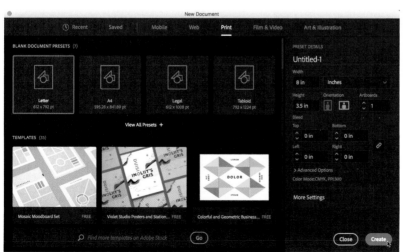

FIGURE 3.6 Select the Print category, and set the width and height to 8 by 3.5 inches.

WORKSPACE › ESSENTIALS CLASSIC Open Illustrator and set the workspace to Essentials Classic by choosing it from the menu in the Application bar or by choosing Window > Workspace > Essentials Classic.

FIGURE 3.7 Drag from the
left ruler onto the artboard
to create a guide.

2. Press **Command-R/Ctrl-R** to view the rulers, then drag a new guide away
   from the left ruler to the 1-inch mark at the top of the document. Drag
   a second guide from the left ruler to 5 inches. Guides will be placed to
   help you align your work evenly within the divisions created on the page
   (**FIGURE 3.7**). Guides are helpful visual aids, they will not appear in print.

GUIDES: HIDE, DELETE, AND MAKE THEM LESS SMART

Guides are helpful when you are aligning elements in a composition. However, sometimes they obscure your view of design elements. It's just as important to know how
and why to draw guides as it is to know how to hide or delete them. Both operations
can be carried out by choosing View > Guides. However, there are three things you
should know:

- The easiest way to hide and show guides is with the keyboard shortcut **Command-
  Semicolon (;)/Ctrl-Semicolon (;)**. Use this one command to hide guides then use it
  again to show them. Simple.

- Deleting guides can be annoying because, by default, Illustrator locks guides. So
  you will need to unlock your guides (View > Guides > Unlock Guides), then select
  a guide with the Selection tool and press the **Delete/Backspace** key on your
  keyboard.

- Smart Guides present alignment guides while you are working. In some situations
  this can be extremely helpful, while in others it is an annoyance. The keyboard
  command shortcut (or hot key) for Smart Guides is **Command-U/Ctrl-U**. It is one
  that is worth committing to memory!

3. Draw a circle, square, and triangle in the left margin of the document
   (between the left edge of the artboard and the guide set at 1 inch) using a
   fill and no stroke. I used a red fill, you can use any color.

FIGURE 3.8 The Delete Anchor Point tool is contained in a stack of tools under the Pen tool.

 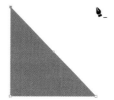

FIGURE 3.9 When an object is selected, its anchor points will be highlighted. Click an anchor point with the Delete Anchor Point tool to remove it, thereby changing the structure of the shape.

FIGURE 3.10 The Polygon tool is contained in a stack of tools with other basic shapes.

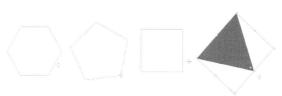

FIGURE 3.11 Drag to create a polygon, and notice the number of sides. While the mouse is depressed, pressing the Down Arrow key decreases the number of sides by one.

SHAPE TIP There are many ways to create a triangle. If you used the Pen tool, you made more clicks (and therefore more work for yourself!) than was necessary! Draw a square then use the Delete Anchor Point tool (**FIGURE 3.8**) to convert a four-point into a three-point shape by removing one of the four anchor points (**FIGURE 3.9**). You will probably have to reform your triangle using the Direct Selection tool. Alternatively, use the Polygon tool (**FIGURE 3.10**) to create a triangle by dragging to create a multi-sided shape, then (without releasing the button) press the Down Arrow key to reduce the number of sides of the shape. For instance, if it begins as a six-sided shape you will have to press the Down Arrow key three times (**FIGURE 3.11**).

4. Select all three shapes then choose Align To Selection from the Align To menu on the Control panel (**FIGURE 3.12**). Use the Align and Distribute buttons to center the three basic shapes along their vertical axes and distribute them evenly.

5. To group the three shapes so they can be aligned as one unit, select them then press **Command-G/Ctrl-G**. This time choose Align To Artboard from the Align To menu and click the Vertical Align Center button to center the grouped shapes between the top and bottom page margins.

FIGURE 3.12 The Align buttons will yield different results depending on how you set the Align To menu. Align these three shapes as they relate to each other by selecting them and choosing Align To Selection. Then use the Horizontal Align Center button to center them along a shared vertical axis.

6. Fill the background of the area
containing the three shapes.
Create a new rectangle and fill it
with a tint chosen from the Color
Guide panel (**FIGURE 3.13**). Set it
behind the three shapes, and
resize it so it is the height of the
artboard. Those three shapes will
be used to create more complicated forms while completing the
next exercises in this chapter.

7. Select the grouped shapes and
the fill that you placed behind
them. Choose Align To Selection
once again. Use the Align buttons
to center the grouped shapes in
the tinted background field.

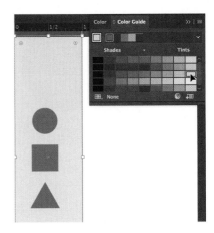

FIGURE 3.13 The Color Guide shows shades and
tints that relate to the colors visible on the
artboard.

ARRANGING THE STACKING ORDER OF PATHS IN ILLUSTRATOR

To change the stacking of elements on the page, select a path then choose one of
these commands from the Object menu > Arrange submenu. (The keyboard shortcuts
for arranging elements on the page are extremely handy):

- **Bring Forward** to move the object one level higher in the stack: **Command-]/Ctrl-]**

- **Bring To Front** to move the object to the top of the stack: **Command-Shift-]/
Ctrl-Shift-]**

- **Send Backward** to move the object one level lower in the stack: **Command-[/Ctrl-[**

- **Send To Back** to move the object all the way to the bottom of the stack:
Command-Shift-[/Ctrl-Shift-[

If you simply remember that positioning an element from front to back on the page
involves selecting the element and pressing some combination of Command-Bracket/
Ctrl-Bracket (adding Shift to go all the way), you can move items efficiently.

 COMBINING SHAPES

1. Select the group of shapes in the left margin, and press **Command-Shift-G/
Ctrl-Shift-G** to ungroup them. Click anywhere off of the group of shapes to
deselect them.

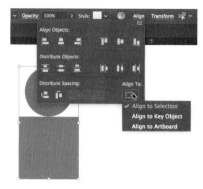

FIGURE 3.14 Choose Align To Selection before aligning the circle and square shapes.

FIGURE 3.15 Holding the Shift key as you resize a shape will constrain its proportions. Adding the Option/Alt key will resize the shape concentrically around its central anchor point. The second rectangle will scale down on top of the first because you pasted a new one in front of (or on top of) the original.

FIGURE 3.16 The new square is horizontally center-aligned and vertically bottom-aligned with the original red square.

2. Copy your circle into the middle section of the artboard. Scale the circle to about an inch for its width and height. You are now creating the graphic icon for the Men's room door in the photo.

3. Copy your square into the middle section of the artboard, and scale its width and height to about 1.25 inches. Place the circle above the square.

4. Select the circle and the square. Choose Align To Selection from the Align To menu, and center the circle and the square on the vertical axis (FIGURE 3.14).

   In Steps 5 through 9 you will make and use a new rectangle in order to cut the missing rectangular shape from the bottom of the square. I am going to demonstrate this process using a longer method than is technically necessary to show how I arrive at the size of the "hole" or the negative space in the final icon.

5. Select the square. Press **Command-C/Ctrl-C** to copy it, then press **Command-F/Ctrl-F** to paste its copy in front of the original square (directly on top of it); finally press **Option-Shift/Shift-Alt** as you drag to scale this new square down from its center point (FIGURE 3.15).

6. Before the square is deselected, change its fill color to any other color so you can see the new shape clearly (mine is cyan). Move the smaller square so it is in the bottom middle of the larger square (FIGURE 3.16).

7. Look closely at the negative space in the final icon; it is not a square. Its height is larger than its width. I estimate that it is about the size of a square plus half of the square's height. With that in mind, you could measure the smaller square and adjust its height in the Control panel. Instead, you will do this in a way that makes the measurement choices even more visually obvious. Select the smaller square with the Selection tool. Press **Command-C/Ctrl-C** to copy it, then press **Command-F/Ctrl-F** to paste it in front. While the second square is still selected, press Shift and the Up Arrow key to move the second small square above the first (**FIGURE 3.17**).

8. Create a guide by dragging from the ruler at the top of the artboard to the mid-point of the top square (**FIGURE 3.18**).

9. Use the Selection tool to drag the top edge of the square down so it aligns with the guide making the square into a rectangle (**FIGURE 3.19**).

10. Select both the original small square and the new rectangle. In the Pathfinder section of the Properties panel, click the Unite button to combine these two shapes (**FIGURE 3.20**). If you do not see the Pathfinder options in the lower-right side of the application window, choose Window > Pathfinder.

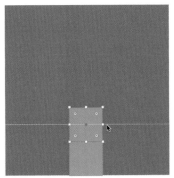

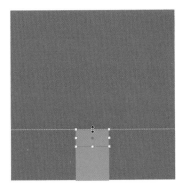

FIGURE 3.17 Place a copy of the small square on top of the first one.

FIGURE 3.18 Drag a guide to the middle of the top square to create a visual placeholder at half of the height of the square.

FIGURE 3.19 Drag the top edge of the square down to align it with the guide.

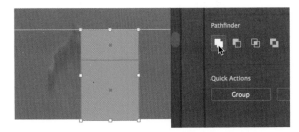

FIGURE 3.20 Hover your mouse over the various buttons in the Pathfinder area of the Properties panel to see different ways to combine shapes. Uniting two shapes converges them into one path. Grouping shapes makes multiple paths "hold hands," but keeps their individual path properties. When you want to treat two or more paths as if they are one shape (for instance, to make them one color or to change their overall contour), they should be united rather than grouped.

FIGURE 3.21 The Minus Front button extracts one shape from another. This is especially helpful when you want the negative space to preserve transparency or opacity of one of the objects.

11. Select the small, united rectangle and the large, red square, then center them using the Horizontal Align Center button.

12. With the smaller rectangle and larger square selected, click Minus Front in the Pathfinder section of the Properties panel (**FIGURE 3.21**).

    Minus Front excludes the top selection from the shape it covers. So in this case, the smaller rectangle will become the negative space cut away from the larger square.

13. Finally, center the two shapes that comprise the body and the head, and unite them using the Pathfinder panel.

DISAPPEARING PATHFINDER If Pathfinder went missing from the Properties panel, you may not have two paths selected.

EXERCISE 3 DUPLICATE THE ARTBOARD AND ADD ANCHOR POINTS

Because you will use the Option/Alt-drag key combination to duplicate the artboard, you will want to see a lot of space in the application window before making a copy. Zoom out if you need to by pressing the **Command-Minus/ Ctrl-Minus** keys or use the Zoom tool while pressing the Option/Alt key.

1. Use the Artboard tool to see the specifications of the current artboard in the Control panel. Hold the Option/Alt and Shift keys as you drag a new page beneath the current artboard (**FIGURE 3.22**).

2. Rename the artboard **Artboard 2** in the Control panel (**FIGURE 3.23**). Click the Selection tool to return to editing your document. Complete steps 3–9 on the second artboard in your Illustrator document.

COPYING TIP You can Option/Alt-drag the new artboard to the top, right, bottom, or left of the original. Always use the Shift key to constrain the alignment of artboards, paths, and objects.

FIGURE 3.22 Duplicate the artboard with the Artboard tool by Option-Shift/Shift-Alt-dragging.

FIGURE 3.23 Rename the artboard in the Control panel.

3. In the second artboard, select the body and head and ungroup them (**Shift-Command-G/Shift-Ctrl-G**). Delete the body. Copy the triangle from your set of basic shapes in the left margin to the body area to make the female icon.

4. Scale the triangle so it is a little larger than the head, and center align the two shapes.

When you placed the image it probably landed on top of the shapes you drew. Send the image to the back by selecting it and choosing Object > Arrange or pressing the keyboard shortcut, **Shift-Command-[/Shift-Ctrl-[**.

5. Choose File > Place to insert **icons.jpg**, the photograph of the doors with the icons, onto the artboard. Arrange it so it is behind the vector graphics (like a template), and scale the image so the female icon appears in the middle section of the document (**FIGURE 3.24**).

In the next steps, you will modify a basic shape (a triangle) into a complex, organic form (a pigtail).

6. Copy the triangle from the left set of basic shapes, and paste it on top of one of the pigtails. Because my triangle is red and the icon is red, I will change my vector art to cyan so it is easy to see my shapes when they are on top of the original image. You can make the hair on the left side of the head or the right side, then duplicate and reflect your work. I will demonstrate this by working on the right pigtail first. Rotate the triangle so it seems to point in the direction of the pigtail (**FIGURE 3.25**).

FIGURE 3.24 Place the image of the door icons behind the vector shapes.

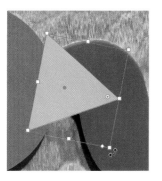

FIGURE 3.25 Adjust the triangle so it gestures towards the new shape you will make. You are converting a basic shape into one that is much more organic. Work in small steps during this conversion process.

FIGURE 3.26 Use the Direct Selection tool to reposition the anchor point and lengthen the sides of the triangle.

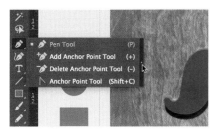

FIGURE 3.27 The set of tools related to the Pen tool can be detached from the Tools panel by clicking the right-facing arrow.

FIGURE 3.28 Once the Pen tools float in their own panel, you can move them so they are close to where you are working in the artboard.

7. Deselect the triangle, then use the Direct Selection tool to click the anchor point nearest the end of the pigtail and stretch it so it is at the curve closest to the margin (FIGURE 3.26).

8. Expand the Pen tools by clicking the triangle icon to the right of the tools (FIGURE 3.27), and move the free-floating panel of Pen tools close to your pigtail/work area (FIGURE 3.28).

9. Prepare this basic shape for the addition of curves by adding anchor points to its path where you will insert the curves of the pigtail. Add four anchor points by clicking the path of the triangle with the Add Anchor Point tool. Click the places (approximately) where the curve of the pigtail changes (**FIGURE 3.29**). Be sure to click directly on the path of the triangle—if you mis-click you will see a warning message.

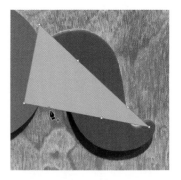

FIGURE 3.29 Add four additional anchor points on the two longer sides of the triangle. You can always reposition these anchor points using the Direct Selection tool as you work.

 ## EXERCISE 4 — CONVERT ANCHOR POINTS FROM STRAIGHT EDGES TO CURVES

1. A straight line can only become a curve if there is an anchor point indicating its direction with Bezier handles. With the Direct Selection tool, drag the four new anchor points made in Step 9 of Exercise 3 so they sit along the contour of the image of the pigtail in places where the line changes direction, often between two curves or in the middle of a curve (**FIGURE 3.30**).

2. Because you started with a shape made of angles, additional anchor points add hard angles and edges to the shape until they are further modified with the Convert Anchor Point tool (the tool at the far right of the Pen tools palette). Use the Convert Anchor Point tool to change the hard edges of the four new anchor points to curves by placing the mouse pointer over each one and dragging slightly away from it (**FIGURE 3.31**). You will have to start to drag directly on the anchor point in order to modify it with the Convert Anchor Point tool. The direction that you drag the mouse influences the curve of the path—if you find the path getting "tangled" into itself, drag the mouse in the opposite direction! You are gesturing towards the shape of the pigtail as the basic triangle become more pigtail-like, but it needs more work.

You can alter the order of the last two steps. Instead of using the Direct Selection tool to push the anchor points along the contour before adding the curves with the Convert Anchor Point tool, you can convert the anchor points before moving them. New learners have a better view and understanding of the process when it is made visible.

3. Each curve is governed by the Bezier handles that extend outward from its anchor point. Complete the pigtail by using the Direct Selection tool to move the position of the anchor points and the Bezier handles. Try to make your illustration match the image (**FIGURE 3.32**).

FIGURE 3.30 Push the anchor points near the curves. You will still see hard edges. You are slowly gesturing towards a new shape.

FIGURE 3.31 Change the hard-edged anchor points to curves by dragging on the anchor point with the Convert Anchor Point tool.

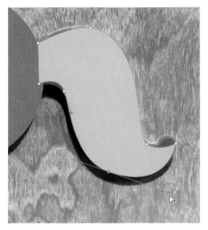

FIGURE 3.32 Change each curve by modifying the Bezier handles associated with it using the Direct Selection tool. Pushing a handle in close to an anchor point steepens its incline, while pulling it far away from the anchor point produces a more gentle curve.

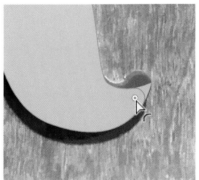

FIGURE 3.33 Drag the Live Corner widget to modify all of the corners of a shape so they are rounded.

4. In the image, the tip of the pigtail is rounded; however, in the vector shape it comes to a point. To modify this anchor point, start by choosing the Direct Selection tool and clicking the shape to select it. Live Corner widgets appear at each corner point. Drag the Live Corner widget nearest the tip of the pigtail inwards, away from the point (FIGURE 3.33). All three of the angles are rounded. You will hide the two near the head by moving them behind the circle.

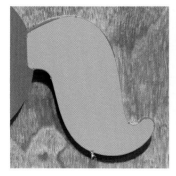
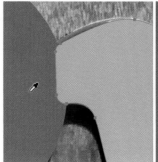
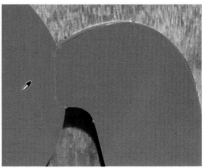

FIGURE 3.34 Make final shape adjustments by modifying anchor points and Bezier handles with the Direct Selection tool.

FIGURE 3.35 Use the Eyedropper tool to sample a color that is already in use on your artboard and apply it to a selected path.

5. Use the Direct Selection tool to move the anchor points of the rounded tip of the pigtail into position. You will have to modify the anchor points and the Bezier handles to make the shape align on top of the image (**FIGURE 3.34**).

6. Finally, if you are working with a shape that is not red, change its color to the same red used for the head and body by selecting the shape with the Selection tool then clicking the red head or body with the Eyedropper tool (**FIGURE 3.35**).

SCREENCAST 3-1 MODIFY PATHS WITH THE PEN AND DIRECT SELECTION TOOLS

The Pen and its related tools can be difficult to master. Working with anchor points is not as intuitive as drawing with a pen (perhaps the tool is misnamed). In this online extra the author demonstrates adding and modifying anchor points and Bezier handles.

All screencasts are available on the companion website, www.digitalart-design.com, or on the Vimeo playlist, bit.ly/foundations-demos.

 EXERCISE 5 REFLECT AND COPY A SHAPE

1. Use the Selection tool to select the pigtail shape. Select the Reflect tool in the Tools panel. It hides beneath the Rotate tool so you may need to press and hold the mouse on the Rotate tool before dragging to select the Reflect tool (**FIGURE 3.36**).

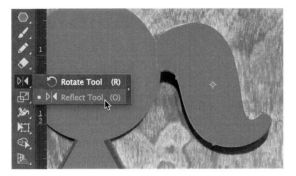

FIGURE 3.36 Select the Reflect tool. You will use this tool in a unique way: by double-clicking the tool in the Tools panel.

FIGURE 3.37 Reflect the image across a vertical axis. Be sure to click the Copy button.

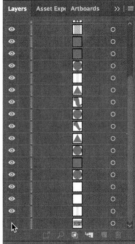

FIGURE 3.38 Clicking the eyeball icon associated with a sublayer (Illustrator) or a layer (Photoshop) is a common method for making artwork visible or invisible. Remember how you made a shape by leaving some of the dots invisible and the remaining dots visible in the Chapter 1 exercises? This issue of visibility is native to digital art and design. Sometimes creativity is inspired by subtractive efforts.

2. Double-click the Reflect tool in the Tools panel. In the Reflect dialog box, check the Vertical radio button, make sure the angle is set to 90 degrees (the default) and click the Copy button (FIGURE 3.37). Because you are making a copy, the second pigtail will appear; however, it may be misplaced.

3. Hold the Shift key as you move the pigtail into position using the Selection tool.

4. In the Layers panel, click the eyeball icon next to the image of the bathroom door to make it invisible. Now you should see the iconic shape you made without the image of the door that you used as a guide (FIGURE 3.38).

EXERCISE 6 · SAVE A MULTI-PAGE PDF

1. Save the master (.ai) file. Next you will save the same file as a PDF—this is a two-step process.

2. Choose File > Save As, and choose Adobe PDF (pdf) from the Format menu (macOS) or choose Illustrator PDF (*PDF) from the Save As Type menu (Windows). Notice that you can save a range of pages because the document contains multiple artboards. Leave the default radio button for All selected; you will want to see both pages in your PDF (FIGURE 3.39). Click the Save button.

3. In the Save Adobe PDF dialog box, choose Marks And Bleeds from the left side menu. In the Marks section of the dialog box, check the box next to Trim Marks (FIGURE 3.40). Click the Save PDF button.

FIGURE 3.39 Be sure to save all of the pages in the file in Adobe PDF format.

FIGURE 3.40 Apply trim marks in the Save Adobe PDF dialog window.

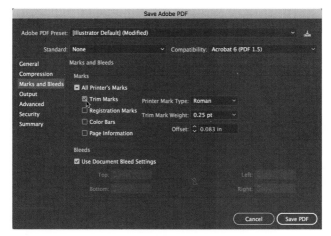

4. Open the PDF to see your icons appear on two pages, demonstrating the exercises in this chapter. In the future, you might use this technique to create a multi-page document demonstrating several compositions for one project, different stages of an interactive work, or frames of an animation. Notice the trim marks in your PDF (**FIGURE 3.41**). When you print the file you can use the trim marks as guides while cutting the print from the standard printing paper size, such as 8.5 by 11 inches, to the size you specified in your Illustrator file: 3.5 by 8 inches.

5. If a printer is accessible to you, print the document and cut it to size. Use an X-Acto knife and a ruler to be precise. Mat board cutters are very tempting. I have made more mistakes with mat board cutters, however, than I have with an X-Acto and a ruler.

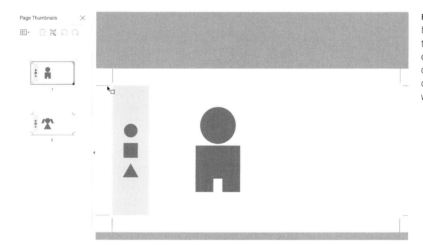

FIGURE 3.41 In Adobe Acrobat Reader you will see the trim marks saved in your document—they appear as cross-hairs or guides you can use to trim the page when it is printed.

 LAB CHALLENGE

Collage photographic elements with these icons to personalize them in the third section of the artboard. For instance, add your hair, glasses, jewelry, or clothing item to the icon. Try to use the photographic imagery as a template while you create icons by modifying basic shapes using the Pen tools. Alternatively, consider making an icon for a gender-neutral bathroom or a gender-inclusive bathroom. What would such an icon look like, and how would you use basic shapes to create it?

FIGURE S2.1 In Santa Monica, California, you can walk into a room-sized camera obscura to see a view of the Santa Monica pier projected onto a disk. The top image portrays the room's ceiling, where the lens in the roof collects light that's projected onto the disk beneath it via carefully positioned mirrors.

SECTION 2
DIGITAL PHOTOGRAPHY

THE GREEK ROOTS of the word photography loosely translate to "drawing with light." In this sense, digital photography is no different than photography using analog methods, but of course the digital camera lets you save files rather than negatives and create prints without a wet lab. Photography developed as an art form at the intersection of the sciences and technology. The camera obscura (FIGURE S2.1), a forerunner of the camera we know today, was a dark room that projected a scene onto its wall as a result of distributing light through a hole in the building (or later, a box). It was used as a drawing aid by such Renaissance artists as Leonardo da Vinci.

Kodak developed the Brownie camera, one of the first snapshot technologies in the early 1900s. As the company's advertisement demonstrates (FIGURE S2.2), it was so easy to use that even a woman could operate the device (sarcasm intended in my interpretation). Digital art and design students have access to a broad range of tools. Some use a digital single lens reflex camera (DSLR), while others primarily rely on a smartphone camera to create their imagery.

FIGURE S2.2 An original advertisement for Kodak's Brownie camera. Adjusted for expected inflation in 2019, the cost for each camera was approximately $30. Shawshots / Alamy Stock Photo.

This section will heighten an artist's or designer's awareness of the digital photographic image, regardless of the capturing device used. The process of creating a photograph is nearly the opposite of the process of creating vector illustrations (reviewed in the first section of this book). For instance, when you begin to create a vector illustration, you start with a blank page (or a white Adobe Illustrator artboard). Vector illustration is an additive process—you add dots, lines, or shapes to the composition. Photography necessitates a process of selective reduction. Instead of adding to the empty canvas, photographers frame their surroundings to capture just the right moment in time. Compositional design elements are still active within the frame, but technological components relating to the camera—we might call this the "hardware"—play a large role in the resulting image. The chapters in this section will help you understand the interplay between composition and lighting by first teaching you the mechanics of your digital camera and then by explaining how to identify the compositional attributes that apply specifically to the photographic

frame and how to adjust the digital histogram that renders the tonal scale within the image.

Of course, photographs (digitized by the camera or the scanner) are made of pixels, and you'll edit or manipulate pixels in Adobe Photoshop. If you're new to pixel-based imagery, this section of the book may be your first experience with bitmap images. It would be convenient if I could assert that the pixel is to the digital photograph what the anchor point is to the vector illustration, but that just isn't accurate. The two systems of image construction are so different that an analogy is not possible. A pixel is a single unit of color, sampled from the original image. If the bitmap image is created with a digital camera, then each pixel is sampled from the scene at the time of the photograph, according to the specific lighting conditions and camera settings. If a bitmap image is created by scanning a print, then the pixel is a sample taken at the time of scanning according to the input specifications in the scanner software. Pixels are finite. You can resample pixels, and there are ways you can add pixels to a document, but for most people who operate some version of Photoshop and want to print on their home inkjet printer, you'll have only as many pixels as were sampled at the time the bitmap image was created. This means that unlike vector art, bitmap images are not infinitely scalable.

In the mid-twentieth century, Ansel Adams developed the famous zone system with Fred Archer: an 11-step scale (counting step zero) to delineate, pre-visualize, and understand the relationship between the luminance of the scene, the density values of the negative, and the final printed image. Using Roman numerals to avoid confusion with so many other numbers on the camera, the scale starts at Zone 0, a black part of a photograph with no texture or image details. It ends at Zone X (ten) where white appears in the print with no texture. The middle point, Zone V (five), is considered middle gray, though it's about an 18% gray value. (When we review the zone system for digital photographers, you'll learn that this percentage decreases a bit.) Although the zone system directly helps photographers with the craft of printing, and although "negative densities" may not seem relevant to digital images, understanding the zone system will help you see what Adams describes as a "practical interpretation of sensitometry" [1]. Because the zone system is so specifically related to value, I've included a study of an adapted zone system for digital photographers in Chapter 5, *Resolution and Value.*

Contemporary artists continue to use the zone system as a method for understanding the values and tonal range in a photographic image. Terry Flaxton's *In Re Ansel Adams* was created in homage to one of Adams's seminal photographic images—the resolution of the digital image is more robust than the tonal range in the original print (FIGURE S2.3). Add the movement of the video and the soundtrack of the waterfall, and the scene comes to life (FIGURE S2.4).

The exercises in Chapter 4, *Creating and Organizing Digital Photographs,* will teach you to use settings that might be available on your digital camera. You'll also learn to organize your files using Adobe Bridge, which can be especially helpful as you're editing the many photographs you'll take while exploring your camera.

REFERENCE [1] Ansel Adams, *Camera and Lens* (New York: Morgan & Morgan, 1970), 22. If you really love it, you can check out Adams's series, *The Camera, The Negative,* and *The Print.* The zone system is most thoroughly explicated in *The Negative.*

The exercises in Chapter 5 will help you learn to see the zone system in a digital photograph. You'll understand the image's histogram and learn to modify the tonal range to increase the contrast of the composition.

FIGURE S2.3 Terry Flaxton
operates a high-resolution
camera during the making
of his *In Re Ansel Adams*.

FIGURE S2.4 Scenes from
In Re Ansel Adams.
You can view Terry
Flaxton's complete video
at www.seditionart.
com/terry-flaxton/
in-re-ansel-adams.

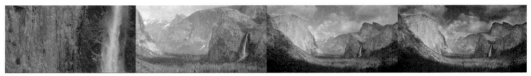

The exercises in Chapter 6, *Color Models*, will
help you understand
essential properties of
color, including harmony,
contrast, and digital
color modes.

In the days of analog photography, working in color was vastly different from shooting, processing, and printing with black-and-white film. For most photographers, working in color implied that they were unable to process their own film and necessitated the use of a color lab for printing. This was not nearly as affordable as a black-and-white darkroom you could rig in your home. Shifting to color typically changed the experience for the photographer from working in solitude with complete control over film processing to working in a shared lab with far less control over film processing. The digital camera, especially the DSLR, has mostly returned photographers to solitude (if they wish to work in this manner), where post-production takes place on a home computer. Shooting in color, from the perspective of processing, is the same as shooting in black and white—in both situations, you will "process" the images on your computer. Color is a basic design element that should be learned alongside value. In the chapters ahead, you'll study color with bitmap images, although the same principles of color apply to vector graphics.

REFERENCE [2] Adams,
Foreword to *Camera
and Lens*.

LINK The Masters of
Photography website, www.
masters-of-photography.
com, provides a substantial
introduction to historically
relevant photographers of
the twentieth century.

In these three chapters, you'll work with the foundation elements of digital photography—the photographic image, value, and color—and you'll be encouraged to think about the relationship between these design elements and digital technologies. As Ansel Adams wrote, "With photography we touch the domains of science, illustration, documentation, and expressible art" [2]. Keep the lessons of the first three chapters in mind, too. You'll continue to see dots (maybe in the form of pixels), lines, and relationships between shapes while you're interpreting value and composing with the rule of thirds.

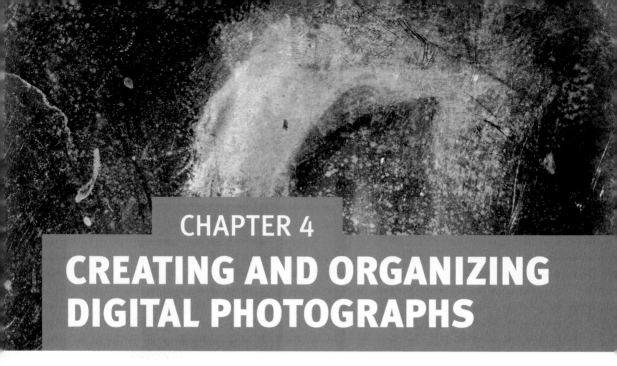

CHAPTER 4
CREATING AND ORGANIZING DIGITAL PHOTOGRAPHS

THE EXERCISES IN this chapter will explain the camera mechanics involved in creating a photograph and demonstrate how to organize, rename, and set up a digital "contact sheet" via a PDF of your images. You'll explore your camera and use your files or those from the companion website to learn some of the best file management tools available in Adobe Bridge.

Light is essential for creating a photographic image. How the light is measured and captured in the camera will affect the resulting image. In this chapter, you'll learn to control how much light is rendered in your "light drawing" or photograph. In the following chapters, you'll learn to compose within the frame of the viewfinder and to adjust the tonal range during the post-production process. Because outdoor light is a direct product of the sun and moon, the amount of natural light in a photograph also relates to the time of day. Conceptually, time, considered as both duration and as the shift in lighting as day passes to night, is a rich theme for photographers and artists to explore and

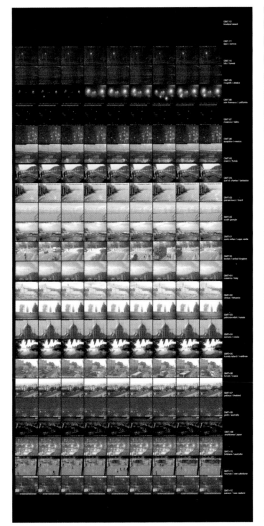

FIGURE 4.1 Thomson & Craighead, *Horizon*, 2009. Screen view, Dundee Contemporary Arts. Image provided courtesy of the artists.

FIGURE 4.2 Thomson & Craighead, *Horizon*, 2009. Installation view, Dundee Contemporary Arts. Image provided courtesy of the artists.

interpret. The new media artist duo Thomson and Craighead (Jon Thomson and Alison Craighead) created an installation titled *Horizon* that displays a representation of the time at one specific location—the horizon (FIGURES 4.1 AND 4.2). On their website, they write:

REFERENCE [1] See thomson-craighead.net/horizon.html

Horizon is a narrative clock made out of images accessed in real time from webcams found in every time zone around the world. The result is a constantly updating array of images that read like a series of movie storyboards, but also as an idiosyncratic global electronic sundial [1].

Your camera may offer you anything from no control over the way light is registered on the digital sensor (which is ultimately responsible for the resulting image file) to complete control in manual mode. Some of the information in the Camera Mechanics exercise won't apply to your situation if you're using a point-and-shoot camera or a mobile device. However, most of my students have access to consumer- or prosumer-level (not quite professional but a step above the consumer level) digital cameras and many have digital single lens reflex (DSLR) cameras. This range offers the photographer some degree of control.

FIGURE 4.3 Harrod Blank, *Camera Van*, 1995 and ongoing. www.cameravan.com. Photo by Hunter Mann.

Photography began as a technical and scientific pursuit of creative and documentary expression. The pervasive nature of digital cameras makes it difficult for some people to conceive of the craft as specialized. For many, the camera is just another gadget. Harrod Blank's *Camera Van* (FIGURE 4.3) includes one of every Polaroid camera ever made along its front grill, and that's just the beginning. The word "SMILE" is printed across the top of the van, each letter formed of Kodak Instamatic cameras (FIGURE 4.4). On the driver's side, a camera-mural of the Kodak Instamatic is made of mounted Instamatics. Do they work? Yes, they do! Screens display photos taken with the van (FIGURE 4.5). Blank showcases image galleries for each set of audiences he's driven past in *Camera Van* (FIGURE 4.6). After learning of the many ways to control the production of a single photographic image, even skeptics should agree that the craft is as rich and complicated today as it was in the days of glass negatives.

FIGURE 4.4 Harrod Blank, *Camera Van*. www.cameravan.com.

FIGURE 4.5 Harrod Blank, *Camera Van*. www.cameravan.com.

FIGURE 4.6 Harrod Blank, *Soy Bean Farmer*, MN. Photograph created by *Camera Van*.

MEASURING LIGHT

PHOTOGRAPHIC VALUES
The zone system for understanding value shifts across the image is more thoroughly covered in Chapter 5, *Resolution and Value*.

The amount of light required to make a photograph is measured with a meter. In the predigital era, some SLR cameras had built-in light meters, while large-format cameras did not. External light meters are still used today in photography studios. Digital cameras include a built-in light meter. The light meter registers the amount of light that's either in the center of the frame, averaged throughout the frame, or—for some cameras with the "spot" option—at a specific location within the frame. Understanding how to adjust your camera settings to comply with the light meter specifications requires you to understand the role of your camera's *f-stop* (which governs the diameter of the aperture) and *shutter speed* (which controls the duration of the shutter release) controls. The light meter reading will show you how much light will be required to make a legible exposure for a balanced combination of f-stop and shutter speed settings (you'll learn more in Exercise 1). Generally, the purpose of your exposure will be to present details at the extreme areas of contrast in the image. That means you'll want to capture details in the highlights and details in the shadows.

If you're shooting in automatic mode or can't control these settings, you'll simply point and shoot, and then hope for the best. Be careful when composing images in high-contrast lighting situations. Avoid shooting at or near noon, when the sun and shadows are strongest. And avoid low-light situations.

If you're working in manual mode, once you know how much light you need, balance the f-stop and shutter speed settings. Your choices about these two settings will depend on the depth of field (in the case of aperture) and movement (shutter speed) you want to include.

Some cameras let you create photographs in *aperture priority* or *shutter speed priority* modes. This means you can choose which of those two features you want to control. The camera will set the opposing lighting variable according to the choice you make.

RULE OF THIRDS

In addition to your camera setting choices, you'll be making decisions while creating a composition. As you can imagine, there are a lot of technical and aesthetic choices to make while creating powerful photographic imagery. In Exercise 5, you'll learn to see the compositional space using crop guides that make visible the *rule of thirds*. This is a common way to understand the photographic frame, which is most often a two-dimensional environment with

FIGURE 4.7 An image composed adhering to the rule of thirds.

GET CLOSER AND WATCH THE EDGES

Additional advice that I offer to new students is not specified by the rule of thirds, but it is important:

- Get closer. By that I mean physically move your body and your camera closer to your subject.

- Watch the edges of the frame. The viewer shouldn't be left in no-man's-land at the edges of the frame. Be conscious about using the full frame to tell your visual story.

a 3:2 ratio. (4:3 and 16:9 are also common ratios among a variety of digital media.) The premise of the rule of thirds is to evenly divide the frame by two horizontal and two vertical lines before composing the subject matter along the intersections of those guides (**FIGURE 4.7**).

One desired result of the rule of thirds is the elimination of the number one newbie mistake: centering the subject in the middle of the frame. You'll also start to see and weigh the visual balance of your subject matter by thirds, bringing more tension and energy to the overall composition. The more you're aware of the compositional space, the more likely you'll be to create a composition that leads the eye to your desired focal point.

RATIOS A ratio is a relationship between pairs of numbers. For instance, if you're cooking rice at a 1:2 ratio with water, you add one part of rice to the pot for every two parts of water. Instead of instructing someone to cook one cup of rice with two cups of water, telling them the ratio of rice to water allows them to scale the recipe to a variety of amounts.

ADOBE BRIDGE

Admittedly, when Bridge was first released for Adobe Creative Suite 2, it was not terribly user-friendly. I didn't use it. My students didn't use it. No one I knew used it. We might have tried it a few times, but it just didn't seem worth the effort. After several revisions, Bridge has become an organizational tool that is absolutely worth learning. Bridge was primarily developed to allow you to organize and view file information relating to all the various types of files you generate using Creative Cloud.

WHAT YOU'LL NEED

Download the following source materials to complete the exercises in this chapter:

✔ The **chapter04-workfiles.zip** file which contains the files you need in the **batch-rename** and **rule-of-thirds** subfolders inside the **chapter04-start** folder. The file also contains the **chapter04-results** folder.

You'll begin the exercises in this chapter by exploring your digital camera.

WHAT YOU'LL MAKE

In the exercises for this chapter, you'll organize your digital photographs in Bridge and create a PDF that showcases a series of images (FIGURE 4.8). This serves the same purpose as and looks similar to the contact sheets that photographers have used for decades. Your PDF will contain images, and it will display your file naming system.

In the following exercises, you'll learn how to rename a folder of files, label (or rate) your files, and generate a contact sheet in a PDF, all at the click of a button. In Chapter 16, *Automation*, you'll use Bridge to apply Photoshop actions.

FIGURE 4.8 Completed PDF contact sheet created in Chapter 4 exercises.

 CAMERA MECHANICS

There's an app for that: If you are shooting with your smartphone, consider installing an app such as VSCO (IOS) or Manual Camera Lite: DSLR Camera Professional (Android). Both allow you to adjust the focus and exposure manually.

Basic operations take place when you create a photograph with your digital camera. If your camera gives you control over them, you may be able to adjust many settings that will have a direct result on the aesthetics of the resulting photograph. Most cameras also have an automatic setting, which lets you simply point and shoot. Even if you're just pressing the shutter button, each of the following steps takes place. Details about each step are included in Exercise 2.

• Before shooting, consider adjusting the white balance, ISO, and file size settings. Or, just let the camera do that work for you. (Your camera might not allow you to control some of these settings.)

• Frame a scene by placing your eye to the viewfinder or by peering at the LCD screen on the back of the camera. Many DSLRs don't allow use of the LCD during shooting. If you have both options, consider the pros and cons of each (TABLE 4.1).

LCD VERSUS VIEWFINDER: WHERE SHOULD YOU LOOK WHILE FRAMING A PHOTOGRAPH?

This choice is dictated by personal preference and limitations presented by the type of camera you're using. When using my DSLR, I always use the viewfinder. However, on my iPhone, I'm forced to use the LCD.

LCD	VIEWFINDER
Accurately represents the framed image space.	Can be slightly inaccurate in consumer cameras due to what is called *parallax* as the viewfinder location is slightly above and to the left of the lens.
Can lead to instability: Because you hold the camera away from your face to see through the viewfinder, the camera is less stable than it would be if you were holding it closer to your balanced body.	Often leads to greater stability: You hold the camera to your face while making the photograph. Remember to square your hips and be still while you shoot.
Drains battery power.	No extra battery power is required for composing through the viewfinder.

TABLE 4.1

- After the image is framed, decide whether to shoot in automatic or manual mode. Do you want the camera to control the amount of light on the sensor, or do you want to control it by balancing the relationship between the f-stop (the diameter of the aperture) and the shutter speed (the quickness of the shutter release)? You'll learn more about f-stop and shutter speed settings in the next step.

- Press the shutter release button. Hold the camera tightly and try to eliminate body movement.

- The shutter will open, and the aperture will enlarge or decrease according to the f-stop settings.

- Light will be recorded on the digital sensor.

- The shutter will close after time has elapsed indicated by the shutter speed settings.

- You can preview your image immediately as it is saved on a memory card.

 CAMERA SETTINGS

The following items are elements you might be able to control when making a photograph. All digital cameras have different user interfaces. I've indicated where these items typically appear on the cameras I've seen in my classroom. Yours might be different. The best thing to do is read your camera's manual, or at least view the page containing the illustration of the camera and its settings! Did you lose it (or throw it away with the box)? Most manuals can be downloaded from the manufacturer's website.

- **File Size, Compression, and/or File Format.** These typically appear in the camera menu or function area.

  Even if your camera isn't terribly fancy, you may have a choice of creating small, medium, or large images, or you might even have a specific set of resolutions, via pixel dimensions or megabytes, to choose from in the File or Camera menu.

  You also might be able to choose to shoot in JPG, HEIC, TIFF, or even RAW mode. Shooting in RAW mode yields the most information and adaptability, but processing a RAW image is outside the scope of this book. (There are plenty of books that deal specifically with Camera RAW, and I encourage photography students to become familiar with these details.) If you can choose between shooting in JPG or TIFF modes, you should know that the JPG will be more compressed (and usually a smaller file size) than the TIFF.

- **ISO**. ISO typically appears in the Camera or Function menu.

  The ISO rating is analogous to what was once referred to as the film speed. Silver nitrate is the light-sensitive chemical found in film. The amount of silver in the film stock directly correlates to its ISO rating.

  - **Low ISO**. A low ISO rating (25 or 50 in special films; 100 or 200 in the kind of film you can purchase at the drug store) indicates that there's little silver nitrate in the film. This in turn means that you'll need a lot of light in order to register the image on the film. If you're shooting outside on a bright day, set the ISO to a low setting. What's the advantage of using a super low ISO setting? In the film world, you'll see less film grain in the resulting print. In the digital world, the same rule applies—though we'll just call the film grain *digital noise*. If you're shooting in a studio and you want to create a high-quality print devoid of noise, use the lowest ISO your camera offers and set up plenty of lights.

  - **High ISO.** A high ISO rating (800, 1600, or 3200 in special films; 400 in common film stocks) indicates that there's a large quantity of silver nitrate in the film. This in turn means that you'll need little light in order to register the image on the film. If you're shooting indoors, in the late evening, or at night, you'll probably need to set the ISO to a high setting. The advantages of using a high ISO setting are that you have greater flexibility in low-light situations. However, you'll see the grain of the film or some digital noise in your files (FIGURE 4.9).

FIGURE 4.9 Although high ISO settings make it possible to create images in low light, they often result in digital noise. Photograph by Thomas Van Deusen.

- **White Balance**. Along with ISO, this typically appears in the camera or function menu.

  Setting the white balance on your camera, if you're able, will ensure that the whites appear as a true white, and that the rest of the colors in the spectrum of the photographs are not the victims of a nasty *color cast*, such as the overall blue or orange tinge seen in **FIGURE 4.10**.

  The following are typical (self-evident) setting labels or icons you might find in a menu or function area. Match the white balance lighting to your situation: Auto (A-WB), Daylight (sunshine icon), Cloudy (cloud icon), Tungsten (lightbulb icon), and Night (moon or flash icon).

- **Aperture.** If you can control the aperture, you'll typically do so with a dial or button near the top of the camera body.

FIGURE 4.10 Three photographs of the same scene made in natural daylight demonstrate the results of different white balance settings. If the white balance setting on the camera does not match the situation, the result may be an unpleasant color cast.

The trick is to remember that the f-stop is a ratio, which means that the f-stop number you select on your camera refers to the denominator of a fraction where the numerator is 1. There is an inverse relationship between the size of the number and the size of the aperture opening. A small denominator corresponds to a big ratio (or a wide aperture).

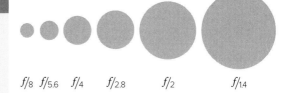

f/8 f/5.6 f/4 f/2.8 f/2 f/1.4

FIGURE 4.11 This illustration demonstrates increasing aperture sizes.

The *aperture* is the size of the opening that light travels through the lens to the digital sensor. The wider the aperture opens, the more light you'll send to the digital sensor; of course, the inverse is true, too **(FIGURE 4.11)**. The aperture's diameter size is controlled by the *f-stop*. Here's the tricky part: the smaller the f-stop number, the wider the aperture is open.

- **Depth of Field.** When the aperture is wide open (for example, *f*/2) the resulting image has a small area of focus; a large f-number (for example, *f*/22) generates a large area of focus in the image. Photographers refer to this optical phenomenon as *depth of field*. Shallow depth of field is created with lower f-stop numbers **(FIGURE 4.12)**, while greater depth of field is seen in photographs made with larger f-stop numbers **(FIGURE 4.13)**. Figures 4.12 and 4.13 showcase the results of using lower and higher f-stop values and the types of visual situations where one is preferred to the other.

FIGURE 4.12 Lauren Thompson, *Snow White* series, 2012. In this image, a low f-stop was used to create shallow depth of field. The focus on the figure's face contrasts with the blurriness of the tree branches she stands behind.

FIGURE 4.13 (RIGHT) Tracey Cole, 2012. In this photograph, a high f-stop is used to capture the details in the glass object.

FIGURE 4.14 Ashley Tingley, *Untitled*, 2012. Photographs captured at a fast shutter speed appear to freeze time.

FIGURE 4.15 David Le, *Untitled*, 2012. Slower shutter speeds record movement.

- **Shutter Speed.** If you can control the shutter speed, you'll typically do so with a dial or a button near the top of the camera body.

  - The *shutter speed* indicates how quickly (or slowly) the shutter will open and close. In automatic mode with a reasonable amount of light, the shutter will probably open for about 1/60th of a second.

  - Anything above 1/60th of a second (which might just be indicated by the number "60" on your digital camera) is considered somewhat fast. A fast shutter speed will appear to "freeze" time, allowing viewers to see a moment that often escapes us. A cup filled with liquid in midair, for instance, can be recorded before it spills **(FIGURE 4.14)**.

  - A slower shutter speed (1/15th of a second, 1/8th of a second, or more) will result in images that record subject matter movement. In **FIGURE 4.15**, the musicians and lights are blurred as they move rapidly on the stage.

SHUTTER SPEED AND SHAKY PHOTOGRAPHS

Your photographs will not display movements due to your physical inability to remain completely still at a shutter speed of 1/60th of a second or less (1/125th of a second, 1/250th of a second, and so on). With practice, you can probably even seem to hold the camera still at 1/30th of a second. Some people claim to be able to get a still image while hand holding the camera at 1/15th of a second (but that has never been the situation for me). If you plan to shoot at a slower shutter speed, use a tripod or steady the camera without human interference.

- **Exposure Value** (**EV or E/V**). If you can't control the f-stop or shutter speed, you may be able to alter the exposure value, typically accessed by a button on the back of the camera near the LCD. This button will normally allow you to take a photograph with slightly lighter and darker exposure values. On some cameras, you can press a Plus (+) or Minus (-) button; on others, you just spin a dial to move across a sliding scale. Altering the exposure value is an essential skill to learn so you can bracket your exposures while you're still learning to create photographs.

 ## BRACKETING

Like the rule of thirds (see Exercise 5), bracketing is one of the first lessons new photographers learn. Because you're drawing with light when you create a photograph, the exposure settings that you choose in your camera—which control the light falling on your film or digital sensor—have a huge impact on the photograph. Bracketing is a method of increasing and decreasing the exposure value on the same scene in order to understand the visual results of an array of exposure values in a particular lighting situation. If you're new to photography, bracketing in as many lighting situations as you can will help you understand how light will register in the image made by your camera.

On any camera where you can control the exposure value, use the bracketing technique by shooting the same scene at least three times (**TABLE 4.2**). First, take a photograph using the most accurate exposure value according to your light meter (built in to DSLRs or likely whatever the automatic mode will indicate on consumer cameras). Then create another photograph of the same scene with one stop of additional light (a single shutter speed setting or f-stop setting). Follow this by creating one more photograph of the same scene by decreasing the amount of light to the sensor by one stop (a single shutter speed setting or f-stop setting in the opposite direction), starting from the "center" or original metered reading (**FIGURE 4.16**).

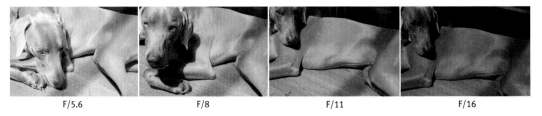

| F/5.6 | F/8 | F/11 | F/16 |

FIGURE 4.16 Bracketed photographs. If you're bracketing with only three images, watch out for digital cameras that include half-stops. It's best to bracket by at least five or even eight exposures if you're brand new to the concept. You'll learn how your camera operates by experimenting.

COMMON BRACKETING SETTINGS

	DSLR If you can control the f-stop and shutter speed settings, use the following list.	**CONSUMER CAMERA** If you simply have the Exposure Value (EV or E/V) button on your camera, use the following list.
Photo 1	Use the most accurate exposure value according to your light meter. You may need to manually adjust your shutter speed or f-stop value, or both to achieve a balanced meter reading.	Use the most accurate exposure value according to your light meter. You'll probably see in the Exposure Value (EV or E/V) area of your camera settings that there's a dotted or dashed line or perhaps a series of vertical straight lines with an indicator (a dot, usually) of the current exposure value. In automatic mode, the exposure value will likely fall in the center of the line. Pressing the EV button (or spinning a dial) will let you register that dot to the right or left of the center mark, which increases or decreases the exposure value.
Photo 2	Lighten the exposure value by one f-stop or by one notch on the shutter speed scale. For instance, if Photo 1 was taken at 1/60th of a second, take Photo 2 at 1/30th of a second to lighten the exposure value by one notch down on the shutter speed scale. (The shutter will remain open longer, allowing more light to register on the digital sensor.) Or, if Photo 1 was taken at f/5.6, take Photo 2 at f/4 to increase the amount of light through a wider aperture.	Lighten the exposure value by one notch to the right of the center on the exposure value line. You'll have to figure out how to add and subtract a notch on the EV scale.
Photo 3	Now decrease the exposure value. Create a photograph that's darker by one f-stop or one notch on the shutter speed scale. For instance, if Photo 1 was taken at 1/60th of a second, take Photo 3 at 1/125th of a second to darken the exposure value by one notch up on the shutter speed scale. Or, if Photo 1 was taken at f/5.6, take Photo 3 at f/8 to decrease the amount of light through a narrower aperture.	Darken the exposure value by one notch to the left of center on the exposure value line.

TABLE 4.2

 BEFORE YOU SHOOT

Before you take off with your camera for a photography session, set aside an intentional moment where you consider some of the camera settings that may not change throughout your shoot:

- Prepare for the lighting situation: Is it daylight? Is it near evening?
  - Set the ISO for the amount of light you expect to capture.
  - Set the white balance for the type of lighting condition.

- Where will the photographs be published or printed? Do you need high-resolution images or are these just "practice shots?" Will the photographs be published strictly on a website?

  - Set the image size or resolution. Use the largest size if you plan to print your images, and use a medium or smaller size for experiments or web content.

  - Set the format of the file. Use RAW only if you know how to process the RAW formatted images. If this is currently beyond your expertise, it may not be worth saving such large image sizes.

- If you have the option, do you want to shoot in full manual mode, shutter speed priority, or aperture priority? Set the mode now.

EXERCISE 5 · RULE OF THIRDS

As you've seen, the rule of thirds is a compositional concept that photographers use while framing the image during its production. Some cameras have a rule-of-thirds grid that you can superimpose in the viewfinder to see the guides while you create the photograph. In this exercise, you'll see how to use this compositional structure in Photoshop to assist you during post-production editing.

1. Launch Photoshop, and open the file **dog-beach.psd** from the **rule-of-thirds** folder.

   I purposefully selected an inactive composition—one with room for improvement—for you to modify in this exercise. Where are the first and second focal points? What's happening at the edges of the frame? Notice that the middle dog and the large branch are two main areas of focus. Where are they positioned in the frame? The top of the frame is full of distracting information: the cone, the volleyball net, and the houses in the background are all unnecessary to the activity in the primary focal area. In the next step, you'll reframe this image.

2. Select the Crop tool from the Tools panel. The default options should appear on the Options bar: Ratio in the first menu, and no sizes are indicated in the image size fields. Check the Overlay Options menu to make sure it is set to Rule Of Thirds (FIGURE 4.17).

Selecting the Crop tool will make the guides available, but they are not visible until you move one of the Crop anchors.

3. Pull the Crop anchor at the middle of the top frame down so the top of the frame touches the tip of the red dog's tail (FIGURE 4.18).

4. Notice where the rule-of-thirds guides are located on the image. The branch is located precisely in the central square. You'd rather see main elements on one of the vertical or horizontal lines than inside what would be a cell if you think of the grid as a table. Move the crop guide on the left edge of the frame toward the middle of the image until the branch is more or less aligned on the left vertical rule-of-thirds guide (FIGURE 4.19).

FIGURE 4.17 The rule-of-thirds grid can be displayed when using the Crop tool.

FIGURE 4.18 Adjust the Crop anchor to eliminate distracting information.

FIGURE 4.19 (RIGHT) Align the subject on the rule-of-thirds grid.

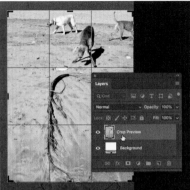

FIGURE 4.22 Starting with Photoshop CS6, you have the option to retain or delete cropped pixels. I prefer to retain pixel information, so I leave the Delete Cropped Pixels button deselected, as seen here. Click the checkmark icon to exit the Crop tool or press the **Return/Enter** key.

FIGURE 4.20 Pay attention to the edges of the photographic frame when cropping the image.

5. Let's eliminate some of the bottom area of the image, just as you did with the top—the information at the bottom is simply distracting the viewer from the activity. Move the bottom crop guide toward the top of the image, keeping the idea of a two-thirds to one-third compositional ratio in mind. I adjusted the bottom crop guide so that the Weimaraner's front left paw is planted on the top horizontal guide (**FIGURE 4.20**).

6. Continue to adjust the crop guides until you're satisfied with the crop. Notice that while you're cropping the image, the Layers panel indicates that you're in a Crop Preview (**FIGURE 4.21**). Click the Commit Current Crop Operation button in the Options bar when you're finished, or simply press the **Return/Enter** key (**FIGURE 4.22**).

7. Save the file as **dog-beach-cropped.psd** to complete the exercise.

 EXERCISE 6 ## BRIDGE WORKSPACES

For the following exercises, which will introduce you to the application Adobe Bridge, you may use the images from your photo shoot or the series of photographs in the **batch-rename** folder. To demonstrate the following exercises, I used 12 daguerreotype images made by Mathew Brady with the words "unidentified woman" in the Library of Congress image title, which I downloaded from the Library of Congress website. Make sure the files are in one easy to find folder.

When I was writing the first edition of this book in 2013, this chapter was one of the most difficult to craft, not for the technology but for the conceptual connection I wanted to make between form and content. The aim of the textbook is to combine three different, yet overlapping areas of thought and practice:

1. The principles of design, such as those taught in the Bauhaus Basic Course

2. Digital practices, such as the techniques you need to know in Adobe Creative Cloud

3. Inspiration from the work of contemporary digital artists and designers

You may notice that none of the chapters are titled with the names or processes of Adobe Creative Cloud applications. Instead, I categorize design learning by concepts and elements, such as dots, paths, lines, color, continuity, and so on. However, this chapter is richly technical because to learn photography you must learn to use the camera. Moreover, an organizational application such as Bridge is an essential tool, but it has not (at least directly) inspired digital art in a way that draws this tool to the subject of the artwork. So, instead, I decided to use the chapter's final three exercises as an opportunity to showcase Bridge as a way to think about downloading and using images found online.

This led me to consider the politics of copyright, copyleft, and alternative licensing models, especially for digital content online. I immediately thought to search the Library of Congress for images that would be either old enough that their copyright is no longer valid or created by an artist while working for the United States federal government (and therefore considered public domain, that is free to download, use, and share).

In the context of the history of photography, Mathew Brady's Civil War photographs were the first to come to mind—many of them are owned by the federal government and, as a result, are in the public domain. What happened next was a result of curiosity and intuition: I began searching through Brady's work in the Library of Congress' digital collection (LOC.gov). In a moment when I was thinking-while-doing, I began to view Brady's online work image by image. I noticed one photo that struck me as unusual among the many war battlefields and portraits of men in uniform: a woman had sat for the camera, but her face was obscured. The title of the work was *Unidentified Women*. I thought this was a poignant visual commentary on the status men held compared to women, which was repeated—right in front of me in 2013—in an online, digital archive. I knew there was a project buried in this thought, but with the book deadline looming, I got about as far along as making the PDF of unidentified women you will complete in Exercise 8.

Five years later, I revisited this creative seed. With a collaborator who studies literature, and a small team of students interested in archives and web development, we expanded those initial ideas to develop *An Archive of Unnamed Women* **(FIGURE 4.23)**.

FIGURE 4.23 A sample entry in *An Archive of Unnamed Women*. xtine burrough and Sabrina Starnaman, with Alyssa Yates (archives and humanities student) and Al Madireddy (computer science student), 2018 and ongoing. This project and many others are collected on my website, missconceptions.net.

This project is a browser-based digital archive juxtaposing nineteenth- and early twentieth-century literature about women with photographs of unnamed or unidentified American women found in the collections of the New York Public Library, including the Schomburg Center for Research in Black Culture. This re-presented archive is a speculative feminist remix project that transforms the algorithmic disadvantages women face embedded in the construction of public library archives into an imaginary, poetic gesture that is both tangible and ephemeral.

FIGURE 4.24 Open a folder for viewing in Bridge by dragging it onto the Bridge application icon.

FIGURE 4.25 In Bridge, the file path to items in the Content panel shows where the file is located on the hard drive.

1. In Exercises 6, 7, and 8 you will learn to use the Bridge workspace to view file information, rename a batch of files, and create a PDF showcasing those images. To begin, you could launch Bridge from the macOS dock or the Windows Start menu, as you would open any other application. However, if you're opening Bridge, you probably have a particular set of files in mind that you want to review. An easy way to start Bridge and view those files immediately is to drag and drop the folder of files you want to view directly on the Bridge application icon. Do this now with the **batch-rename** folder of photographs (**FIGURE 4.24**).

2. To ensure that your Bridge screen looks similar to mine, choose Window > Workspace > Essentials.

3. Notice that the content of the folder you dragged onto the Bridge icon appears in the main window (the second of three columns) beneath a tab labeled Content. The file path to this content appears at the top of the application window (**FIGURE 4.25**).

4. The top of the first column holds a set of tabs for Favorites and Folders. If your folder isn't displaying in the Content panel, you can use one of these two tabs to navigate to the folder you want to view. (For instance, if your folder is located on the desktop, you can click the Desktop icon in the Favorites list and then double-click the appropriate folder in the Content panel.) Locating your files within Bridge is essential because you won't be able to do anything to your files unless you can see them in the Content panel.

BE CAREFUL! Double-clicking a file in Bridge may open that file in a different application, such as Photoshop or Illustrator. You can alter these settings in the Preferences dialog box (**Command-K/Ctrl-K**), by selecting File Type Associations from the list in the left column and choosing an application to use to open files in the JPG format (as in this example) or in other formats.

5. Drag the slider in the lower right of the Content panel to increase or decrease the size of the thumbnail image (**FIGURE 4.26**). Because I have only 12 files in my folder, I zoomed out enough to see all of them on the screen at once.

6. The column on the far right contains the Metadata panel. This panel provides you with the most information about your files. Click once on any of the images in the Content panel—be careful not to double-click, as this may open your file in another application. Meta information (or information about the selected file) appears in the Metadata panel (**FIGURE 4.27**). This panel is especially helpful if the images were created on

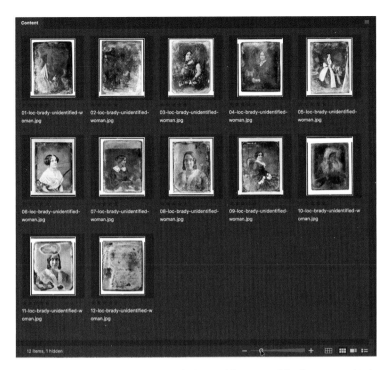

FIGURE 4.26 You can use the slider near the lower-right corner of the Content panel to increase or decrease the size of the thumbnails.

FIGURE 4.27 Information about the file appears in the Metadata panel. If I'd used my DSLR to take these images, I would also see f-stop, shutter speed, and ISO information.

a digital camera that stores metadata within the image file. (For instance, DSLR cameras store this information.) If the files were downloaded from a website (as mine are), the top areas in the panel may not show much information. The File Properties section inside the Metadata panel, however, enables you to learn about the file's format (or document type), size, pixel dimensions, color mode, and more. Quick access to this type of information can be extremely helpful when you have a folder with many similar files.

 EXERCISE 7

BATCH RENAME

The tool I use most in Bridge is Batch Rename. This command lets you assign a new file name to a group of files. You can rename an entire folder of files or just a few files selected within a folder.

1. The file names that I've assigned to the 12 photographs are long. I included a number, the source ("loc" for "Library of Congress"), the photographer's last name, and the name of the series. Let's assume that you're going to select half of these original files to modify in your own work. You want a

KEYBOARD SHORTCUT
Press **Command-A/
Ctrl-A** to select all the
files in the folder (that
is, all files present in
the Content panel). Use
the Shift key to select
files that are next to one
another. If you acciden-
tally include a file in your
selection, press and hold
the Command/Ctrl key
while clicking it once
to deselect it from the
group.

BE CAREFUL! I usually
rename my files in the
same folder rather than
copy my files to a new
folder. But, consider
this a warning: When
you rename files in the
same folder, you'll have
lost the original names.
You can't undo a batch
rename.

new folder for your work, and you want to rename the files with your first
initial, last name, and a sequence number (for example, **x-burrough01.jpg**).
Before applying a batch rename, decide on a system for renaming the files.
Start by selecting the files you want to use. I selected every other file by
holding the Command/Ctrl key as I clicked each of them in the Content
panel (**FIGURE 4.28**).

2. With the files actively selected (you'll see an outline around the selected
   file thumbnails), choose Tools > Batch Rename. In the next steps you will
   make several choices regarding the Batch Rename process.

3. In the Destination Folder area, click the radio button next to Copy To
   Other Folder because you are going to create a copy of the original files
   with a new name. Click the Browse button and locate the spot on your
   hard drive where you want to save this new folder. I navigated to my
   chapter04-results folder. Click the New Folder button, name the new folder
   (**FIGURE 4.29**), click Create, and then click the Open button.

4. Set the conditions for the new file names:

   A. In the New Filenames area, click the Minus (-) or Plus (+) buttons to the
      right of the text fields until you have two fields.

   B. Change the first field in the New Filenames area to the type, Text and
      then enter **unidentified-woman** in its field.

   C. Change the second field to the type, Sequence Number. Enter **1** as the
      first sequence number, and choose Two Digits from the menu to the
      right of the field (**FIGURE 4.30**).

FIGURE 4.28 To select multiple files that are not positioned next to
each other, press and hold the Command/Ctrl key while clicking
each image once.

FIGURE 4.29 Create a new destination folder during the
Batch Rename process.

5. Review your selections. You should see the proper file path to the new folder. An example of the new file names appears at the bottom of the dialog box, as well as a message about how many files will be processed. If all of this seems accurate, click the Rename button.

6. The new files are renamed and copied into a folder that may be located outside of the current folder on view in the Content panel. If this is true for you as it is for me, in the file path towards the top of the application frame, click the folder outside of the content area you are looking at in order to locate where you saved your files. I clicked once on the **chapter-04** folder, which is two levels up from (or outside of) the content I was viewing (**FIGURE 4.31**). From there, I double-clicked the **chapter-04 results** folder.

7. Double-click the new folder—with your name and **batch rename** as its label—to view its contents (**FIGURE 4.32**). You should see the six renamed files in the Content panel.

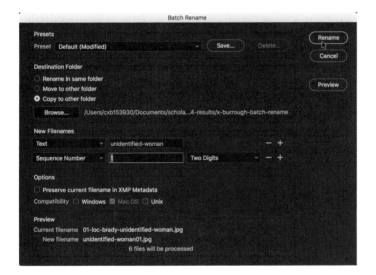

FIGURE 4.30 Set the rules for the new file names using the New Filename fields. You can see the file path to the location of the saved new folder next to the Browse button in the Destination Folder area. Also, you can see a preview of the new file names in the Preview area.

FIGURE 4.31 (BELOW) In the file path at the top of the application frame, click the folder where you saved your batch renamed files to view its contents.

FIGURE 4.32 Double-click the folder in the Content panel to view its contents. Notice the file path at the top of this window area.

EXERCISE 8 GENERATE A PDF TO SHOWCASE YOUR FILES

If you had one or several sheets of negatives to preview, you'd go to the darkroom, press the negatives onto a sheet of sensitized photographic paper with heavy glass, and expose the glass-negatives-paper sandwich with the light of an enlarger. The resulting proof is called a contact sheet because the negative is in direct contact with the paper during the printing process. Digital images can be previewed on the camera, so the need for contact sheets is not as necessary for sharing a view of the files. Yet it's extremely common to share a set of images, mock-ups, or compositions with others in a single file that does not require on-camera viewing or viewing at the time of shooting. Earlier versions of Photoshop (before CS4) included an automated process for creating these types of documents, aptly titled Contact Sheet. Starting with CS4, the Contact Sheet automated task was transferred to Bridge. In current versions of Bridge the name Contact Sheet has been lost but the process remains. In the following exercise, you'll create a PDF to showcase thumbnail (or larger)-sized images using Bridge's Output Workspace.

1. In Bridge, view the contents of the folder you created in Exercise 7, during your batch renaming process.

2. Change the workspace from Essentials to Output.

3. Notice that the Content panel has moved towards the bottom of the application. The central part of the interface is called the *Canvas*. This is where you will organize content for the PDF you will create. Click the first thumbnail image in this area. Press **Command-A/Ctrl-A** to select all of the files. Press the Command/Ctrl key while deselecting any folders or files you don't want to include in the PDF (FIGURE 4.33).

4. When you drag one of the selected files to the Canvas, the group of selected images will move. Click and hold on any one of the selected files, and drag it to the Canvas in the Output Preview panel (FIGURE 4.34). Because the default template has room for four images, an additional page is added.

FIGURE 4.33 To select all the files, click one of them then press **Command-A/Ctrl-A**.

FIGURE 4.35 Change the document settings for the PDF you will export from Bridge.

FIGURE 4.34 Select files in the Output workspace, and place them on the Canvas before saving a PDF.

5. In the Document section of the Output Settings panel, change the Page Size to Letter (FIGURE 4.35). Check the boxes for the Include Filename and Include File Extension options.

6. Notice there are other options you can use or ignore in the Output Settings panel. The Grid And Margins section enables you to adjust how many cells appear on each page. The Header And Footer, Watermark, and PDF Properties (notably with security features) sections are clearly labeled should you want to add those features to your document. Collapse the sections you don't want to use by clicking the sideways arrow to their left.

7. Click the Export To PDF button near the bottom of the panel. Name the new PDF **contact-sheet-untitled-women.pdf** and save it in your batch-rename folder. To view it, open it in Adobe Acrobat or any application you use to view PDF documents (FIGURE 4.36).

8. View the PDF file in your **batch rename** folder. Check the PDF file size on your operating system. On a Mac, you can see the file size by viewing the files in list format or by clicking the file once and then choosing File > Get Info in the Finder or Desktop area. On a PC, you can right-click the file and view the file size in the Properties area. My document, which showcases 6 images, is less than 2 megabytes—a reasonable size for emailing or uploading the file.

 LAB CHALLENGE

Find or take a series of photographs to demonstrate the theme of time passing. This is a classic photography assignment for which many people have photographed a flower throughout its growth and death stages. Don't choose to document a flower! What other visual references to the passing of time can you develop? (Stretch your imagination to avoid imagery of clocks, too). Make several images based on one idea, and place them in a single PDF using Bridge.

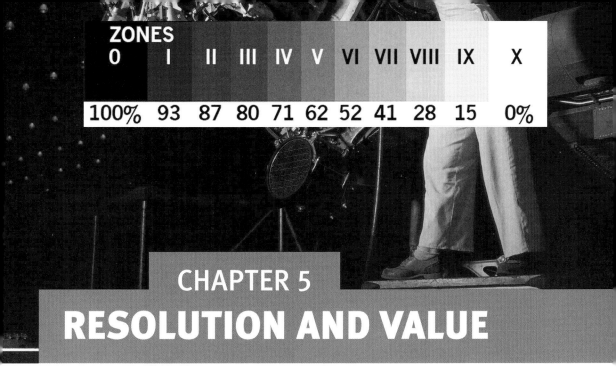

ZONES										
0	I	II	III	IV	V	VI	VII	VIII	IX	X
100%	93	87	80	71	62	52	41	28	15	0%

CHAPTER 5
RESOLUTION AND VALUE

THE EXERCISES IN THIS CHAPTER will provide a technical lesson and a set of aesthetic exercises focusing on values that make up the tonal range of a composition. In Adobe Photoshop, you'll explore the file size and resolution of a bitmap image to understand an image created by pixels. Then you'll study the values in a grayscale digital photograph. You'll learn to apply a zone system to gray values and to use a digital camera with this system in mind, for readers who opt to shoot in manual mode. Finally, you'll apply a Levels adjustment layer to the photograph to increase contrast in its tonal range.

REDISTRIBUTING AND RESAMPLING PIXELS VIA RESOLUTION

The Image Size dialog box in Photoshop (choose Image > Image Size to open it) will be the main area of study in the first exercise. This dialog box allows you to control the file resolution in relationship to your output preferences. Remember, the number of pixels captured is determined at the moment the digital photograph or scan is made. If you need to change the file's resolution, you will have to decide whether you want to redistribute or resample those pixels.

In the first exercise, you'll review or modify the way that the pixels are distributed within the file in the Image Size dialog box. Most people think of Image Size as the place where you adjust the file resolution. To avoid confusion, think of this as the place where you adjust the size of the file, in onscreen (pixel) units or printed media (inches or centimeters, for example) units, by redistributing or resampling the pixels in the file.

To *redistribute* pixels is to compress or spread out the existing pixels, those native to the document. You can tell the document to pack pixels more sparsely or more densely into each inch of screen or printed space, but redistributing will not add or subtract pixels from the total number in the file. Therefore, when you redistribute pixels, the file size will remain the same. Because the number of pixels remains the same, you cannot change the pixel dimensions of the file when you are redistributing pixels.

As you may have noticed, the Image Size dialog box does not contain a "Redistribute" option, but it does offer a Resample option. If Resample is off (not checked), then changes in the other Image Size dialog box settings will redistribute pixels. If Resample is unchecked, you essentially *freeze* the number of pixels in the document. So, modifying the resolution will result in redistributing the existing pixels by spreading them over more (if you decrease the resolution value) or fewer (if you increase the resolution value) inches. This, in turn, changes the printed size of the image. This process also puts a finite limitation on how much you'll be able to increase the image size and still get acceptable printed results. Depending on the values you see in the Image Size dialog box, you might not want to modify the size at all.

To *resample* pixels is to either throw them away (therefore reducing the document file size) or add new pixels, which generally is not a good idea. You should resample the image only if you need to throw away pixels to decrease the size of the document. If you do, you can turn on resampling by checking the Resample option in the Image Size dialog box.

VALUE AND THE TONAL RANGE

Following the exercise on resolution, you'll learn to see values in a bitmap image by reading its *histogram*, a graphic display of the range of values. You'll apply an adjustment layer to an image to alter its set of values, or the *tonal range*. The ability to control the tonal range in a photographic image enables you to express a mood or atmosphere. The tonal range might be a result of purposeful play between light and shadow, or it may be limited by the printing technique selected by the artist.

During the 1920s (the same decade that Walter Gropius led the Bauhaus school in Weimar and delivered a paper on unity among art, science, and technology), the artist Man Ray created a series of "rayographs" in reference to his version of the popular camera-less image-making process, the *photogram* (which he called the "Rayograph"). Man Ray's work influenced László Moholy-Nagy, who taught at the Bauhaus and also made photograms, but these were not the first set of light and object studies created with the photogram process. More than 70 years earlier, Anna Atkins created a book of cyanotype prints titled *Photographs of British Algae: Cyanotype Impressions*. These images are a result of placing an object (or objects) directly on sensitized paper before exposing the paper-object combination to light (**FIGURE 5.1**). The white imprint of the image (its *there-ness*) is mildly set apart from the cyan negative space where unobstructed

FIGURE 5.1 Anna Atkins, *Cystoseira foeniculacea*, in *Photographs of British Algae: Cyanotype Impressions, Part I*. 1843–53. Courtesy of the Spencer Collection, The New York Public Library, Astor, Lenox, and Tilden Foundations.

paper receives a full exposure. A short shadow may be visible due to the close proximity between the object and the paper. The presence and absence of the representation of the object(s) might remind you of the binary nature of computing, where a bit is either "on" or "off." Of course, objects with some level of transparency (fruit slices, mesh fabrics, tracing paper, and so on) will also have an effect on the tonal range of the image. The digital version of a photogram is a scanogram, wherein objects, rather than prints, are placed on the scanner bed.

Stark images with high contrast have a shallow tonal range. They can express an intensity, as seen in Kevin McCarty's 2006 series *I'm Not Like You*. His portraits of young punks with spiky, dark hair showcase tonal values at the low and high ends of the zone, but few in the middle gray area. For example, in **FIGURE 5.2** the viewer is drawn to the contrasting tones in the subject's face and the bright hue of her neck scarf.

If high-contrast images with sharp contours and few tones imply an ideological position, those with a soft, full tonal range may suggest uncertainty. For instance, Christopher James's 2010 portrait *Nelske* has a dreamlike aesthetic quality (**FIGURE 5.3**). In this wet plate collodion print, the artist painted a

FIGURE 5.2 Kevin McCarty, *Monster*, from the series *I'm Not Like You*, 2006. Photograph courtesy of the artist.

FIGURE 5.3 Christopher James, *Nelske*, 2010. Photograph courtesy of the artist.

sodium thiosulfate concentration in specific sections of the plate before baking it in the summer sun. The result is a range of gray values that spread across the subject's face and hair before blending into the background. Where the face of the subject in *Monster* is harshly defined, in *Nelske* it is soft. Her eyes remain unknowable.

You might notice similarities between controlling the set of values in an image and using a square, circle, or triangle as a primary shape in a design. The tonal range informs the viewer (consciously or subconsciously), just as basic shapes signify visual meaning. In the following compositions, you'll learn to control the tonal range in the camera and see how it affects human perception.

ZONE SYSTEM REDUX

As mentioned in the introduction to this section, Ansel Adams first published a method for determining photographic values in his series of books, *The Camera*, *The Negative*, and *The Print*. The zone system is referenced in all three books, but it's most thoroughly described in *The Negative*. You'll learn about the zone system for digital cameras briefly here. Depending on the level of control you have over your camera exposure settings, however, you currently may not be able to use the discussed guidelines.

For a more lengthy explanation of the zone system for digital photographers, see Chris Johnson, *The Practical Zone System for Film and Digital Photography* (Waltham, MA: Focal Press, 2012).

The zone system enables photographers to divide a subject into 11 areas of value from black to white, as seen in FIGURE 5.4. The first, Zone zero, is pure black. The last, Zone X, is pure white. (Zones are traditionally labeled with Roman numerals.)

If you can shoot in aperture priority, shutter priority, or full manual mode, you'll use your light meter to determine how much light is required to obtain an exposure, resulting in visible details in the highlights and shadows. Typically, this metering is averaged throughout the scene, and the exposure values you choose will likely place middle gray in the Zone V area. In other words, the traditional (analog film) method for utilizing the zone system was to expose the film for middle gray. The digital "rule" is to use the zone system to expose for the most important highlight values (usually occurring in Zone VII). The reasons for this rule are expressed eloquently by Chris Johnson

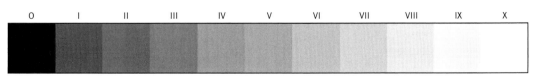

FIGURE 5.4 Zones 0 through X (11 values) between black and white are seen in this traditional scale representing the zone system.

in *The Practical Zone System for Film and Digital Photography* (referenced in the margin). This is a major paradigm shift for those who learned to use the zone system with film and have converted to digital media. If the zone is new to you, then you can simply learn the digital zone and work with a system whereby exposing for Zone VII will give you the most flexibility with your digital file. To do this, you'll need to either fill the frame with a Zone VII element in the shot, or set your camera metering to *spot*. In Exercise 3, you'll learn to recognize the zones throughout a photograph, and in Exercise 4, you'll see why a slightly overexposed digital file will produce better results with digital processing.

WHAT YOU'LL NEED

Download the following source materials to complete the exercises in this chapter:

✔ The file **chapter05-workfiles.zip** which contains the images you need in the folder **chapter05-start**. One image is a photograph I downloaded from the Library of Congress and then resized. The download also includes the **chapter05-results** folder.

You could also use your own digital photographs, although your settings will undoubtedly differ from mine. You'll benefit from the ability to see changes in value across all areas of the image.

WHAT YOU'LL MAKE

In the exercises in this chapter, you'll create a study of value by noticing and placing the zone system on a photograph (FIGURE 5.5). You'll also learn to modify the tonal range in a photograph using a Levels adjustment layer (FIGURE 5.6).

FIGURE 5.5 (ABOVE) The exercises in this chapter will help you see the values in a photograph using the zone system.

FIGURE 5.6 (BELOW) The adjustment layer for Levels is added to the photograph on the right. Notice the difference in the tonal scale between the original (left) and adjusted (right) images.

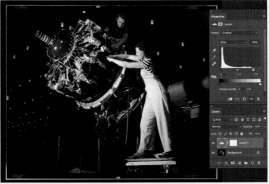

EXERCISE 1

REDISTRIBUTE PIXELS FOR PRINT RESOLUTION

1. Download the **chapter05-workfiles.zip** file from the companion website and open the **chapter05-start** folder.

2. The **chapter05-start** folder includes an image file (**chapter05-start.jpg**) and a digital representation of the Zone System named **zone-scale.jpg**. Open **chapter05-start.jpg** in Photoshop. Set your workspace to Photography by choosing Window > Workspace > Photography.

3. This photo was captured in color, but for these exercises we'll focus on the tonal range, which is much easier to see in grayscale. Choose Image > Mode > Grayscale. Click the Discard button to lose color information.

4. Choose Image > Image Size to evaluate the pixel dimensions and resolution of the file (FIGURE 5.7).

5. Make sure that the Resample option is not checked, so in the Image Size dialog box you can redistribute, rather than resample, the pixels that comprise the image file. Let's assume that you want to print this image on a home inkjet printer as large as it can be printed without compromising the quality of the print. If your viewers will experience your file on paper or through some other printing process, then the file resolution should be approximately 300 pixels per inch (or PPI). Most consumer inkjet printers will produce a fine print from a 240 PPI image (often given as 240 DPI, or *dots per inch,* when speaking of putting ink on paper), so there's a little wiggle room for files that aren't quite large enough at the time of printing.

The start file for Chapter 5 exercises is preserved in the Library of Congress. The photograph was made by Alfred T. Palmer for the Farm Security Administration in 1942. The name of the photograph is *"Women are trained to do precise and vital engine installation detail in Douglas Aircraft Company plants, Long Beach, Calif."* The reproduction number is LC-DIG-fsac-1a35357. I downloaded this image from the LOC's Flickr photo stream: www.flickr.com/photos/library_of_congress/2179925802

MODE SUBMENU Notice that all of the modes of color, or digital color spaces, are listed in this submenu of the Image menu.

REMINDER You'll learn to add an adjustment layer for Levels in Exercise 4. When you're comfortable with adjustment layers, you can choose whether you want to discard color information as you did in Step 3 of Exercise 1 or hide the color information by using an adjustment layer. When the color is discarded, it is literally removed from the file.

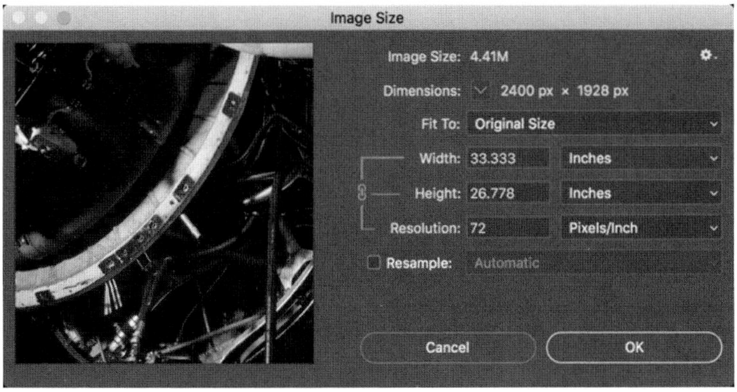

FIGURE 5.7 Notice the Width, Height, and Resolution fields are linked together as the Resample option is not checked.

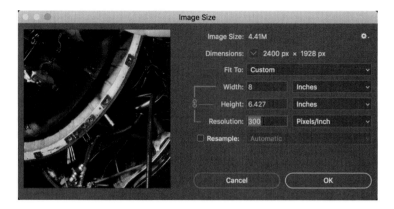

This image is very large when only 72 pixels are packed into each inch—it is nearly 33 by 27 inches! However, at 72 DPI, you would need very large paper to print on and the resulting image would be pixelated or blurry. Make sure the Resample checkbox is not checked, because you don't want to add or subtract pixels to or from the document. Then redistribute the pixels within the document: Change the file resolution to 300 PPI, and notice that the largest print you can make is now 8 inches wide **(FIGURE 5.8)**. Click OK to exit the dialog box, and notice that nothing appears to change because your file still contains the same number of pixels—you simply specified how to distribute the pixels at the time of printing.

6. Choose File > Save As and save the new file as **chapter05-print.psd** when you choose Photoshop from the Format menu in macOS (or the File Type menu in Windows).

PRINTING RESOLUTIONS

If you're printing with a commercial lab, always ask the printer for the correct file resolution specifications before setting up and sharing your documents. The paper and printing process may both have an effect on determining the best resolution (or dots printed in an inch). For instance, most newspapers specify that the file should be saved between 150 and 200 DPI, which is lower than the resolution you'll use on your home inkjet printer, because the printing process and paper qualities are both different. I can print decent-quality inkjet prints at home at a resolution of 240 DPI, while the laser printer in the lab where I teach has generated decent prints at 180 DPI (although those are noticeably less fine than prints sent to the laser printer with a file resolution of 300 DPI). Although this chapter is about resolution and value, and you will learn more about color relationships in the next chapter, it would be negligent not to mention that you should also ask the print technician about the color mode that best fits the printer you will be using.

RESAMPLE PIXELS FOR SCREEN RESOLUTION

Now assume that instead of formatting the image for printing, you want to format it for sharing on the web. If your viewers will experience your file on a screen (for instance, on a webpage, tablet, mobile device, digital video, and so on), then the file resolution could be less than 300 PPI. In most cases, a file resolution of 72 pixels per inch (or PPI) is appropriate. Mobile media is more complicated, but if you are saving your file to share it online then 72 PPI is a reasonable resolution. The smaller the file resolution, the fewer the pixels that occupy one inch of space, and therefore the file size is smaller. When the file size is small, the image or video can be more quickly downloaded and so more easily shared over a network.

SCREEN RESOLUTIONS

A basic website will contain images that could be saved at 72 PPI. Sometimes people share large files (perhaps the additional information or precision of the bigger file is more essential than a shorter download time), so 72 is not exactly a magic number. Moreover, the resolution in PPI is not as important as the width and height of the file in pixels—this actual file size is what the viewer will see as digital devices control the display of the file. In Photoshop, choose View > 100% (**Command-1/Ctrl-1**) or double-click the Zoom tool to see the size of the file at 100% (or its *actual* size on your digital display). Finally, screen resolutions vary enormously from one mobile device to another; but, most graphic design for mobile is created with vector art that is easily scaled. Designing for mobile devices falls outside of the scope of this chapter.

1. While **chapter05-print.psd** is still open, choose Image > Image Size or press **Option-Command-I/Alt-Ctrl-I**.

2. In the Image Size dialog box, you'll likely see the same settings you just left at the end of Exercise 1. Make sure the Resample option is turned off, and then redistribute the pixels to place only 72 pixels in an inch (**FIGURE 5.9**). Notice that at this resolution the document size is gigantic—just over 33 by 26 inches. This digital image would expand larger than most web browsers, as it takes up a lot of screen space. Of course, a print made at 72 DPI would lack quality due to blurriness or pixelization. Click OK.

3. Return to the Image Size dialog box (**Option-Command-I/Alt-Ctrl-I**). In addition to redistributing pixels in order to modify the file resolution, you'll also throw away some pixels because this file has a larger width than webpages are designed to fit. Check the Resample box. From the adjacent menu, choose Bicubic Sharper (Reduction), and then change the units

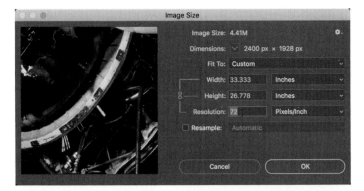

FIGURE 5.9 Screen resolution is 72 dots or pixels per inch (DPI or PPI). Notice how the document size increases when pixels are redistributed for screen resolution.

FIGURE 5.10 With the Resample option checked, it is possible to remove pixels from the document in the pixel dimension area of the Image Size dialog box.

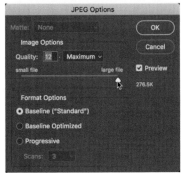

FIGURE 5.11 The JPG quality slider appears when you choose the JPG format from the Save As option in the File menu.

next to the Width and Height values to Pixels. Change the width to about 900 pixels **(FIGURE 5.10)**. Notice that your file size will be approximately 635 KB, nearly one-seventh the file size of the original (4.41 MB).

4. Click OK to exit the dialog box. Your file should have been visibly reduced in size because you threw away pixels by using the Resample option inside the Image Size dialog box. Press **Command-1/Ctrl-1** or choose View > 100% to see your file at 100% and confirm its digital size.

5. Choose File > Save As, and save this file as **chapter05-web.jpg** by choosing JPEG from the Format menu. Click the Save button and then drag the quality slider to 12 to save this image with the highest quality setting **(FIGURE 5.11)**.

6. Look at the difference in file sizes: My print file is 4 MB while my web file is 276 KB (less than half a megabyte). The web file has far fewer pixels saved within the document, and it was saved in a format that further compresses the file size. Print files are typically larger than files saved for viewing on a screen because they require larger file resolutions to maintain their quality.

ANALYZE A PHOTOGRAPH USING THE ZONE SYSTEM

EXERCISE 3

1. Redistribute pixels in **chapter05-web.jpg** by changing its resolution to 240 DPI without resampling the image (**FIGURE 5.12**). Click OK to exit the dialog box and nothing should appear to change on your screen.

2. Let's use an image of the zone system created for use in a digital file within this document. To expand the space in your image document for the next steps, choose Image > Canvas Size. Here you can add space to any or all sides and specify where the extra space will be added in relation to the image by placing an *anchor*. Change the Height value to 4 inches. On the Anchor grid, click the middle box in the top row. This tells Photoshop that you want the image to remain in the center (horizontally) and at the top of the space (**FIGURE 5.13**). Because you're not adding to the Width value, you'll simply see new document space at the bottom of the image.

3. Open the file **zone-scale.jpg** in Photoshop, and notice that the file opens in a new tab.

You'll know you've resampled rather than redistributed pixels when the file becomes visibly larger or smaller on your screen. If you didn't intend to add or delete pixels, choose File > Undo or press **Command-Z/ Ctrl-Z** to step backward and try the process again.

CANVAS COLORS The added canvas space will be transparent if the document was originally set up with a transparent background, or it will use the background color set in the Tools panel.

THE ZONE SYSTEM SCALE

I created the zone system scale by following Lee Varis's steps from a tutorial on his website, www.varis.com. The tutorial, called "Digital Zone System-Part I," can be downloaded at varis.com/PDFs/DigitalZoneSystem-Part-1.pdf

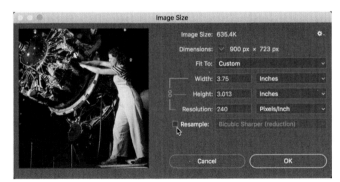

FIGURE 5.12 Redistributing pixels in the Image Size dialog box. (Notice the Resample option is not checked.)

FIGURE 5.13 The anchor in the Canvas Size dialog box is used to position the page opposite the location of the added canvas (or document) area.

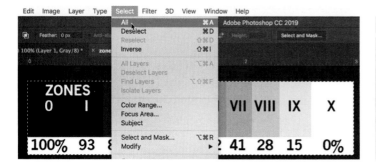

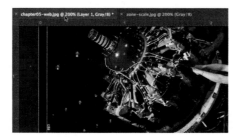

FIGURE 5.14 It's common to select all pixels on a layer in one Photoshop document, copy them, click the tab for a different document, and paste the copied material. Memorize this process using the following key commands: **Command-A/Ctrl-A** (Select All), **Command-C/Ctrl-C** (Copy), **Command-V/Ctrl-V** (Paste).

4. In this step, you'll select, copy, and paste. Because Photoshop reads the entire image as a collection of pixels, the copy action is available only when something is selected. So, first press **Command-A/Ctrl-A** or choose Select > All to create a selection of the entire image. (I prefer using the keys for such common, repeatable actions.) Press **Command-C/Ctrl-C** or choose Edit > Copy to copy the selection. Click the **chapter05-web** file tab to bring that image to the front. In this file, press **Command-V/Ctrl-V** or choose Edit > Paste to paste the image that you copied (**FIGURE 5.14**).

LAYERS When you paste new content in a Photoshop document, it is placed on a new layer. You'll learn more about using, moving, and modifying layers in Chapters 6, 7, and 8.

5. The image of the zone scale will be pasted into your document window on a new layer. It will be visible on top of the photograph. Move the zone scale to the bottom area of the composition by dragging it with the Move tool (the first tool in the Tools panel). Hold the Shift key while you move the scale, and it will remain centered in the document. When you save the image now, you will be prompted to save a Photoshop (PSD) file because your document contains two layers (as the Layers panel shows). In order to save a file with more than one editable layer, you need to save it as a PSD image. Choose File > Save As, and save the file as **chapter05-zone.psd**.

6. Notice that the zone system demonstrates each zone, 0 through X. The darkest shadows are on the low end of the zone. Zone 0 is as close to pure black with no image details as you can get—most of the time you won't want to see Zone 0 in your photographs. Zone X, likewise, is as close to pure white with no image details—another zone you probably don't want

to see in your images. Zone V is approximately middle gray. In some images, you'll want a compacted tonal range, with values that fall into only a few zones. In other images, you may want to see a tonal range that spans Zones II through IX. The photograph appears dark in value overall, because of the large dark area around the women workers. However, the tonal scale is widely used in this image, as you will see in this exercise.

MOVE TOOL The Move tool acts only on the active layer. If you've made a selection, it will move only the selected pixels or object. If you haven't made a selection, the entire layer will be displaced.

WHY IS THE ZONE SYSTEM LABELED IN ROMAN NUMERALS?

Ansel Adams labeled the zones in Roman numerals to set them apart from so many of the other numbers that photographers dealt with during the camera, negative, and development phases of the photographic process.

7. Notice that the zone system includes a range of percentages below the shades of gray from black to white. The percentages indicate the amount of black value present in each zone. Zone 0 is 100% black, while Zone V is 62% black in Grayscale color mode. Zone X is 0% black. The zones are not evenly distributed in Grayscale color mode. Different digital color modes will register the zones with slightly different percentages. Middle gray is consistently a little higher than 50% in RGB, CMYK, and Grayscale color modes.

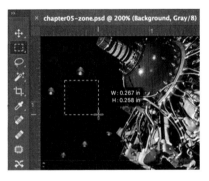

FIGURE 5.15 A rectangular selection of a dark tone in the image.

8. Evaluate parts of the image that fall into particular areas of the zone system. Click once on the **Background** layer in the Layers panel to activate it. Use the Rectangular Marquee tool (second from the top of the Tools panel) to select a small area of the image containing a consistent value in what you believe will be Zone 0 by dragging a box around it **(FIGURE 5.15)**.

9. Press **Command-C/Ctrl-C** to copy the portion of the image you selected on the **Background** layer. Then press **Command-V/Ctrl-V** to paste it. You might think nothing happened, but look in your Layers panel. Pasting part of an image will place that part on a new layer. The pasted image is directly on top of the copied image (mine is named Layer 2). Trust that it's there, and use the Move tool to move the image part beneath the zone system scale **(FIGURE 5.16)**. I placed mine beneath Zone I for this dark gray area of the photograph.

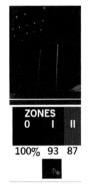

FIGURE 5.16 Move the pasted image selection beneath the zone scale, nearest to the zone in which the value belongs.

10. Try this again to match Zone II in a slightly different way. This time, create a rectangular selection that matches the width of Zone II. It doesn't matter what layer is active while you're dragging to create the selection. Once the selection is in place, be sure to click the **Background** layer to activate it **(FIGURE 5.17)**.

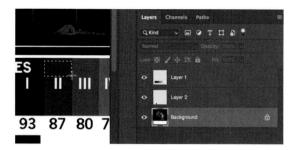

FIGURE 5.17 A selection is created that matches the width of the Zone II box.

FIGURE 5.18 After a selection is created, it can be moved by dragging with any of the selection tools. Here, a selection was made to fit the width of the Zone II box, and then it was moved to a location in the photograph that includes a dark area.

11. When a selection has been made and while you're still using a selection tool (such as the Rectangular Marquee tool), you can place the tool inside the selection and then drag to move the selection around the image. *This is different from moving an image—instead, you're moving a selection on an image.* Put the Rectangular Marquee selection tool inside the box, and drag to move it to an area of the photograph that you think registers Zone II values **(FIGURE 5.18)**.

SELECT, COPY, AND PASTE

Remember that to copy part of an image, you must first select it. To select part of an image, you must identify and select the appropriate layer. It's very common for learners to forget to click the layer first and then select the image. If you see a warning that "No pixels were selected," check to see which layer is currently active.

SCREENCAST 5-1 USE THE INFO PANEL TO CHECK YOUR EYE AGAINST IMAGE DATA

Was it hard for you to see the different gray values in Exercise 3? You can "cheat" (or be extremely precise) by using the Info panel. Watch the video online to learn more.

All screencasts are available on the companion website, www.digitalart-design.com or or on the Vimeo playlist, bit.ly/foundations-demos.

FIGURE 5.19 Selections from the photograph are pasted beneath the zone scale to showcase grayscale tones.

12. Press **Command-C/Ctrl-C** to copy this part of the image and **Command-V/ Ctrl-V** to paste it. Click the Move tool, and move the new, pasted image to the bottom of the composition along the Zone Scale **(FIGURE 5.19)**.

13. Eek! You might be pasting your images behind the image on **Layer 1** (which contains the zone system scale). If this is a problem for you, drag **Layer 1** down in the Layers panel so it's just above the **Background** layer (**FIGURE 5.20**). You can adjust the layer stacking order by dragging layers above or below one another. This will in turn adjust how the viewer understands which image is "on top of" another or closer to the eye. While you're making Layers panel adjustments, rename **Layer 1** to remind yourself that it's the layer containing the zone system scale. Double-click the text "Layer 1" in the Layers panel, and, when the field turns blue, type the words "zone scale" (**FIGURE 5.21**).

14. Continue repeating Steps 10 through 12 to find as many parts of the zone system as you can in this digital photograph. I placed image swatches near Zones I through IX.

15. Rename your layers to match the zones you placed them in (**FIGURE 5.23**).

FIGURE 5.20 (LEFT) The stacking order of the Layers panel can be modified by dragging a layer to a new position above or beneath a different layer.

FIGURE 5.21 (RIGHT) Rename a layer by double-clicking the layer name. Be careful. If you double-click the layer outside of its name, you will open the Layer Style dialog box. If this happens, click the Cancel button to close it and try again.

TIP FOR SELECTION CONSISTENCY

If you want to keep your selection boxes the same size, you can use a key command to select the first image portion you pasted and then use that selection to copy a new area of the image. In the Layers panel, simply press the Command/Ctrl key and click the Layer thumbnail to make a selection of items on that layer (**FIGURE 5.22**). Once the layer is selected, use a selection tool (such as the Rectangular Marquee tool) to move the selection to an area of the digital photograph you want to copy. Then be sure to activate the **Background** layer before pressing **Command-C/Ctrl-C** to copy.

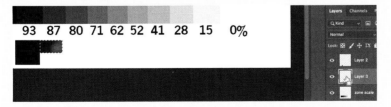

FIGURE 5.22 Command/Ctrl-click a layer's thumbnail icon to select everything on the layer.

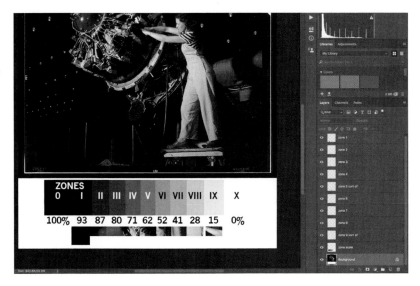

FIGURE 5.23 The Layers panel displaying layers copied and pasted from the original background layer and renamed to fit the zone of each copied selection.

EXERCISE 4 MODIFY THE TONAL RANGE WITH A LEVELS ADJUSTMENT LAYER

The tonal range of this photograph spreads across the zones. This photograph was exposed for the midtone values, but the black level in the shadows could be darker in this digital file. The negative may have been a little flat. In the printing process, the contrast would have been boosted with a filter. Because we are viewing a digital scan of the negative, we will now adjust the tonal range to increase contrast in the image and darken the lower zones.

1. Select the Crop tool (the fifth down in the Tools panel). Crop the image to include the photograph only and delete the zone system scale by dragging the bottom, middle crop anchor to the bottom edge of the photograph (FIGURE 5.24).

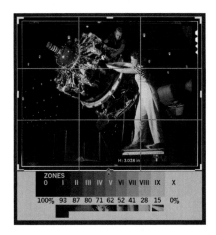

FIGURE 5.24 Drag the anchors at the edges of the Crop tool selection to frame the new crop of the document.

2. Confirm the crop by pressing the **Return/Enter** key or by clicking the checkmark icon at the right end of the Options bar. You can always start anew by pressing the **Escape** key or by clicking the Cancel button on the Options bar.

REMINDER You can review the Crop tool in Chapter 4, Exercise 5.

"AW, SNAP"—THE CROP TOOL

If you are trying to crop an image but the tool won't quite allow you to get to the edge, the Snap command is probably working against you. Look in the View menu, is Snap on? I call this an "Aw, snap!" moment. Snapping is often a powerful way to keep image elements aligned. But "with great power, comes great responsibility,"[1]— sometimes Snap is unknowingly irresponsible, and works against you. While you are dragging the Crop tool, press and hold the Control/Ctrl key to release snapping. This will enable you to align the edge of the Crop tool to any location in the image. I found myself using this key shortcut when cropping the photograph in Step 2.

3. Delete the zone layers you created by dragging them to the Trash icon in the Layers panel. You can Shift-click the top zone layer and the bottom one to select and delete all of them at once (**FIGURE 5.25**). Save your file as **chapter05-levels.psd**.

4. If the crop edges are showing, click any other tool to hide the crop edges from your view. (I usually click a selection tool when I'm not working with a particular tool.) The **Background** layer is active now, as there are no other layers.

5. You've analyzed the range of gray values within this photograph by comparing selections of the image to a scale of values put forth by Ansel Adams's zone system. Now you will visualize the same range as a digital graph called a *histogram*. The Histo-

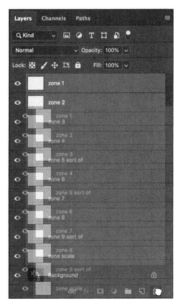

FIGURE 5.25 Shift-click to select all of the zone scale layers and drag them to the Trash icon in the Layers panel to delete them.

REFERENCE [1] This common phrase was popularized by Stan Lee in the Spider-Man comic books. Its exact origins are not clear, but there is evidence of this phrase recorded in British Parliament in 1817 and before that, during the French Revolution in the late 1700s. See *The Parliamentary Debates from the Year 1803 to the Present Time*, Vol. 36, *Comprising the Period from the Twenty-Eighth Day of April to the Twelfth Day of July, 1817*, "Habeas Corpus Suspension Bill," Speaker: Mr. Lamb (William Lamb), Date: June 27, 1817, Start Column Number 1225, Quote Column Number 1226 and 1227, Published Under the Superintendence of T. C. Hansard, Fleet-Street, London; and *Collection Générale des Décrets Rendus par la Convention Nationale*, May 8, 1793 (Du 8 Mai 1793), Quote Page 72. Chez Baudouin, Imprimeur de la Convention Nationale. A, Paris.

gram panel should be open in the top right area of the Application frame. If you do not see it, choose Window > Histogram. The histogram graph represents how many pixels exist at each gray value within the image. Typically, you'll be dealing with 8-bit images that have a tonal range of

FIGURE 5.26 The Histogram graphs the amount of information in each of the 255 gray tones in a bitmap image. The left side of the graph maps the shadow areas (Zone 0, for instance), and the right side maps the highlights (Zone X).

FIGURE 5.27 With **Background** selected as the active layer, click the Levels adjustment layer icon.

256 gray values from black (0) to white (255). This accounts for all of the continuous tones that happen throughout the zone system. The human eye requires only 200 shades of gray to perceive a continuous tone.

Notice that the Histogram panel (FIGURE 5.26) displays the most information on the left side of the graph. The taller the vertical bar, the more information there is at any particular value. The values start at 0 on the left side of the x-axis (black) and increase to 255 (white) on the right side of the x-axis. This histogram tells us what we already know just by looking at the image: Most of the image information is compacted in the darker ranges of the composition.

6. Click the Adjustments tab to pull this panel in front of Libraries, and click the second icon (its icon looks like a bar graph) to add an adjustment layer for Levels (FIGURE 5.27). Levels will open in the Properties panel. If you don't see the Adjustments panel, choose Window > Adjustments. All panels can be accessed from the Window menu.

7. The Levels display in the Properties panel will resemble the histogram you just studied in Step 5. The difference is that you're able to adjust the highlights or shadows, resulting in a reorganization of the tonal range. Because the digital scan of the negative made in the creation of this image lacked contrast in the shadow areas, this panel lets you process the image to increase contrast in those areas. The slider on the left side relates to the shadow areas of the image, the slider in the middle relates to the midtones, and the slider on the right side relates to the highlights. Push the left slider (the shadows) to the right (towards the middle of the graph), and then push the right slider (the highlights) to the left. How far should you push the sliders? The answer depends on your aesthetic choices. I pushed the shadow slider until it reached a new level of 9, and I repositioned the highlight slider to the new level, 213 (FIGURE 5.28). You could click the Auto button and then decide whether you want to use what Photoshop provides as the best adjustment (FIGURE 5.29). When I clicked the Auto button, I noticed the levels remained similar to what I had produced just by looking at the image.

8. Look at the histogram now. It should show a new graph representing the changes you made with the Levels adjustment layer.

9. When you're happy with your adjustment, simply close the Properties panel (FIGURE 5.30). The beauty of an adjustment layer is that you can access and modify it at any time. The changes to the tonal range you implemented in Step 7 can be removed or modified because they're

contained on their own layer. So if you printed this image and realized that you pushed the highlights too far toward the shadows (or not far enough), you could always open the adjustment layer and alter its settings. To open the Levels adjustment layer, double-click its Layer thumbnail icon in the Layers panel.

10. Press **Command-S/Ctrl-S** to save your file.

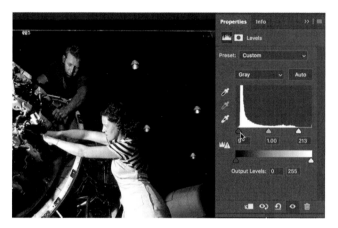

FIGURE 5.28 Modify the Levels by dragging the slider on the right to reposition the highlights in an area of the image where pixel content exists.

FIGURE 5.29 Click the Auto button to allow Photoshop to adjust the levels automatically. For this image, it produced a similar histogram to the one that I created by manually adjusting the tonal range.

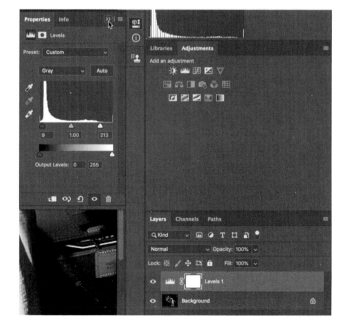

FIGURE 5.30 Close the Properties panel by clicking the small double-arrow in the top-right corner, and notice the new Levels layer in the Layers panel.

 **LAB CHALLENGE**

While visualizing the values in the zone system, take a series of photographs making use of different lighting situations in which you expose the image for the highlight areas. Bracket these exposures so that you can then open the images and create a Levels adjustment layer to recover the shadows and expand the tonal range.

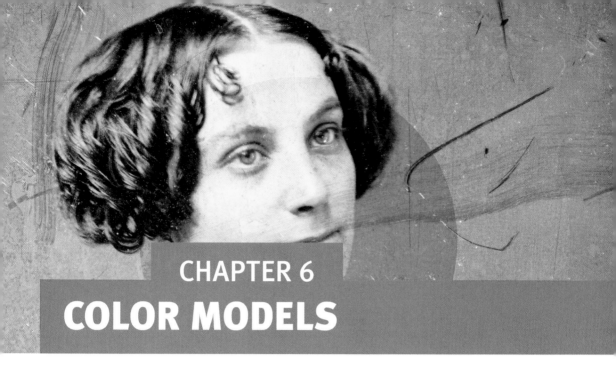

CHAPTER 6
COLOR MODELS

THE EXERCISES IN this chapter will encourage you to consider color as a relational element in your compositions. Just as values relate to one another—one value can't be considered "lighter" without being compared to another value—color is dependent on its surrounding context. Color can be studied in vector graphics or bitmap art. Because adjusting color in a digital photograph is more complex than adjusting color in a flat graphic, you'll learn about color through the lens of photo editing (forgive the pun). You'll use adjustment layers and explore the Color Picker while learning the basic tenets of color theory. Then you will color correct the same image in Adobe Photoshop and Adobe Lightroom Classic.

Color is really a combination of three properties: hue, saturation, and luminosity (HSL). *Hue* specifies what we typically think of as the color, such as blueness or redness. *Saturation* refers to the grayscale value or chroma. *Luminosity* refers to the degree of brightness, referred to in Adobe applications as *lightness*.

SUBTRACTIVE PROCESSES

In an elementary art course, you may have learned about the relationships between primary and secondary hues using an RYB (red-yellow-blue) color model (FIGURE 6.1) to predict the result of mixing paints. You might have tried to mix equal portions of red, yellow, and blue to produce a rich brown. My failed attempts always resulted in a murky gray.

This *subtractive* process involves two players: the surface on which the paint is applied and the pigment. In this case, the surface reflects the light that's transmitted to your eye. Let's assume the surface is white. A white surface will reflect all colors of light in approximately equal proportion. When red paint is applied to the surface, you may think that the color red is being "added" to the white surface. However, all the colors of the spectrum are present, and the white surface is reflecting back to your eye all colors except those that are sub-

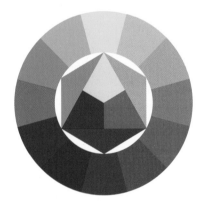

FIGURE 6.1 Johannes Itten, *Farbkreis* (Color Wheel), 1961. Image from Plateresca/Shutterstock.

tracted by the particular pigment. A more precise translation of this experience is that the red pigment absorbs the other hues that are already present. So the red pigment subtracts those hues from your visual experience.

I've always found the subtractive process hard to wrap my head around and the paint and brush ridiculously difficult to control. So I'm grateful that computer graphics are made up of light and no pigments are involved.

ADDITIVE PROCESSES

Because the computer screen projects light to your eye, the process of combining hues to create color is an *additive* process, whereby color is a result of mixing projected light. When there's no light, you are in darkness. Any color at all is produced by adding light.

RGB

The primary hues for this additive process are red, green, and blue (FIGURE 6.2). These hues of light exist at specific wavelengths and cannot be created by mixing any other lights together. When all three hues are present in equal amounts, the result is light with no hue in a range from dark gray to white. (This might remind you of the zone system.) When none of the hues are present, there is no light. The obvious result is black.

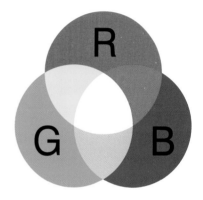

FIGURE 6.2 Additive RGB color diagram. Original version by Mike Horvath (Wikipedia name SharkD) (2006); new version by Jacobolus (2007). Courtesy of Wikimedia Commons. From Kagan Kaya/Shutterstock.

Because red, green, and blue are the primary hues in the additive process, any image that you open in Photoshop from your digital camera (or that you scan) will automatically be set in RGB color mode. If you're preparing images or graphics for presentation on a screen (for instance, the web, a video monitor, or a kiosk), you'll most likely continue working in RGB mode. The final viewing location will use the RGB spectrum, so it makes sense to prepare images for RGB display.

A RETURN TO HISTOGRAM VALUES

Remember viewing the tonal scale in Photoshop's Histogram panel (or even in the Levels adjustment layer in the Properties panel) in the Chapter 5 exercises? The tonal range was computed from the number 0 to 255, as there are 256 possible shades of gray present in any 8-bit graphic. Now that you know about the additive process, think more deeply about this concept: When the gray value is 0, you should see black. That's why the 0 value on the left side of the chart is indicative of the shadow areas in a bitmap image. The value 255 is essentially white light. This is when the light is on full-blast.

The complementary hues for each primary hue are as follows:

- Red is the complement for cyan.
- Green is the complement for magenta.
- Blue is the complement for yellow.

This is illustrated by the hues' positions on the RGB "wheel." (This isn't a terribly accurate term, but these are the hues you'll find when the primary hues overlap.) You'll experience this in Exercise 2.

There are other color modes that you can choose while working on your files. For instance, in Chapter 5, you converted the original colored image to grayscale by changing the mode to grayscale.

CMYK

If you're preparing images for commercial printing (meaning that you're sending the file to an offset or digital printer), set the image to CMYK color mode. (Choose Image > Mode > CMYK.) In this printing process, the file contains four color channels that each store the separate values for the primary pigments: cyan, magenta, yellow, and black.

The aim of this book is to guide you through basic exercises relating to design principles and theories. Offset printing is slightly outside the scope of this text, but a good rule to follow is to always communicate with the printer. She will tell you what the specifications are for printing on her press and may even provide directions for converting RGB images to CMYK mode.

FIGURE 6.3 Vincent van Gogh, *Irises*, 1890. The blue flowers are in extreme contrast with the yellow in the background, as these complementary colors are opposites on the color wheel. From Photosublime/Alamy Stock Photo.

PRIMARY AND COMPLEMENTARY COLOR RELATIONSHIPS

The strongest contrast is created when the primary hues are placed near their secondary hue counterparts (FIGURE 6.3). Traditionally, secondary or complementary hues directly oppose the primaries on the color wheel. In the RGB model, the complementary hues are a mixture of two of the pure primary light hues. (In other words, mix red at a level of 255 with green at a level of 255, and you'll arrive at yellow, the complement to blue.) Another way of explaining this is when one of the three RGB hues is set to zero and the other two are fully present, the result is the complement of the absent RGB primary (FIGURE 6.4).

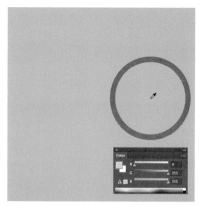

FIGURE 6.4 Red, green, and blue (the left column) are the primary colors in the additive process. To the right of each color is its complement: cyan, magenta, and yellow. Notice the Color panel atop each complementary color. The missing hue is the primary to its left. For instance, cyan is created by mixing two of the three primaries (green and blue) and leaving the red value at zero.

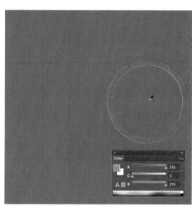

COLOR AS SUBJECT

When Josef Albers created his *Homage to the Square* paintings, his presentation was more meaningful than you might expect. His placement of colored paint as the subject of the painting, rather than the tool for expression, transformed how artists experimented with the boundaries between media and subject, or process and expression. This emphasis on formal properties, such as color, as the subject of a work of art has been further explored in new media works of the late 20th and early 21st centuries.

In Brian Piana's online project *Tweeting Colors*, Twitter messages are transformed into a collection of colors **(FIGURE 6.5)**.

Jack Hughes's *Colour Clock* **(FIGURE 6.6)** also transforms information into colors. The browser or screen application converts hours, minutes, and seconds into hexadecimal values relating to the red, green, and blue values that can be displayed online. Visit thecolourclock.co.uk to see Hughes's clock in action. (Note: the *Colour Clock* project requires that the Flash Player be installed in your Web browser.)

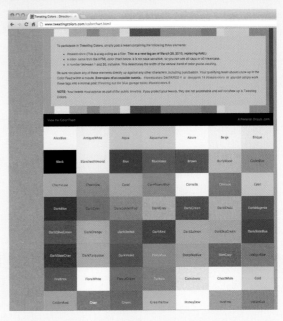

FIGURE 6.5 Brian Piana, *Tweeting Colors*, 2010. Image courtesy of the artist.

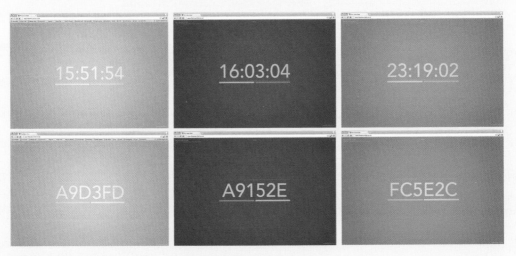

FIGURE 6.6 Jack Hughes, *Colour Clock.* Image courtesy of the artist.

WARM AND COOL

Hue can also be used to dictate how the viewer perceives the depth of an image. Warm hues appear closer to the viewer, while cool hues tend to recede into the background. This phenomenon is demonstrated in Paul Cézanne's still life painting: the warm hues in the center float to the foreground as the cool blue tones at the edges of the watermelon and back wall fade to the background (FIGURE 6.7). In the RGB model, when the image is more blue than red, the hue will be cooler. When images contain more red than blue, the hue will be warmer. The green value will influence the degree of warmth or coolness and, of course, the hue itself.

Additive and subtractive processes do not affect the warmness or coolness of a hue.

SIMULTANEOUS CONTRAST

Bauhaus teachers Josef Albers and Johannes Itten developed color studies and theories that influenced abstract, op (short for optical), and conceptual artists' perception of color and its role throughout the mid-20th century. Albers's *Homage to the Square* series, consisting of hundreds of paintings of nested squares, illustrates his idea of halation, sometimes referred to as *simultaneous contrast* (FIGURE 6.8). You'll learn more about halation in Exercise 2.

LINK See Richard Nelson's *Albers Homage to the Square: An Explanation* on Vimeo at www.vimeo.com/25215702.

In the exercises in this chapter, you'll create various color studies using the selection tools and adjustment layers.

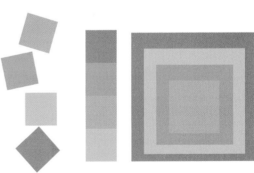

FIGURE 6.7 Paul Cézanne, *Still-Life with a Watermelon and Pomegranates* from The Walter H. and Leonore Annenberg Collection, Gift of Walter H. and Leonore Annenberg, 2001, Bequest of Walter H. Annenberg, 2002/ Metropolitan Museum of Art.

FIGURE 6.8 A still from Richard Nelson's *Albers Homage to the Square: An Explanation* on Vimeo.

WHAT YOU'LL NEED

Download the following source materials to complete the exercises in this chapter:

✔ The **chapter06-workfiles.zip** file which contains three images in the **chapter06-start** folder.

You could also use your own digital photographs, although your settings will undoubtedly differ from mine.

WHAT YOU'LL MAKE

In the exercises in this chapter, you'll create both harmony and simultaneous contrast using Hue/Saturation adjustment layers (FIGURE 6.9). You'll also learn to color correct a photograph using two methods: the Levels and Curves adjustment layers in Photoshop and the Edit panel in Adobe Lightroom Classic. You'll see how to apply color to a black-and-white photograph in Photoshop in the Screencast.

FIGURE 6.9 The results of the exercises in this chapter include a study of harmony (top left), contrast (top right), and color corrections ("before" on the bottom left and "after" on the bottom right).

 EXERCISE 1

HARMONY IN RECTANGLES WITH ADJUSTMENT LAYERS FOR HUE/SATURATION

Harmony is achieved when colors near one another on the color wheel or within the color model are juxtaposed in an image. For the following exercise, the starting file is a black-and-white image. You'll convert it to RGB mode and then apply color using a series of Hue/Saturation adjustment layers.

Adjustment layers enable you to create and save modifiers to the layers stacked beneath them. Adjustment layers modify image data such as contrast (Brightness/Contrast, Levels, and Curves adjustment layers), tone (Exposure, Vibrance, and Hue/Saturation adjustment layers), and color balance (Color Balance, Black & White, Photo Filter, and Channel Mixer adjustment layers); and there are a few other adjustments included. Because each adjustment is stored on a layer that is separate from the image information, the adjustments remain editable after they are applied. This is helpful for on-screen viewing, but it is especially necessary when you plan to print. You may notice that the available light in different locations changes how a print appears to the viewer. With this in mind, you might revise the tone or colors by editing the adjustment layers in the file and create a new print that is optimized for viewing in a certain space and time.

In the following exercise, you will add three Hue/Saturation adjustment layers to the image to create color harmony within the composition.

1. Open **harmony.psd** from the **chapter06-start** folder. This may look familiar, as it's one of the images you used in the Adobe Bridge exercises in Chapter 4. Set the workspace by choosing Window > Workspace > Photography, or choose Photography from the workspace switcher in the Application bar.

2. Choose the Rectangular Marquee tool, and try to draw a rectangle that follows the white frame surrounding the photograph. You'll notice that it isn't possible because the frame is slightly tilted (FIGURE 6.10).

SELECTION TOOLS The Rectangular Marquee tool is sometimes referred to as the Rectangle selection tool because all of the marquee tools are used to select parts of a bitmap image.

3. Deselect this area by clicking anywhere outside the selection or by pressing **Command-D/Ctrl-D**.

4. To follow the edge of the frame, redraw the selection using the Polygonal Lasso tool. This tool enables you to define selections along straight lines from any point to any point. Load it from the Tools panel (FIGURE 6.11). Click just once inside one of the four corners of the frame. Move to the next corner of the frame (move in a clockwise or counterclockwise direction), and again click once. Repeat this until you've clicked three of the four corners. To return to the fourth corner, zoom in and click with the Polygonal Lasso tool in the same location where you began this selection. When you hover over the correct location, you'll see a small circle next to the bottom of the tool icon, indicating that you're closing the selection (FIGURE 6.12).

FIGURE 6.11 The Polygonal Lasso tool is grouped with the Lasso and Magnetic Lasso tools in the selection area of the Tools panel.

FIGURE 6.12 End the Polygonal Lasso selection by clicking on the location where you started the selection.

FIGURE 6.10 The Rectangular Marquee tool creates square and rectangular selections. Because the frame of the image is slightly tilted, the selection does not fit the frame.

ZOOM ZOOM

To zoom in or out easily, you can use the keyboard shortcuts **Command-+(plus)/Ctrl-+(plus)** to zoom in or **Command- –(minus)/Ctrl- –(minus)** to zoom out. You can also press **Command-Spacebar/Ctrl-Spacebar** (zoom in) or **Command-Option-Spacebar/Ctrl-Alt-Spacebar** (zoom out). Using the **Command-Spacebar/Ctrl-Spacebar** shortcut loads the Zoom tool, so you can click exactly the area you want to magnify. **Command-+/Ctrl-+** (or –) simply enlarges (or reduces) the magnification while leaving the center of the image in your viewing area.

5. This image is a grayscale file. To add the first wash of color to it, you will use the Adjustments panel: Click on its title to pull it in front of Libraries. Notice that if you try to click the icon to add an adjustment layer for hue, you will receive a tooltip notice that it is unavailable **(FIGURE 6.13)**. You can't add color to an image until you're working in a color mode that supports color information—and this image contains only shades of gray. Choose Image > Mode > RGB Color to convert the bitmap image from Grayscale mode to RGB.

6. Click the Hue/Saturation adjustment layer icon now that it is available. Inside the Properties panel, you can adjust the hue, saturation, and lightness of the selected area of the image. Notice that your selected edges have disappeared; the selection has been converted to a layer mask, which you will learn about in Chapter 8. Click the Colorize option toward the bottom of the Hue/Saturation panel, and drag the Hue slider toward a warm orangish-yellow or *sepia* **(FIGURE 6.14)**.

FIGURE 6.13 To add a Hue adjustment layer, click the first icon in the second row in the Adjustments panel. When the Hue/Saturation icon is dimmed, color is unavailable.

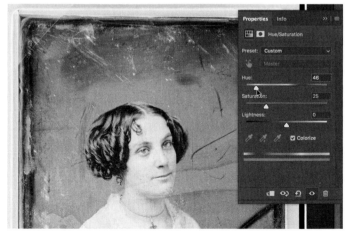

FIGURE 6.14 Selecting the Colorize option applies a wash of color to parts of the image affected by the Hue/Saturation adjustment layer.

7. The Hue/Saturation adjustment layer is saved in the Layers panel. Notice that the adjustment layer has two thumbnail icons on it: the layer thumbnail and the layer mask thumbnail. The mask is where the original selection you made in Step 4 has been saved. The adjustment for hue and saturation has been applied only to that area. Press and hold the Command/Ctrl key while you click the icon for the layer mask (FIGURE 6.15). The Properties panel changes and the mask properties are displayed as the selection based on the mask is loaded in the document.

8. In reference to Josef Albers' *Homage to the Square*, you are creating a series of rectangles related in a progression of sizes to see an interaction of colors applied using the Hue/Saturation adjustment. You will start with the selected area of the largest rectangle (currently active) and transform it in Steps 9 and 10 to make two smaller rectangular selections used to modify the hue. Choose Select > Transform Selection.

9. Scale the selected area: This won't scale or transform the image, just the selection rectangle around parts of it. Press and hold the Option/Alt key while you drag one of the selection edges in toward the center of the image. You will decrease the size of the selection around its center point (FIGURE 6.16). Press the **Return/Enter** key when you're satisfied with the new selection—keep in mind that you will do this one more time to create an additional hue adjustment. To abandon this selection and start anew, press the Escape key.

When any of the selection tools is loaded, you can move a selection around the image without transforming the image or the selection size by dragging from within the selection. The selection tool will transform to a white arrow with a small selection marquee to its bottom right.

FIGURE 6.15 Press the Command key or Ctrl key while you click the icon of the layer mask on the Hue/Saturation adjustment layer to create a selection based on the mask.

FIGURE 6.16 The Photoshop interface for transforming a selection looks similar to the interface for transforming a layer or image. Notice that the selection, represented by the "marching ants" or dashes, has decreased in scale while the image remains the same size.

10. Return to the Adjustments panel, and add a new Hue/Saturation adjustment layer. Activate the Colorize option, and drag the Hue slider to the left of the warm yellow to add an orange hue to the selected area, then increase its saturation until the hue noticeably separates from the background (FIGURE 6.17).

11. Repeat Steps 7 through 10 to make a third rectangle inside the second one. Adjust the selection to include a deep magenta wash of color using another Hue/Saturation adjustment layer (FIGURE 6.18).

12. Save your final file as **harmony-final.psd**. Notice how each of the colors you applied to the composition are situated near one another on the left side of the Hue slider in the Hue/Saturation Properties panel. These colors create harmony because they are near one another on a color wheel or, in the case of a digital interface such as Hue/Saturation, nearby on a slider.

FIGURE 6.17 A second Hue/Saturation adjustment layer is added on top of the first within a smaller selection area.

FIGURE 6.18 A third Hue/Saturation adjustment layer is added on top of the first within a smaller selection area.

SIMULTANEOUS CONTRAST IN CIRCLES

EXERCISE 2

Simultaneous contrast or *halation* is achieved when complementary colors are juxtaposed within an image. In this exercise, you'll convert the starting file to RGB mode and then apply a primary hue and its complement within "parent" and "child" circles using the Layers panel and the Color blending mode.

1. Open **harmony.psd**, the same file you started with in Exercise 1. Convert the mode to RGB Color (see Step 5 of Exercise 1), choose File > Save As, and save the file as **contrast.psd**.

2. Select the Elliptical Marquee tool from the Tools panel. It's nested under the Rectangular Marquee tool, so you may need to click and hold on the tool that's displayed to find the Elliptical Marquee tool (FIGURE 6.19).

3. Drag to create a circular selection while pressing the Shift key. The Shift key constrains the proportions, so the ellipse will be drawn as a circle. Center the selection, and try to fill as much of the frame as you can (FIGURE 6.20). After you make the selection, you can nudge it up, down, left, or right by using the arrow keys. Add the Shift key with the arrows to move the selection ten pixels at a time. For greater movement, place the Selection tool inside the selected area, then drag to reposition the selection.

4. Click the Create A New Layer icon at the bottom of the Layers panel (FIGURE 6.21). Rename Layer 1 by double-clicking the name **Layer 1** and entering a new name. I named my layer **blue**. Press the **Return/Enter** key to set the name of the layer.

> **YIKES!** If you double-click the layer outside the layer's name, you'll open the Layer Style dialog box. Close it, and try to rename the layer again. You have to double-click right on the name to do this.

FIGURE 6.19 The Elliptical Marquee tool is grouped with the Rectangular Marquee tool in the Tools panel.

FIGURE 6.20 Fill the frame with your elliptical selection.

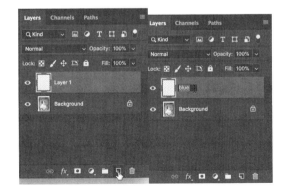

FIGURE 6.21 Add a new layer by clicking the button next to the Trash icon in the Layers panel, then rename Layer 1.

FIGURE 6.22 The Color Picker displays a range of chroma values for a selected hue from the top right of the window to the bottom left (in this case, blue from highly chromatic or saturated in the top-right corner to desaturated gray in the bottom-left corner). The hue shifts in value from top to bottom (from white/light at the top to dark/black at the bottom). Choose a hue by dragging the slider in the rainbow strip of colors.

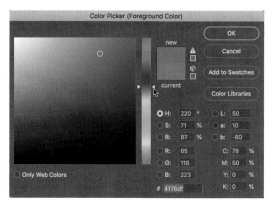

FIGURE 6.23 Warning icons in the Color Picker window let you modify color choices based on your final output. The top warning is for the printing gamut: Click the square below the exclamation point to select a similar color that can be printed. The bottom warning is in regards to colors available on the web.

5. Click the Foreground color chip at the bottom of the Tools panel to open the Color Picker dialog box. Use the slider on the thin rainbow of hues to zoom in on a blue hue. The square on the left side of the dialog box shows you what that hue looks like as it increases in value from top to bottom. (Notice pure white in the top-left corner and black in the lower-right corner.) It also shows the hue with a gradation of saturation from the top-right corner where it's most heavily saturated to the lower-left corner where it's desaturated. As you drag the circular color selection icon around this square, the hue loads in the New color field of the Color Picker dialog box (**FIGURE 6.22**). There are two icons to keep an eye on next to the New color field in this dialog box. One is an exclamation point in a triangle, which gives you information about colors that are out of the printing gamut (will not print). The other is a cube, which lets you modify your color selection so that it's part of the web-safe palette. You needn't be concerned with web-safe colors now, but get in the habit of clicking the exclamation point icon or the color swatch below the out-of-gamut warning as a best practice (**FIGURE 6.23**). Click the OK button to exit the dialog box.

KEYBOARD SHORTCUT
Instead of Edit > Fill, I use **Option-Delete/Alt-Backspace** to fill with the foreground color. Press **Command-Delete/Ctrl-Backspace** to fill with the background color.

6. Before filling the circle with blue, check on two items: You should still see your selection edges because you haven't yet deselected the circle, and the layer named **blue** should be active (highlighted, or selected) in the Layers panel. If both of these are true, choose the Edit menu > Fill. Contents should be set to Foreground Color, Blending Mode to Normal, and Opacity to 100%. Click OK.

7. Deselect the circle by pressing **Command-D/Ctrl-D**.

All the selection tools follow a similar working methodology:

- When you press the Shift key while dragging out your initial selection, the rectangle or ellipse will conform to a perfect square or circle. *Release the mouse before you release the Shift key.*

- When you press the Option/Alt key before you begin dragging, you can "draw" the selection from its midpoint outward. You can combine the Shift and Option (or Shift and Alt) keys if you want to, as well.

- While you're dragging the mouse to draw the selection, press the Spacebar to move the position of the selection around the image. I find this especially useful when I'm trying to align a selection with a specific part of an image.

8. Drag the **blue** layer to the Create A New Layer icon (**FIGURE 6.24**). Rename the resulting **blue copy** layer to **orange**. Two blue layers are in the same location, one on top of the other. It seems as though there's only one, but you'll modify the image in the next steps and see that there are two.

9. While the **orange** layer is active, press **Command-I/Ctrl-I** to invert the color of items on the layer. The blue circle will become orange because orange sits opposite blue on the color wheel. The command, "invert," comes from the language of photography. If you were to invert a color negative showcasing a blue sky, the sky would turn orange.

FIGURE 6.24 Drag a layer to the Create A New Layer icon to duplicate it in the Layers panel.

10. This time, instead of transforming the selection, you'll transform the orange shape. Choose Edit > Free Transform, or press **Command-T/Ctrl-T**. As of Adobe Creative Cloud 2019, this command automatically constrains proportions, so there is no need to use additional key commands to maintain original proportions. However, you should press the Option/Alt key while you drag one of the corners toward the middle of the shape to reduce its size from its center point (**FIGURE 6.25**). Press the **Return/Enter** key to confirm the transformation, or click the Commit Transform checkmark in the Options bar.

11. Repeat Steps 8 through 10 to create a new layer named **cyan** with these exceptions: Duplicate the **orange** layer this time, and instead of pressing **Command-I/Ctrl-I** (which would simply load the same blue as the outer circle), you'll need to change the hue to cyan using a different method. Click the Lock Transparent Pixels icon

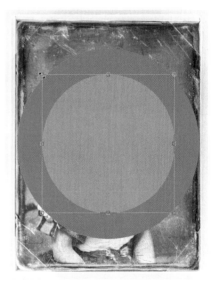

FIGURE 6.25 Press and hold the Option/Alt key while transforming a shape around its center point. There is no need to hold the Shift key to maintain proportions while scaling items as of Photoshop CC 2019.

FIGURE 6.26 Lock the transparency of a layer by clicking the Transparency Lock icon in the Layers panel.

FIGURE 6.27 Color is one of many blending modes you can choose from the Blending Mode menu in the Layers panel.

in the Layers panel to prevent changes to the transparent parts of the **cyan** layer (FIGURE 6.26). Then load cyan into the Foreground color chip using the Color Picker or the Color panel. The RGB values for cyan are R:0, G:255, B:255. Enter these values in the RGB fields near the bottom right area of the Color Picker, or choose any shade of blue that looks similar to cyan. Apply the new color to the circle using the key commands (see the Keyboard Shortcut note near Step 6).

12. The grand finale: you'll now apply these colors to the photograph by changing their blending modes. Make all three of the new layers active by pressing the Shift key as you select them. Then set the three layers to the Color blending mode using the menu on the left side of the Layers panel (FIGURE 6.27). If you modify each layer, one at a time, the total effect won't be visible until all three are set on Color mode. Layer blending modes are used to determine how each layer interacts with the ones beneath it in the stacking order of the Layers panel. The Color blending mode transforms filled color areas into a wash of color applied to the texture of the bit-mapped image.

13. Save the file as **contrast-final.psd.**

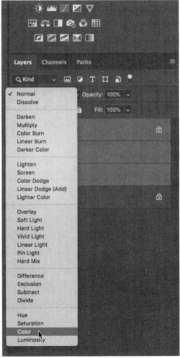

COLOR COMPARISON

Open the two final files, **harmony-final.psd** and **contrast-final.psd**, to view them side by side. If you open both files in Photoshop (with nothing else open), choose Window > Arrange > Tile All Vertically (**FIGURE 6.28**). Can you see how the image containing contrasting colors has a tension and feels smaller, while the image where the hues create harmony seems bigger? The circles recede into space, whereas the rectangles make the woman's face pop out toward the viewer. The way that colors relate to one another will affect the viewer's perception. When you're finished studying the results of these two exercises, close both files.

FIGURE 6.28 A side-by-side comparison of the final files showcasing harmonic colors in rectangles and contrasting colors in circles.

COLOR CORRECTION WITH ADJUSTMENT LAYERS FOR LEVELS AND CURVES

Color photographs, whether they're captured digitally or on film, often require some degree of color correction in the printing or production process. In this exercise, you'll alter the color in the photograph **correction-start.jpg.** You could do this using Levels and Curves adjustment layers in Photoshop, or you could do this using the Quick Develop panels in Adobe Lightroom Classic. Because both methods are relevant, and one of the purposes of this book is to expose (pun intended) new learners to various applications in the Creative Cloud, this exercise and the next will demonstrate how to correct the color in the same photograph—first in Photoshop and then in Lightroom Classic.

FIGURE 6.29 The Levels adjustment opens in the Properties panel and adds a new adjustment layer to the Layers panel.

1. In Photoshop, open the file **correction-start.jpg** from the **chapter06-start** folder. This photograph was taken in a gallery with white walls and ample light. Nonetheless, it has a warm color cast and would benefit from a boost in contrast.

2. Begin by adjusting the tonal range. Because this is a color photograph, you'll adjust each color channel individually within the Levels panel. Click the Levels icon in the Adjustments panel **(FIGURE 6.29)**.

3. Don't adjust the tonal range on the RGB composite. Instead, use the menu just to the left of the Auto button (the "channel" menu) to choose the Red channel and adjust the tonal range for only the red parts of the image **(FIGURE 6.30)**. To adjust the levels, you will use the sliders beneath the shadows (left side), midtones, and highlights (right side) towards the position on the histogram where data is present. Remember that the complement of red in an RGB image is cyan. So you'll not only place the shadows into a position where there's image information (move the left slider toward where information begins on the histogram), but also adjust the midtone slider slightly. This may be difficult to see at first, but the midtone areas have a green cast because of the way the light bounced off the green cage. Move the midtone slider to the left. You will see a shift throughout the midtones that will begin to correct for the green color cast, even though the image will appear warmer **(FIGURE 6.31)**.

4. Use the channel menu to choose and adjust the green channel. Set the shadows, then adjust the highlights and midtones. Don't panic, it will look green temporarily **(FIGURE 6.32)**.

BE CAREFUL! Your adjustments should be minor, not major deviations. You should just barely be able to see the changes you're making to the image. Instead of pushing or pulling the midtone sliders, I usually place my cursor in the midtone box and use the **Up Arrow** and **Down Arrow** keys to adjust this part of the tonal range in increments of one.

FIGURE 6.30 The Levels Properties panel displays levels for each separation of colors. In an RGB image, you'll see the RGB composite histogram, as well as one for each color: red, green, and blue.

FIGURE 6.31 Set the sliders in the shadows and highlights to positions in the histogram where there is data—that is, where the graph begins to rise above zero—in the red channel of the Levels adjustment layer. Adjust the midtone slider based on your aesthetic judgement of the colors in the image.

FIGURE 6.32 Adjust the green channel in the Levels adjustment layer.

5. Use the channel menu to adjust the shadows and highlights in the blue channel as you did the red and green channels, then make a slight adjustment to the midtones by pushing the middle slider to the left (FIGURE 6.33). Exit the Properties panel when you're done by clicking the double-arrow in the top-right corner of the Properties panel. You can always reenter the Levels adjustment layer by double-clicking the adjustment layer thumbnail icon in the Layers panel.

6. Next you will increase the overall contrast with a Curves adjustment layer—click its icon in the Adjustments panel. (It's just to the right of the Levels icon.)

FIGURE 6.33 Set the shadows and highlights in the blue channel of the Levels adjustment layer, then make a minor adjustment to the midtone slider.

FIGURE 6.34 Set two anchor points on the Curve graph.

FIGURE 6.35 Apply an S-shaped Curve adjustment to increase contrast.

7. When you first add a Curves adjustment layer, its "curve" isn't a curve at all, but a straight diagonal line. To increase the contrast, you'll add a couple of bends to make it more like an "S" shape. The tiny Curves icon on the Adjustments panel bears a microscopic S-shaped graph just like the one you're going to create. To begin, click the graph of the straight line to add a first anchor point where there is information in the shadow area on the left side, and a second anchor point in the highlight portion of the graph on the right side (**FIGURE 6.34**). Drag the first anchor point slightly down in the shadow area to darken the shadows. Repeat this action in the highlight area on the right side, but pull the anchor point up to brighten the highlights (**FIGURE 6.35**). Don't drag either anchor point too far! You don't want to push your shadows or highlights to the point that there's no image information in those areas. Close the Properties panel when you're done.

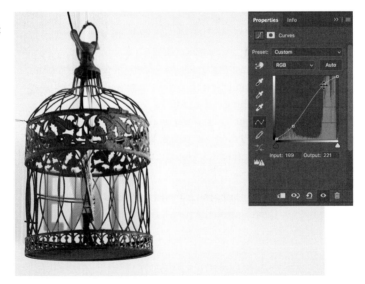

8. Save the file as **correction-adjustments-final.psd**.

9. Finally, preview your before-and-after color correction by hiding and showing the adjustment layers in the Layer panel. Click both of the eyeball icons to the left of each layer to hide the adjustments, then click in that part of the Layers panel again to show each layer **(FIGURE 6.36)**. Alternatively, leave the layers showing and open the start file. View the files side by side as you did in Exercise 3, and pat yourself on the back. Quit Photoshop as you will open Lightroom Classic in the next exercise.

FIGURE 6.36 View the document with and without the adjustment layers by toggling the eyeball icons for those layers in the Layers panel.

EXERCISE 5 COLOR CORRECTION IN ADOBE LIGHTROOM CLASSIC

Similar to Exercise 4, in this exercise, you'll alter the color in the photograph
correction-start.jpg. You may have just completed this task using the Levels
and Curves adjustment layers. In this exercise, you will use the Light and
Color panels in Adobe Lightroom Classic to adjust the image exposure and
remove the color cast.

FIGURE 6.37 Add photos
to your library to work on
them in Adobe Lightroom
Classic. Notice that the Add
option is active.

1. Launch Adobe Lightroom Classic. Choose File > Import Photos And Video,
   and browse through your hard drive on the left side of the screen to the
   chapter06-start folder. You will be prompted with thumbnail icons of
   each image in that folder. Deselect the files to leave **correction-start.jpg** as
   the only file with a checkmark in its upper-left corner. Make sure the Add
   option at the top of the screen is activated, then click the Import button
   (FIGURE 6.37).

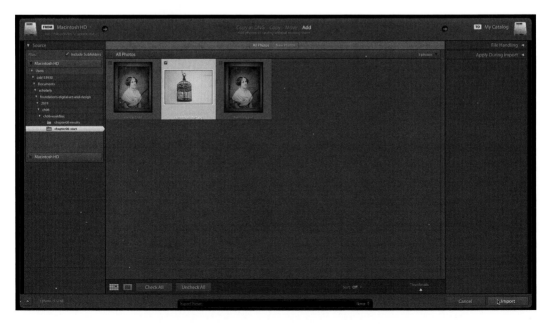

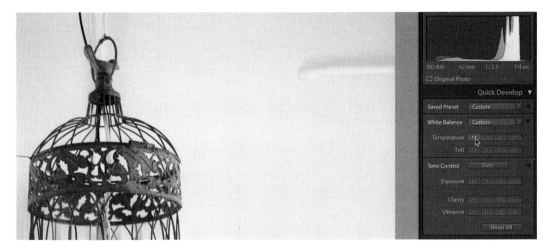

FIGURE 6.38 The Temperature buttons in Adobe Lightroom Classic adjust how warm or cool an image appears. Because this photograph was made with warm room lights, you will balance the color cast by making it cooler.

2. Double-click the thumbnail of the image to open it in the Library panel in the center of the screen. Again, we see a photograph taken in a gallery with white walls and ample light that presents a warm color cast and would benefit from a color correction and boost in contrast.

3. Expand the Quick Develop panel on the right side of the application and expand the White Balance section. Begin by removing much of the warm color cast by modifying the temperature. If you don't see the four Temperature buttons, click the disclosure arrow to the right of the White Balance menu to reveal them. From left to right, these buttons indicate "make cooler" (with two dots), "make cooler" (with one dot), "make warmer" (with one dot), and "make warmer" (with two dots). The dots represent applying the effect in small (one dot) or large (two) increments. I clicked the button closest to the word "Temperature" to make the image significantly cooler (FIGURE 6.38).

4. Adjust the image's exposure and clarity settings. The button interface for this area is similar to Temperature. I clicked the third Exposure button from the left to increase the exposure by a small amount. When you color correct an image with a strong color cast, you should also look at the tonal range in the image and consider increasing the level of contrast. I followed my exposure adjustment by clicking the fourth Clarity button from the left to add a significant amount of contrast (FIGURE 6.39).

FIGURE 6.39 The Clarity modifier adjusts the contrast in the image's midtone values.

5. In Photoshop, view the **correction-adjustments-final.psd** you completed in Exercise 4 (or from the **chapter6-results** folder available on the companion website), and toggle back to Lightroom Classic to see how close your adjustments are to one another. Mine was still much warmer in Lightroom. I re-adjusted the temperature by clicking the less significant "make cooler" button (one dot) and by adjusting the exposure and clarity to make the image slightly darker with more contrast.

There are many methods of accomplishing art and design goals in the Adobe Creative Cloud. You will learn more than one way to work with color, or to make or save selections or alpha channels, for instance. Finding the method that works best for you is the fun part of learning new tools.

6. Press **Command-E/Ctrl-E** or choose Photo > Edit In > Edit In Adobe Photoshop 2019, then select the Edit A Copy With Lightroom Adjustments option and click OK. Choose Window > Arrange > Tile All Vertically to see the two images side by side in Photoshop. Save and name the new file **correction-lightroom-final.psd** (FIGURE 6.40). The corrections I made in Lightroom Classic appear a little flat to my eye, but it would be easy to make additional adjustments in Photoshop from here.

7. Toggle back to Lightroom Classic, and when you are satisfied with your adjustments, quit the program. If an alert asks if you really want to quit, click Yes; and if another alert asks whether you want to back up the Library, click Backup. Your changes will be saved with the original image in the Library.

FIGURE 6.40 Re-open in Photoshop an image that you edited in Lightroom Classic.

 ## LAB CHALLENGE

Create a series of digital photographs in various lighting situations, such as warm room light, outdoor light, low lighting, candle light, and so on. Open and edit the images in Photoshop and/or Lightroom to correct for color imbalances. If it is available to you, load Adobe Capture on your mobile device (it is available for iOS and Android). Open the app, and take a photo of your face to see the color palette Capture assigns to your self-portrait composition.

FIGURE S3.1 Nicéphore Niépce, *View from the Window at Le Gras*, 1825–27. This printed photograph, taken with a camera obscura, shows a view of the roof and surrounding area of Niépce's estate during an eight-hour exposure. Unless it is traveling, you can view the original image at the Harry Ransom Center on the campus of the University of Texas at Austin. The Picture Art Collection/Alamy Stock Photo.

SECTION 3
DIGITAL MANIPULATION AND ~~FREE~~ FAIR USE

DIGITAL MANIPULATION of images is rooted in the art of photo manipulation, and photo manipulation is nearly as old as the advent of printed photographs. Nicéphore Niépce created one of the earliest known photographs in 1825 and then produced the well-known *View from the Window at Le Gras* photograph (made with a camera obscura) sometime between 1825 and 1827 (FIGURE S3.1). The 1830s through 1850s were a time of advancement in photographic and printing technologies, including the daguerreotype process (1837), which made possible the fixed development of printed images; Alexander Wolcott's first American patent for a camera (1840); William Henry Fox Talbot's calotype process (1841), which permitted multiple prints to be made from one negative; and Frederick Scott Archer's collodion process (1851), which lessened the time of image exposure to just two to three seconds. While the technology of the art form grew, artists and experimenters also pushed the boundaries of photography's aesthetic possibilities.

LINK Explore the Metropolitan Museum of Art's microsite about *Faking It*, the first major exhibition devoted to the history of manipulated photography before the digital age, at www.metmuseum.org/exhibitions/listings/2012/faking-it.

REFERENCE [1] Dawn Ades, *Photomontage* (London: Thames and Hudson, 1976), 9.

REFERENCE [2] For more on the Hurricane Sandy viral photograph, see *Clouds Over Lady Liberty* in "7 Fake Hurricane Sandy Photos You're Sharing on Social Media" mashable.com/2012/10/29/fake-hurricane-sandy-photos/

FIGURE S3.2 Henry Peach Robinson, *Fading Away*, 1858. The artist used five different negatives to create this combination albumen print. Gift of Donato Esposito, 2016/Metropolitan Museum of Art.

In the exercises in Chapter 7, *Repairs and Hoaxes*, you'll learn to perform digital photographic repairs and create a simple hoax in Photoshop using the Spot Healing Brush tool, selection tools, Clone Stamp tool, Burn and Dodge tools, and Layers panel.

In the 1830s, Talbot and Anna Atkins made cyanotype prints of found objects on paper (refer back to Figure 5.2). In her book *Photomontage*, Dawn Ades considers these a type of photographic manipulation that predates and inspires the photogram (or Rayogram or Schadograph) works by Man Ray, Christian Schad, and László Moholy-Nagy in the 1920s. By the 1850s, Hippolyte Bayard, Henry Peach Robinson, and Oscar Gustav Rejlander had developed combination printing as a pictorial approach to photography in which the medium was used for storytelling, as opposed to documenting. Bayard relied primarily on the combination technique to create separate exposures for different parts of the image. (Ansel Adams's zone system had not yet been conceived.) Robinson and Rejlander created combination prints to bring multiple images into one frame, expanding the narrative of the photograph by way of juxtaposition (**FIGURE S3.2**). Many thought these images were deceitful, as photography was considered to be a scientific process that captured the truth of a moment. Ades writes, "The members of the Photographic Society in France were banned from exhibiting composite works" [1]. In the age of Adobe Photoshop, I probably don't have to convince you that the photographic image can tell multiple truths, and it can create a deceptive illusion at the whim of the photographer. Photographic hoaxes brought nor'easter storm clouds both to Henry Peach Robinson's 1890 photograph (*Nor'Easter*) and the viral image of the Statue of Liberty in the aftermath of Hurricane Sandy in October 2012 [2].

Following the photographic manipulations of the late 1800s, the Russian Constructivists (the Soviet group of photo collage artists) and Dadaists of the 1920s assembled works of photomontage that are remembered today for their political and disruptive anti-art aesthetics.

PHOTOMONTAGE AND COLLAGE

During the 1910s and 1920s, there were multiple ways of conceptualizing the collage or photomontage. Soviet Russian architect El Lissitzky "renounced self-expression in art, along with easel painting" [3]. His use of photography and collage demonstrated his belief that artists should be grounded in the technological processes relating to industry. His contemporary Aleksander Rodchenko supported the concept of *faktura*. In relationship to photography and collage, faktura was a theoretical belief in discovering a "medium's distinctive capabilities by experimenting with its inherent qualities" [4]. Rodchenko, Lissitzky, and other Russian Constructivists used the manipulation of photographs through juxtaposition to experiment with the medium and combine images of man, science, industry, and the future with typography, lines, and basic shapes. These works were largely utilized for political propaganda.

During the same time period, the Dada art movement spread throughout Europe and to New York. Dada artists also utilized collage and juxtaposition to create works of anti-art. Though factions of the Dadaists had their differences, the work of the avant-garde was largely created in reaction to the political interests leading to World War I and the art historical subjectivism inherent to the Expressionist movement. While the Dadaists rejected logic, capitalism, and rules, they embraced the technology that the Expressionists were responding to with their moody, human, nonrealistic paintings. The anti-logic of Dada is articulated in Tristan Tzara's *Dada Manifesto* of 1918 [5]:

> I am writing a manifesto and there's nothing I want, and yet I'm saying certain things, and in principle I am against manifestos, as I am against principles.

The impact made by Tzara and other Dada manifesto authors is evident in responses from artists and philosophers spanning the last century. In 2016 McKenzie Wark wrote a "RetroDada Manifesto" to celebrate the Dada Centenary, which I designed as a door hanger for readers of the *Visual Communication Quarterly* in 2017 (FIGURE S3.3).

The truthfulness of the photographic image is a subject that has a rich textual history. See especially the first essay in Susan Sontag's *On Photography* and Roland Barthes's *Camera Lucida*.

REFERENCE [3] Mary Warner Marien, Photography: *A Cultural History* (Upper Saddle River, NJ: Prentice Hall, 2002), 244.

REFERENCE [4] Marien, 245.

REFERENCE [5] See Tristan Tzara's *Dada Manifesto of 1918* at 391.org/manifestos/1918-dada-manifesto-tristan-tzara/

FIGURE S3.3 *RetroDada Manifesto Door Hangers*, xtine burrough, text by McKenzie Wark, 2017. As I wrote in the *Quarterly*: "It is important to note that this tribute is published as an open source text. I designed it to be distributed on door hangers to suggest that a 'RetroDada Manifesto' might be your next business calling card or a message to Housekeeping: Please do disturb and disrupt! You, or perhaps your students, are also invited to reimagine other ways to reprint it. Feel free to share, remix, and to clean house" (Vol. 24, No. 2, 86–7).

LINK See "A Photographic History of Collage" at www.eyeem.com/blog/collage-photography.

The Berlin Dadaists agreed that the term *photomontage* best described their efforts, as the word "monteur" translates from German to "mechanic" and from French to "assembly." Much of the photomontage or collage work created in this time period has an edgy, aesthetic quality: Words and images overlap, chaos is preferred to logic, and dynamic movements are prevalent. Photographs are cut and pasted together from preprinted or found source materials, such as newspapers and magazines. Instead of painting a blank canvas, the role of the artist was transformed into that of a collector of raw data and an assembler of new messages using materials of mass communication. These images are not meant to deceive the viewer into believing an alternate reality. Instead, they're meant to demonstrate a quality of rebellion or disobedience and co-optive authorship. The edges of the cut-and-pasted images are apparent. Outlines around separate images are unworthy of blending, as their separateness is central to understanding the politicized message.

MARCEL DUCHAMP'S FOUNTAIN

In 1917, French artist Marcel Duchamp (who was affiliated with the New York Dadaists) entered his *Fountain*, a urinal he had signed with the pseudonym R. Mutt, in the Society of Independent Artists exhibition **(FIGURE S3.4)**. The work was rejected from the show, but it had far-reaching implications for generations of artists that followed. Duchamp challenged the role of the artist: He selected an everyday object (what he called a "readymade"), positioned it as a work of art (by entering it into a fine arts exhibition), and treated it as would the maker of an art piece by adding his signature. Although the Society of Independent Artists did not appreciate Duchamp's mind game in 1917, *Fountain* would go on to become one of the most celebrated works of conceptual art of the 20th century.

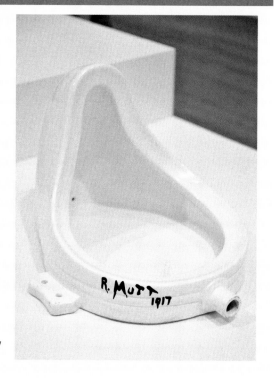

FIGURE S3.4 Marcel Duchamp, *Fountain*, 1917. Photography by Nils Jorgensen/Shutterstock.

Of course, the collage style seen in Dadaist works has been used by artists and designers throughout the 20th and 21st centuries. The opening title of *Monty Python's Flying Circus* showcases Terry Gilliam's detailed animation collages that draw visual parallels to works by Hannah Höch [6]. The deconstruction movement in typographical layout of the 1990s also takes its cue from the perspective of Dada disorder.

REFERENCE [6] View the opening credits to *Monty Python's Flying Circus* on YouTube. This link is active at the time of writing: www.youtube.com/watch?v=2AxiATxLofk.

PRECURSOR TO PUNK

Although you may have never heard of the Dadaists before, the works of George Grosz, John Heartfield, Hannah Höch, El Lissitzky, Aleksandr Rodchenko, Kurt Schwitters, and others might remind you of the punk movement that began in the 1970s. A similar attitude and aesthetic lineage can be traced from the latter to the Dadaists and Russian Constructivists and even to the Italian Futurists who came before them.

SURREALISM

The first of two Surrealist manifestos was written in 1924 by French artist André Breton. The Surrealists were less politically charged than the Dadaists and more interested in exploring the unconscious. If the Dadaists wanted to instigate social change of the outer world, the Surrealists aimed to develop human consciousness through an examination of perception in the inner mind. The movement spread through diverse forms of production to include photography, painting, film, acting, musical composition, and writing.

REFERENCE [7] You can often find the full version of *Un Chien Andalou* on YouTube.

Un Chien Andalou (*An Andalusian Dog*) was written and directed by Luis Buñuel and Salvador Dalí in 1929 [7]. The silent film is more of a dreamscape than a narrative, often demonstrating a double-exposure where film clips are montaged.

REFERENCE [8] You can see the first part of Sergei Eisenstein's *Strike* (1925) on YouTube at youtu.be/ VtjKauYAqMM. Notice the transformation from the man to the owl near the end of the clip.

During the same time period, Russian filmmaker Sergei Eisenstein developed montage-editing techniques that he wrote about in articles and books. Dubbed the "father of montage," Eisenstein used repetition, symbolism, juxtaposition, rhythm, and double-exposure in his films. Similar to the Constructivists who used photo collage for propaganda purposes, Eisenstein was a Bolshevik artist who utilized new filmmaking techniques for political purposes [8].

In the exercises in Chapter 8, *Select, Copy, Paste, Collage,* you'll learn to create a cut-and-paste style photo collage with selection tools, the Pen tool, the Magic Wand tool, and the Layers panel in Photoshop. Later, in Section 4, *Typography,* you'll use Adobe Illustrator to add text to this collage. The subject of the collage is the film *Un Chien Andalou.*

Of course, just as photo manipulations occurred long before the avant-garde movements of the 20th century, *A Trip to the Moon* (1902) by Georges Méliès predates the Surrealists and films by the Soviet father of montage by more than 20 years. The silent 14-minute science fiction fantasy is loosely based on Jules Verne's novel *From the Earth to the Moon* and H. G. Wells's *The First Men in the Moon.*

DIGITAL MANIPULATION

Of course, manipulation doesn't start and end with the Dadaists and the Surrealists. The advent of the networked society calls for new tools for interacting with our various linked screens. User interface (UI) designs for interactive media can be created with pixels or with vector art (see Section 1, *Bits, Pixels, Vectors, and Design*). For this reason, many UI designs are developed in Illustrator or Photoshop. Over the years, Photoshop has expanded its primary function as a bitmap application to include a collection of vector shape tools. These tools are often used for digital creation and image manipulation (by way of juxtaposition and/or masking).

FAIR USE AND APPROPRIATION

Not all visual works are protected by copyright laws. In your collages and photo manipulations, you're free to use images that are in the public domain. These include official media created by the U.S. government, much of the content in the Library of Congress (LOC), and works that have an expired copyright (the death of the author plus 70 years for U.S. authors). Online collections including the LOC website and its Flickr stream, NASA's image gallery, as well as Wikimedia Commons are excellent resources for finding and downloading these types of images or media, although it is always your responsibility to determine the copyright.

In addition to the public domain and expired copyrights, some artists actively contribute to a growing collection of media licensed with alternative mechanisms to the traditional U.S. copyright. GNU and Creative Commons licenses allow artists to set specific guidelines in regard to how their work can be shared, transformed, or redistributed, both commercially and noncommercially.

IMPORTANT! I am not a lawyer, and I'm not offering legal advice. I'm simply summarizing a portion of copyright law in the United States as I understand it.

FAIR USE

The fair use doctrine is important for media makers because it's the part of the U.S. copyright law that permits the use of previously published materials, provided that a particular set of conditions are met. When you use previously published work in your new creation, it's considered to be a *derivative* of the original. Here are the four criteria that a judge or jury would use to determine if your use is legitimately fair:

1. *The purpose of the derivative work.* For instance, a collage made by an instructor that will not be sold or distributed beyond the classroom is probably fair, but one inserted into a commercial publication is likely to be ruled in violation.

2. *The nature of the content of the original.* Factual content can legitimately be reused, whereas creative content is considered to be intellectual property.

3. *How much of the original work is used in the derivative.* For visual works, there is no set guideline for how much you are allowed to use. But, if the transformative quality (not quantity) of the new work is hard to recognize, your work may be so similar to the original that it seems to use "too much" of it.

4. *The effect of the new work on the actual or potential market value of the original.* If the new work defames the original or lessens the value of the original work, the use would not be considered fair.

Commercial artists and designers must be very careful in regard to using prior published works. As a general rule, you should always seek permission from the author, even if the work is licensed in a way that suggests redistribution is permissible. Some of the images you will use in the following chapters may appear to be licensed relatively freely. Nonetheless, I contacted all authors to ensure that we have permission to use the media included in this text.

APPROPRIATION

You'll download and use images that are licensed with a "copy left" (Creative Commons or GNU license) or are in the public domain in the first two chapters of this section.

Appropriation is a conceptually rich practice of borrowing, reclaiming, and transforming an original work of culture that informs and inspires artists who work in a variety of media formats. Though appropriation can be found in visual culture throughout recorded history, many artists learn of the concept through early 20th century art: Pablo Picasso and Georges Braque's mixed-media Cubist collages and Marcel Duchamp's ready-mades (see the sidebar on Duchamp's *Fountain*), or mid-century works such as Andy Warhol's *Campbell's Soup Cans*. The intentional act of appropriation as a means of creating transformative visual culture has become even more prevalent in the age of digital media.

REMINDER If you're creating appropriated work for commercial purposes, be sure that you have permission to modify the original work.

Artists and designers often borrow images, media, formats, or ideas from prior recognizable works in visual culture. The word "appropriation," however, means more than just the simple action of borrowing. To appropriate is to borrow *and* to transform. In this way, appropriation (when successful or obvious) will help your work meet the third criterion in the fair use test.

VERISIMILITUDE

REFERENCE [9] Unilever, *Dove Evolution of Beauty* (video), 2006. youtu.be/iYhCn0jf46U.

REFERENCE [10] Simon Willows, *Slob Evolution*, 2006. youtu.be/lV8JardV74w.

Verisimilitude is a scientific, theoretical term that is generally used in the arts to allude to a quality of truthlikeness. If your aesthetic intent is to trick a viewer into believing in an alternate reality, then verisimilitude is present. Layering, blending, and matching lighting sources and tonal differences will be key to your process of assembling the image. Almost any advertisement in any medium relies on these techniques. Dove deconstructed this process in its *Evolution of Beauty* commercials [9]. The Dove campaign showed the advertising industry's use of verisimilitude to sell a particular "truthfulness of beauty" to their female demographic. In 2006, Simon Willows's parody, *Slob Evolution*, was nominated for a Daytime Emmy Award [10]. Willows's work appropriates Dove's style and format while inverting the message. This video is an example of verisimilitude (its truthlikeness as an advertising campaign with a production quality similar to Dove's original) and appropriation (the act of borrowing the visual culture reference and transformation of the message).

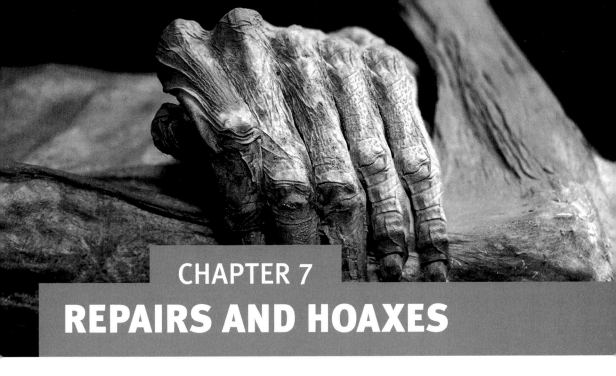

CHAPTER 7
REPAIRS AND HOAXES

THE EXERCISES IN this chapter will provide technical lessons using Adobe Photoshop and Adobe Lightroom Classic and teach you to match textures and values to create photographic illusions in two compositions. You'll explore various tools for *healing* and *cloning* parts of an image, as well as add a simple layer mask to blend image features for a quality of verisimilitude.

DIGITAL REPAIRS

LINK For more information on the repair tools in Photoshop, see the Adobe Photoshop help page: helpx. adobe.com/photoshop/ using/retouching-repairing-images.html.

The repair tools are stacked in a series in the Photoshop Tools panel, starting with the Spot Healing Brush tool beneath the Eye Dropper tool. The tools I use most often to make repairs are the Spot Healing Brush tool and the Clone Stamp tool. The Patch tool can be hard to control or predict, and the Red Eye tool does what you think it does. (It's certainly useful.)

The Spot Healing Brush tool functions as a fix-it paintbrush. You simply click any part of the image, and the brush attempts to *repair* (or correct uneven tones in) the area based on a sample of nearby pixels. Of course, it's never a good idea to modify your original image. So when using these tools, I recommend copying the background layer to preserve the original file. You'll learn more about *non-destructive* editing in Chapter 8, *Select, Copy, Paste, Collage.*

HEALING BRUSH This tool is essentially a combination of the Spot Healing Brush tool and the Clone Stamp tool: It lets you sample a source and tries to even out adjacent tones and blemishes based on nearby pixel information.

The Clone Stamp tool is also a brush. Cloning is a two-step operation: Photoshop needs to understand what you're cloning and where the clone should be applied. So you'll need to sample an original source (the *what* part of the question) and then brush the sample into a new location (the *where* part). The sampling part of the Clone Stamp operation can sometimes be tricky to learn, but once you master the tool you'll be able to repair just about anything.

Before Photoshop, artists manipulated images during the photo shoot, in the darkroom, or on the print, for instance, with SpotTone, a specialty ink used to correct or fill in white areas of photographs for dust spots. This seems like a lost art now that basic photo repairs can be made so quickly using software. However, manipulating photographic imagery has ethical implications for photojournalists and media contributors in the digital age. For instance, the National Press Photographers Association (NPPA) Code of Ethics includes the following statement:

REFERENCE [1]
See nppa.org/code-ethics.

"Editing should maintain the integrity of the photographic images' content and context. Do not manipulate images or add or alter sound in any way that can mislead viewers or misrepresent subjects" [1].

You can see both images of O. J. Simpson on the cover of the two magazines side by side in the entry "O. J. Simpson murder case" on Wikipedia.

Instances of photo manipulation to "get a better shot" have led to firings (for instance, Bryan Patrick from the *Sacramento Bee*) and loss of credibility (the infamous *National Geographic* cover of the Egyptian pyramids in 1982 where a horizontal image was smooshed into a vertical cover space). They've also led to increased criticism within the field. Take a look at two shots of O. J. Simpson published in June 1994 by *Newsweek* and *Time* magazines: the *Time* photograph was manipulated to make Simpson's skin appear darker than it actually is.

CREATING A HOAX

Although visual reporters need to handle digital manipulations with caution and care, artists often use these tools to create commentary on popular media and historic subject matter. For instance, Josh Azzarella's still and video works use manipulation to revise historic events by way of deletion. In his still image, *Untitled #15 (Tank Man)*, Azzarella re-creates the scene from Tiananmen Square, originally photographed by Associated Press photographer Jeff Widener. In Widener's image, the man is face-to-face with several Type 59 tanks during the Tiananmen Square protests of 1989. However, in Azzarella's image, the tanks are removed, and the man is left isolated in the middle of the street, seemingly out of the way of danger (FIGURE 7.1). Similarly, *Untitled #7* (16mm) is an 11-second loop showing President John F. Kennedy driving near the grassy knoll but never experiencing the fatal bullet wound. The footage of JFK riding in the car is haunting for contemporary viewers who know where the drive leads, even though it never quite gets there [2]. These examples of revision and manipulation aren't meant to hoax or deceive the viewer (after all, we know what the artist is up to), but the strategies for image manipulation are the same as those used to create a photographic hoax, which you'll do in Exercises 4 and 5.

REFERENCE [2] See Josh Azzarella's videos on his website: www.joshazzarella.com.

FIGURE 7.1 Josh Azzarella, *Untitled #15 (Tank Man)*. This image is a single frame in Azzarella's video. Image appears courtesy of the artist.

FIGURE 7.2 A portrait of President John F. Kennedy before and after digital repairs.

WHAT YOU'LL NEED

Download the following source materials to complete the exercises in this chapter:

✔ The **chapter07-workfiles.zip** file which includes **repair-start.psd** and **hoax-start.psd** in the **chapter07-start** folder.

✔ Alternatively, you can download the two photographs you'll need for this chapter from their source repositories online (see the sidebar *Downloads*). Save them in a folder named **chapter07**.

You'll benefit from the ability to see changes in values and textures across all areas of the image.

WHAT YOU'LL MAKE

In the exercises in this chapter, you'll repair a dusty portrait of JFK (**FIGURE 7.2**) and create an "extra finger" mummy hoax (**FIGURE 7.3**). The repairs and hoax share the aesthetic quality of verisimilitude—they deceive the viewer into believing your manipulated version of reality.

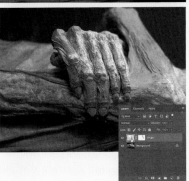

FIGURE 7.3 A mummy hoax includes an extra finger.

Image credits for the source photographs President John F. Kennedy, head-and-shoulders portrait, facing front (1961) appears and is used in this chapter courtesy of the Library of Congress [LC-USZ62-117124]. Hand of Guanajuato Mummy appears and is used in this chapter courtesy of Tomás Castelazo.

To begin the exercises in this chapter, you'll use two images that are, for different reasons, free to you. The portrait of JFK has two listings that let me judge that the image is in the public domain:

- Rights Advisory: No known restrictions on publication.

- Notes: U.S. Navy photo.

Because there are no known restrictions and this was a U.S. Navy photo (and government media is typically in the public domain), I have assessed that the image is fair to use. Also notice that the Library of Congress includes the following in red letters: "Rights assessment is your responsibility."

The mummy image is licensed under the Creative Commons Attribution-Share Alike 2.5 Generic license. Because the image has a Share-Alike component (and this book is not licensed with a CC-BY-SA license, as it would be written in shorthand), I contacted the author for permission to use the image.

DOWNLOADS: HIGH-RESOLUTION IMAGES FROM THE LIBRARY OF CONGRESS WEBSITE AND WIKIMEDIA COMMONS

1. The photograph of President John F. Kennedy is available on the Library of Congress website—search for image LC-DIG-ppmsca-38698 on loc.gov. Beneath the thumbnail of the image on the left side of the page, you'll see a link to download the 32.1 MB TIFF file of the image. This is the largest image available, and it's the one you should download, because you can always scale down but you can't add pixels. 32 MB is a large black-and-white file! It's approximately 17 by 21 inches at 300 DPI. I downloaded this image and then scaled it down to 9 inches vertically at 300 DPI for the **repair-start.psd** file that I've included in the files on the companion site. If you want your brush sizes to match mine during the exercises, do the same or use the files on the companion site.

2. The file **Placid death.jpg** is available from Wikimedia Commons. The highest resolution file can be downloaded by clicking the "Original file" link that appears beneath the image on the file page. If you click the image itself to open it in a separate window, you'll view the largest image. Then you can right-click the image (Control-click on older Macs) to open a contextual menu from which you choose Save Image As to download the image. Download the original file and save it as **hoax-start.jpg.**

EXERCISE 1 REMOVE DUST AND HEAL JFK'S BLEMISHES WITH THE DEVELOP PANEL IN ADOBE LIGHTROOM CLASSIC

There are multiple ways to repair skin tones with digital tools. In this exercise, you will use the Spot Removal tool in Lightroom Classic. In Exercise 2, you will use similar tools in Photoshop.

See Chapter 6 Exercise 5 to learn about importing images to Lightroom Classic.

1. Launch Adobe Lightroom Classic, and import the **repair-start.psd** file to your Lightroom library. Make sure the Add option is active before you click the Import button.

2. Double-click the image preview, and change the module from Library to Develop by clicking the Develop button in the Module Picker at the top of the screen **(FIGURE 7.4)**.

3. The tonal range and contrast in this photograph do not appear to need significant adjustments, however digital artists often touch-up portraits to soften wrinkles, even skin tones, and remove blemishes. Zoom in on JFK's face either with the mouse wheel (or touchpad) or by pressing the **Command-+/Ctrl-+** keys. Inspect the surface of the skin, looking for places where wrinkles appear to be especially deep as a result of shadow/highlight contrast. Also look for spots or blemishes. Load the Spot Removal tool from the set of buttons beneath the Histogram **(FIGURE 7.5)**.

FIGURE 7.4 Open the **repair-start.psd** file in the Adobe Lightroom Classic Develop module.

FIGURE 7.5 Load the Spot Removal tool in Lightroom Classic.

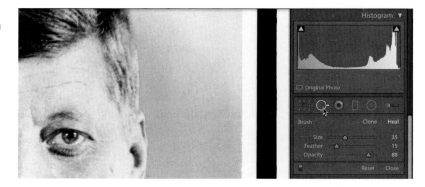

4. Notice the Brush options that appear beneath the Spot Removal tool when this tool is loaded. This tool operates like a brush: It has controls for its size, feather (that is, edge sharpness), and opacity. You can work with this tool in Clone or Heal mode. If you are cloning, you need to sample a source to clone from before you begin brushing with the tool. If you are healing, simply click with the brush and Lightroom Classic will work its magic by automatically selecting a source based on a similar area of the image according to its tone and texture. Be sure that Heal mode is selected as you will work with the brush in this mode in the next steps (FIGURE 7.6).

5. Practice zooming in and out and moving the image around in the application window. I use hot keys for all of this, as when I use my trackpad or mouse wheel (or a touchpad), I often end up resizing the brush by accident. I use **Command-+** and **Command-–** to zoom (**Ctrl-+** and **Ctrl-–** for Windows users), and I press the **Spacebar** to engage the Hand tool, which I use to move the surface of the image around. When I am repairing or modifying the image data, like you are about to do in this step, I like to see that information in detail, which means that less of the image appears on screen at once. You will quickly develop kinetic memory in your hands to change the zoom level and location of the image on the screen without having to look down. While the image of JFK's face fills the screen from his forehead to his lips, look for a dark spot on his cheekbone (his left, your right side). Move the Spot Removal tool so the brush hovers over this area. Is the brush too small, too large, or just the right size for repairing this dark spot? The circular brush tip should be just a little larger than the spot. Mine happened to be exactly the same size as the spot, so I increased my brush by about 15 pixels. I did not use the Size slider in the Brush panel, instead I used the key commands. Press the **Left Bracket** ([) key to decrease the size of the brush and the **Right Bracket** (]) key to increase its size. When the brush size is set correctly, click the dark spot (FIGURE 7.7).

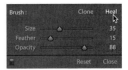

FIGURE 7.6 Set the Spot Removal brush to Heal.

HAND TOOL Use the Hand tool to move the image around the screen while you're zoomed in. You're not moving any part of the image file; you're simply changing your view when you use the Hand tool. Access this tool by pressing the spacebar. This tool is useful in many Adobe applications, including Lightroom Classic, Photoshop, and Illustrator.

ZOOM TOOL You can easily access the Zoom tool while working with most other Adobe Creative Cloud applications by pressing the **Command/Ctrl keys** with the **Equal** or **Minus** key. (I always think of zooming in as **Command-+** even though the Shift key is not involved).

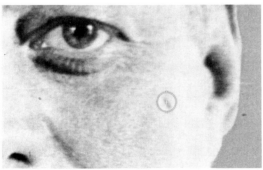
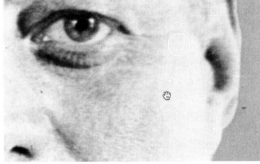

FIGURE 7.7 Click the Spot Removal tool on a dark spot or blemish to replace it with similar tones selected from another part of the image. Use a brush size that covers the spot.

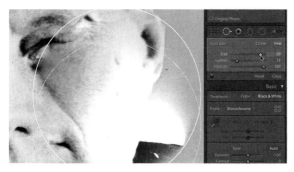

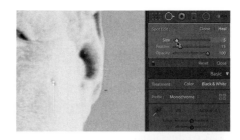

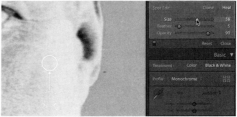

FIGURE 7.8 When the brush is too large (above) or too small (top right), your image edits will draw more attention to the spots you are trying to hide. When the brush is the right size (right), you should consider adjusting the feather and opacity until the new image information fools the eye.

6. Did the spot disappear? Are you happy with the tonal adjustments Lightroom Classic, selected for you? You can still edit this spot because Lightroom edits are *non-destructive*. All of the information in the original image is preserved, and modifications made in the Develop panel are saved separately. In addition to your repair, you should see two circles connected by a thin arrow on top of the image. One circle shows the location Lightroom chose to sample repair information for the dark spot. The arrow grows from this circle to another one. At the end of the arrowhead is the second circle, where you made the repair. Notice how the Spot Removal tool's appearance changes depending on where you place the pointer on the image. When you hover the tool over either of the circles, it changes to a hand pointer. In all other parts of the image, the circular brush remains active for the tool, so you can repair or remove additional spots. Click the circle over the dark spot you just removed. Modify the brush settings; they are still active, even after you used them. Change the Size, Feather, and Opacity settings by dragging the sliders all the way to the left and right extremes, just to see how these adjustments control the results of your repair, and then use your best judgment to set them properly. I ended up leaving my settings as seen in the third part of FIGURE 7.8.

7. You can also move the circle that accounts for the sampled part of the image to see different results from the Spot Removal tool. Use the Spot Removal tool, again with the brush set to Heal to drag a line over the darker wrinkle across the middle of JFK's forehead (FIGURE 7.9). You'll modify the results in the next step.

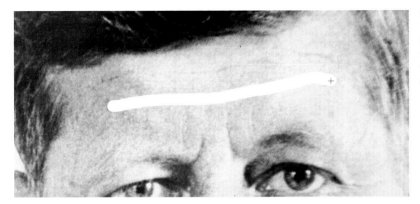

FIGURE 7.9 The Spot Removal tool can be drawn in a line over large areas for repair. Be extra attentive to the Opacity and Feather settings in these cases.

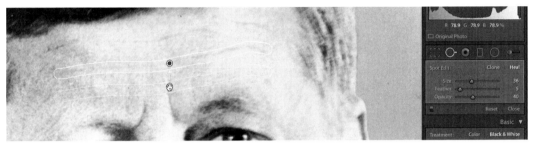

FIGURE 7.10 The location of the sample source can be adjusted once you have made a repair.

8. Wrinkles should not be completely erased. If your Opacity was set to 100 you will have replaced them with smoother skin and you should adjust the opacity downwards. If your brush was too large, you may have sampled the other wrinkles across his forehead, which could have left you in a bit of a mess. Now you should modify the brush options while the area you just painted across is active. (If you deselected it, click the circle attached to the area where you made an adjustment.) I changed the Opacity value to 40, then I moved the sample source to a lower part of the forehead by dragging the circle at the blunt end of the arrow (FIGURE 7.10).

> **FEATHER** You will find a numeric field or slider to control the Feather value in various parts of such Creative Cloud applications as Lightroom Classic and Photoshop. In all cases, this refers to how sharp an edge should appear. When you are using the Spot Removal in combination with Heal mode or the Healing Brush in Photoshop, you will probably choose a small number for the Feather option because you do not want the brush edges to be visible. When you are cloning, however, you may want to start with no amount of feathering so that you clone pixel information precisely. Then you may return to the clone area with some amount of feather applied to the brush to blend the results.

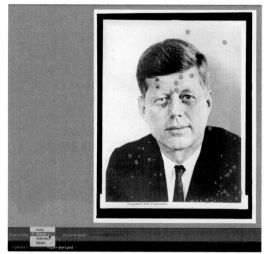

FIGURE 7.11 When the Tool Overlay option is set to Always, it is easy to see all of the locations where repairs have been made.

FIGURE 7.12 Changing the Tool Overlay option to Never allows you to see results of the repairs you made without being distracted by the interface.

FIGURE 7.13 Finish your repairs, and click the Done button.

TOOL OVERLAY In the Toolbar at the bottom of the image is the Tool Overlay menu. This lets you control the visibility of tools, depending on what you are working on. If you leave it on Always, you will always be able to see the circles created by the Spot Removal tool. This can be helpful for being able to select them and modify them. At other times, you may want to change the menu to Selected or Never, because it can be difficult to see the results of the tool in the context of surrounding pixels when a white trace line interrupts your view.

9. Continue working with the Spot Removal tool set to Heal on the entire image, including the dust in the negative space around JFK's head and the bags beneath his eyes. Choose the Tool Overlay option Always to see all of the locations where you have modified the image (**FIGURE 7.11**); choose Never to see the results of your work (**FIGURE 7.12**).

10. When you are finished, click the Done button in the lower-right side of the image window (**FIGURE 7.13**).

11. Choose File > Export to save a file with all of your adjustments. In the Export One File dialog box, choose Export To: Hard Drive from the first menu. In the Export Location section of the dialog box, choose Same Folder As Original Photo from the Export To: menu, and in the File Naming section, choose Filename-Sequence from the Rename To: menu. You should see a preview of the file name, **repair-start-1.jpg** (**FIGURE 7.14**). Click the Export button.

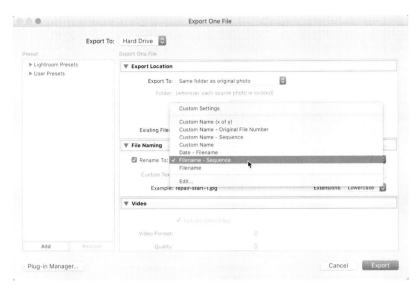

FIGURE 7.14 Export the file containing image repairs to the same folder as the original folder with a sequence number.

12. Quit Lightroom Classic as you will work in Photoshop next.

EXERCISE 2 — JFK'S EYES: TONAL REPAIRS WITH DODGE AND BURN

Now you'll focus on repairing the eye area. Because you've already done a once-over with the Spot Healing Brush tool for dust, scratches, and major blemish repairs, you'll do this additional, localized work on a new layer in Adobe Photoshop. In this exercise, you'll modify a copy of JFK's eyes with the Dodge and Burn tools. If you've never printed a negative in the darkroom, the analogy between this tool and common darkroom practices might not be intuitive. Dodging reduces the amount of light a print is exposed to during image processing in a darkroom, while burning adds additional exposure time (remember that the more light that hits a patch of photographic paper, the darker it becomes). Sometimes a negative needs a full exposure in all areas except for one (for instance, around JFK's eyes—beneath his eyes he had dark rings and his eyebrows are so light they barely register). Photographers dodge prints during the image processing by blocking exposure light on a certain area (or areas) of the paper (to keep them lighter) or by blocking nearly the entire exposure with the exception of a small area in order to "burn" it in (and darken it). In turn, these small portions of the print receive less or more light in comparison to the rest of the projected imagery. When burning an area of the sensitized paper during an exposure to light in a black-and-white wet lab, for instance, a common exposure time for the adjustment might be about 5 to 10 percent of the total exposure. So, in Photoshop, you might start with the

WORKSPACE Choose
Window > Workspace >
Photography for the
remaining exercises in
Photoshop.

Exposure value set at 5% or 10% in the Burn tool options. Of course, this value varies from negative to negative (or file to file), so it's common to make a best guess when using this tool in combination with **Command-Z/Ctrl-Z.**

1. In Adobe Photoshop, open **repair-start-1.jpg**, which you just exported from Lightroom Classic. If you skipped this first exercise, open **repair-start-1.jpg** from the **chapter07-start** folder in **chapter07-workfiles.zip** available on the companion website.

2. Select the Lasso tool from the Tools panel (**FIGURE 7.15**). This tool lets you make a free-form selection around any part of the image. It's not a good tool to use when you need to perform a precise selection, but it's perfect for quickly isolating a general area of the image.

FIGURE 7.15 The Lasso tool is grouped with other selection tools.

3. Draw a loose circle all the way around the left eye area, including a bit above the eyebrows. Be sure to begin and end the selection at the same point so that Photoshop knows the complete area of the selection. You'll see flickering dashed lines surrounding the selected area, often referred to as "marching ants." Now you'll add a selected area around the right eye to the current selection. Press and hold the Shift key while drawing a circular shape around the right eye area with the Lasso tool—the tiny plus sign near the bottom of the tool shows that you're adding to the current selection. You should have two sets of marching ants on the image, one surrounding each eye (**FIGURE 7.16**).

KEYBOARD SHORTCUTS
When copying and pasting from one layer to another, an alternative to
Command-C/Ctrl-C and
Command-V/Ctrl-V is to
use the single command
Command-J/Ctrl-J to
"float" the selected area to
a new layer.

4. Copy the selected eye area and paste it using the keyboard shortcuts **Command-C/Ctrl-C** then **Command-V/Ctrl-V.** In the Layers panel, rename the new layer **eyes.** Choose File > Save As to save the PSD file to your hard drive. I named mine **repair-end.psd** and put it in my **results** folder.

FIGURE 7.16 Start and end the selection with the Lasso tool at the same location in the image. Press and hold the Shift key to add to an active selection. The "marching ants" show a selection around the eye area.

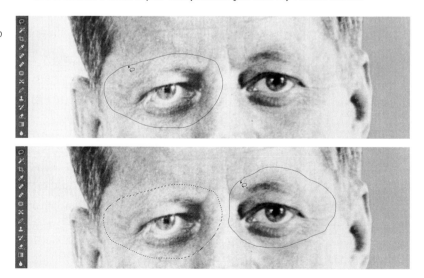

Keep a copy of the original file in the Layers panel when working on repairs. Naming your layers as you work will keep the panel organized and help you work efficiently as the size of the list increases.

5. The bags beneath his eyes were too dark before you lightened them with the Spot Removal tool in Lightroom Classic. In opposition to this, his eyebrows (especially his left brow) are so light they barely register. Because you already corrected for the skin tones under his eyes in Lightroom, load the Burn tool to darken the brows (FIGURE 7.17).

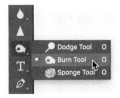

FIGURE 7.17 The Burn tool is grouped with the Dodge and Sponge tools. These tools alter the tonal values and intensity of the hue in an image.

6. Glance at the Layers panel. Nothing should have changed there; you should be working on the **eyes** layer. (Click it to make it active if you noticed that another layer is active.) Always look at the tool options, especially before using a new tool. There are many options for the Burn tool. For now, notice the Brush Preset picker menu, the Range menu (choose Highlights), and Exposure control (set that to 10%). There are other options, too, including the option to enable airbrush style build-up, the Protect Tones checkbox, and an icon that allows the pressure to determine brush size when using a stylus pen. Open the Brush Preset picker menu, and make sure that the Hardness level is set to zero, as you'll want your brush to have a soft edge to allow the burning results to feather or blend into the image. Place your pointer over the eyebrow and use key commands to adjust its size so it covers the eyebrows where they are largest (**Left Bracket** key or **Right Bracket** key, just like in Lightroom). Now you need to estimate a reasonable exposure value. The general rule is that you can always brush these tools over an area more than once, so it's better to err on the side of a lower value. Play with the exposure value (I ended up using 10%), and make a quick brushstroke over JFK's left eyebrow to darken it (FIGURE 7.18). Zoom out to 100% to evaluate your results. I brushed twice over the left brow and once towards the end of the brow on the right side of the image. The modification should not be extreme. Your modification should be believable!

POINTER IMAGE If you don't see a circle representing the size of the brush in Photoshop, check your Photoshop preferences. The brush's appearance is set in Photoshop > Preferences > Cursors/Edit > Preferences > Cursors. Choose Normal Brush Tip. Also, make sure your Caps Lock key is not depressed. Engaging Caps Lock will change the pointer image to a cross-hair.

FIGURE 7.18 Touch up the brow area with the Burn tool. Adjust your settings so you need to brush over this area of the image only once or twice.

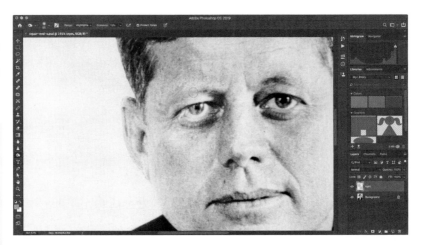

Why not use the Spot Healing Brush tool here? You could work with the Spot Healing Brush tool to correct the eyebrows, but the trouble here is not the pixel information, just the value of the highlight tone. In this situation, correcting the tones by burning and dodging will maintain the integrity of the image.

COPYING IMAGE PARTS

Be extra attentive to the Layers panel when copying selected parts of an image. It's common for new users to attempt to copy part of the image that they can see, but that isn't actually on the selected layer. If you do this, you might get an error message stating "Could not complete the copy command because the selected area is empty." This happens to everyone at some point during image manipulations. Simply click OK to exit the warning dialog, and then activate the appropriate layer before attempting to copy again.

HISTORY IS FULL OF REVISIONS

Repairs will inevitably lead you to over-click with tools such as the Healing Brush or the Dodge and Burn tools in the Photoshop file. It's easy to become click-crazy in the process. Familiarize yourself with the History panel, as you'll come to rely on this handy Photoshop archive. There are three things you need to know about using the History panel:

- Access the History panel from Windows > History or the History icon in the column of panels on the right side of the Application window.

- By default, Photoshop may save only 20 or 50 of your previous clicks or steps. You'll want to increase this when doing repair work. Choose Photoshop > Preferences > Performance/Edit > Preferences > Performance. On the right side of the dialog box, enter 99 in the History States field. The more clicks or previous states you save, the more RAM you'll use. If your computer is slow or lacking RAM, you may want to skip this step.

- To go back a step or two, or five, click once on the name of each of the previous steps in the History panel until your file appears in the state at which you want to begin working anew. There's nothing else you need to click. Simply begin working again, and the History panel will create new steps, overwriting the dimmed step or steps that you're leaving out of your process.

7. Review your modifications at actual size by using the keyboard short-cut **Command-1/Ctrl-1**. Click the eyeball icon next to the **eyes** layer in the Layers panel to hide and show the layer (**FIGURE 7.19**). If you have gone too far, you can reverse your way back through your actions using **Command-Z/Ctrl-Z** or the History panel (see the sidebar). When you are finished adjusting the eye area, save your work and close the file.

FIGURE 7.19 Making the **eyes** layer alternately invisible (top) and visible (bottom) helps preview repairs. You can easily see your repairs by clicking the Eyeball icon on and off in the Layers panel.

EXERCISE 3
IT'S A HOAX! ADDING AN EXTRA MUMMY FINGER

In this exercise, you'll add an extra mummy finger using the Clone Stamp tool. This tool functions similarly to the Spot Repair tool in Lightroom Classic and the Healing Brush tool in Photoshop, but you're responsible for selecting the location of the source area before making repairs. You'll work with a hard-edged and soft-edged brush in this exercise. In the next exercise, you'll clean your work with a layer mask.

1. Open **hoax-start.psd** in Photoshop. Continue to work in the Photography workspace.

2. In the Layers panel, click the Create A New Layer icon. Unless you clicked the icon more than once, the layer's default name is **Layer 1**. Rename it **finger**. You now have an empty layer named **finger** above the locked **Background** layer in the Layers panel.

3. Select the Clone Stamp tool from the Tools panel (FIGURE 7.20). View the Options bar. I set my brush to 250 pixels and changed the Hardness value to 85%. Because you'll be copying pixels with this tool, you'll want to use a brush that isn't too soft. The soft edges often blur the pixel information, which you want to keep sharp, at least during the copying portion of this process. Keep the Mode set to Normal, leave the Opacity and Flow at 100%, check the Aligned box, and set the Sample menu to All Layers (FIGURE 7.21). Remember, you'll first sample with this tool and then clone. If you check the Align box, you're telling Photoshop to keep the sample area aligned with the cloning area. You'll see that it makes sense to keep the source and clone aligned.

FIGURE 7.20 The Clone Stamp tool is grouped with the Pattern Stamp tool in the Tools panel.

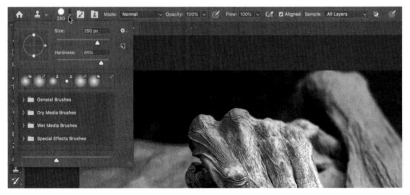

FIGURE 7.21 Brush settings are in the Options bar. The brush hardness is set to 85%. You can also see the other tool options set for cloning in this exercise.

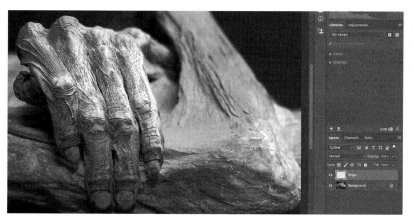

FIGURE 7.22 Sample from the mummy's knuckle with the Clone Stamp tool. Check to make sure the **finger** layer is active.

4. Zoom in using the same key commands as in other Adobe applications, such as **Command-+/Ctrl-+**. Make sure the **finger** layer is active; this is where you want to place your cloned finger. Place the Clone Stamp tool (which basically functions as a brush with an extra sampling step) on top of the last knuckle. Press the Option/Alt key, and click just once in this location (**FIGURE 7.22**). Don't drag the mouse. You just told Photoshop that this is the area that you want to sample as you clone the new finger, and because the option for Sample is set to All Layers, you are allowed to sample from whatever parts of the image this brush covers, on any of the layers. There is nothing to sample on the **finger** layer, so the Clone Stamp tool will sample from the mummy finger on the **Background** layer.

5. Move the mouse to the right of the last knuckle and down a little bit to align it with a plausible location for a new knuckle (**FIGURE 7.23**). The Clone Stamp tool provides a preview of what the cloned image will look like in your composition so you can get the alignment just right before committing to a click. Click and drag downward, tracing the finger, until you reach the end of the fingernail (**FIGURE 7.24**). Save the file as **hoax-end.psd**, which you'll update at the end of the next exercise.

Congratulations! You just added a sixth finger to a mummy. In the next exercise, you'll clean the cloned image data to make the new finger blend with the rest of the composition.

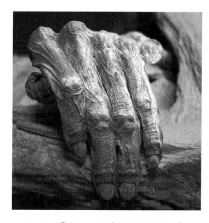

FIGURE 7.23 Paint a new finger using the Clone Stamp tool aligned next to the sampled finger.

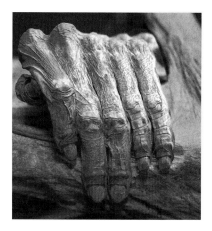

FIGURE 7.24 The new finger in position. The brush hardness ensures that pixels are sampled accurately.

EXERCISE 4 — SOFTENING CLONED EDGES

KEYBOARD SHORTCUT
Because you'll always work with white and black on Photoshop layer masks, you should remember that **X** is the hot key for swapping the foreground and background colors.

Fingers don't stay the same size from the knuckle to the nail, so because there are extra parts of the cloned finger that obstruct the view of the original composition, the viewer can tell that the image has been manipulated. In this exercise, you'll use a layer mask to hide extra parts surrounding the cloned finger. Consider this exercise to be a brief introduction to the layer mask. You'll learn more about layer masks in the next chapter.

1. In the Layers panel, activate the **finger** layer and then click the Add Layer Mask button **(FIGURE 7.25)**. You'll see a new icon in the Layers panel: a white square next to the layer icon of the finger.

FIGURE 7.25 While the **finger** layer is active, click the Add Layer Mask icon to create a mask specific to this layer.

2. The layer mask is used to hide or show parts of a layer. Because the **finger** layer contains only the extra, cloned finger, the mask will affect only this image data. You could work with the Eraser tool to delete image data, but instead it is preferable to work non-destructively, to simply hide (rather than delete) pixels. Layer masks operate in white (show the layer content), black (hide the layer content), and shades of gray (partially hidden). Press **B** to select the Brush tool (or locate it nested with the Pencil tool in the Tools panel), and press **X** to load black into the foreground color chip **(FIGURE 7.26)**.

FIGURE 7.26 The Brush tool is selected with black loaded into the foreground color chip.

3. View the Brush tool options. Set the Hardness value to 0, as you'll want to use a soft-edged brush. Leave the Mode set to Normal and Opacity and Flow at 100%. You will adjust the size using the keyboard.

4. Before using the Brush tool, make sure that the mask is active in the Layers panel. You can click once on the layer content thumbnail or on the mask icon. Notice that whichever is activated is framed with white edges around its icon and near the file name (at the top of the document window) additional information confirms your location in the file's organizational structure **(FIGURE 7.27)**. When you're sure that the mask is active, you are ready to set the size of the brush and then paint black around the edges of the finger where you want to hide the extra image details **(FIGURE 7.28)**.

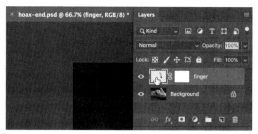 

FIGURE 7.27 Click the layer content icon or the layer mask icon to make adjustments to the layer or its mask. Notice how the information near the name of the file updates depending on which part of the file is activated.

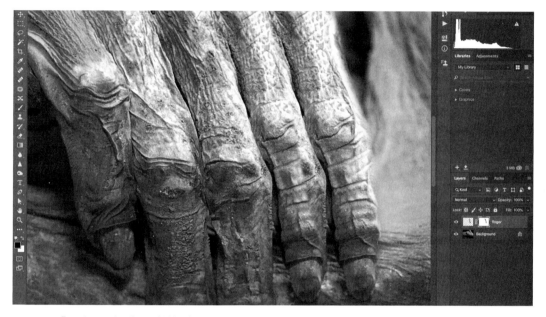

FIGURE 7.28 Extra image details are hidden by painting the mask black in those areas. Here you can see the black brushstroke on the layer mask icon.

5. Notice that the layer mask now contains an abstract black painting on its white background. Option-click/Alt-click the layer mask icon in the Layers panel to show just the mask in your composition (FIGURE 7.29). The black areas of the composition are hidden. The white areas are revealed. Look for gaps between the black and white areas. You may want to review those parts of the composition and add more black or white paint to fill in the gaps. This is an easy way to clean the mask because you can easily see how the image details are being treated. Option-click/Alt-click the mask icon in the Layers panel again to resume the normal working mode and continue to modify the layer mask (FIGURE 7.30).

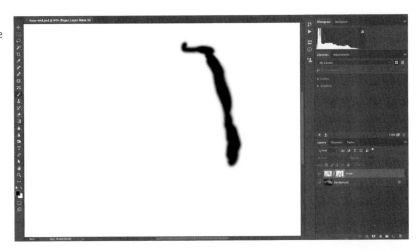

FIGURE 7.29 A view of the **finger** layer mask. The white areas are visible in the document. The black areas are hidden from view (or masked). Any gaps would be filled in with the Brush tool using black.

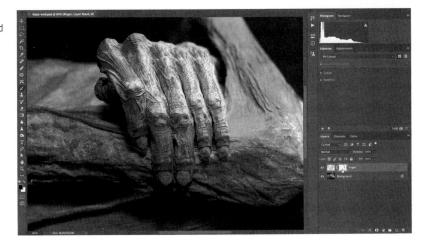

FIGURE 7.30 The mummy finger hoax is complete and visible in normal editing mode.

6. Remember to view the document at actual size and then save the file.

 LAB CHALLENGE

Create a hoax! Modify a current news story by using the repair and clone tools you learned about in this chapter on a fictitious news image. In news photography, the caption is important, too. Don't forget to write a caption to accompany your newsworthy image.

CHAPTER 8
SELECT, COPY, PASTE, COLLAGE

THE EXERCISES IN this chapter will provide technical lessons in photographic collage and teach you about juxtaposition. You'll create a Dada-style photomontage (in which source materials are often made visually apparent) to create a composition that could be used to promote the 1929 Surrealist film *Un Chien Andalou*. You'll explore various tools for precision selecting, copying, and pasting parts of an image. In Chapter 10, *Type and Image*, you'll place this collage in Adobe Illustrator and add typography on top of the photomontage.

PRECISION SELECTING WITH THE PEN TOOL

To make your cutout precise, you'll need a perfectly sharp selection. In most cases, the Pen tool provides the best method for creating this type of selection. Unfortunately, I've found it to be one of the hardest tools in the Adobe Creative Cloud to teach to new students. Part of the problem is the name: This tool does not, despite its name, act like a pen. You won't drag your mouse around a contour to trace it with the Pen tool. However, when the tool is used properly, the result is a perfect tracing of the contour of an image with a path comprising multiple anchor points. The Pen tool is used in Adobe Photoshop and Illustrator (and other Adobe applications). Bundled with the Pen tool are the Add Anchor Point, Delete Anchor Point, and Convert Anchor Point tools, which you used in Illustrator to complete exercises in Chapter 3. I find it more accurate to think of the Pen tool as a "drop anchors" tool rather than a pen.

The second challenge of learning the Pen tool is that you have to predict where the path is going before it gets there. People who excel at using the Pen tool are typically adept at drawing. They can intuit where the contour of the resulting path is headed, which enables them to plot anchor points in just the right places. If drawing isn't your best talent, consider this an opportunity to learn how to see and predict the contour of a shape.

It's important to understand the fundamentals of working with the Pen tool, as follows:

- To add an anchor point, click just once. Then release pressure and move the mouse. Don't click and drag; instead, click, release, and reposition.

- Click again to add the next anchor point, which creates a path between the two points.

- To create a curved path, press and hold the mouse button and drag ever so slightly while plotting the anchor point. You'll see resulting *Bezier handles*, which look like tiny paths with their own anchors originating at your point.

- During the contour tracing, you may need to Option-click/Alt-click an anchor point directly to access the Convert Anchor Point tool. This changes the anchor point from a place where two straight, angular lines meet to one that supports a curve with its Bezier handles. (Or the reverse—Option-click/Alt-click an anchor point to change what would be a curve to a straight line.)

- Curves can be difficult to understand at first. The Pen tool will create an anchor point at the apex of the curve and two Bezier handles that you can use to determine the direction and intensity (hardness or softness) of the curve.

Of course, the advantages of the Pen tool far outweigh the growing pains of mastering it. You'll be able to make crisp paths around image parts, which can then be converted to a selection that you'll eventually use to create a layer mask. For some projects, there's simply no better way to go about masking an image than to start with the Pen tool and convert its resulting path to a mask. This is the first process you'll learn in the following exercises.

MEMBERS SPEAK FOR THEMSELVES

Mark Edwards designed a smartphone/QR code campaign for AIGA (American Institute of Graphic Arts) in 2011. The phone displays video of a designer's talking mouth, which completes its associated postcard **(FIGURE 8.1)**. This interactive campaign is an example of a collage where the precision of the mouth or dissonance of the mouth-to face scale (as you move the phone near or far from the printed piece) is part of Edwards's play with juxtaposition.

FIGURE 8.1 Design and concept by Mark Edwards, *Members Speak for Themselves, 2012.* Postcard series for the AIGA Orange County Chapter in Southern California.

NON-DESTRUCTIVE EDITING

This section could also be called, "Why You Should Use a Mask Instead of the Eraser Tool." I'm so adamant that you should never delete pixels that I won't even demonstrate the Eraser tool. You should, instead, always retain your pixels. Your goal is always to preserve the original image file and edit bitmap graphics on separate masks, adjustment layers, or layer copies. It's not too difficult to stay true to this credo with simple tonal repairs, but when juxtaposing image parts, you'll eventually want to delete part of the image. This is where the layer mask is a necessary part of your arsenal: it is a weapon of massive non-destruction!

The fundamentals of working with layer masks include the following:

In addition to carefully juxtaposing images using Adobe Photoshop, you can learn to see shape relationships by using an app such as Juxtaposer (iOS) or Superimpose (Android). These apps enable you to produce photo collages using images you have taken with the camera on your smartphone.

- A layer mask can be applied to an unlocked layer. If you want to add a mask to a digital photograph opened directly from your camera, double-click the name **Background** in the Layers panel to rename and unlock that layer.

- When a layer mask is applied, it's linked to the layer thumbnail (or content) by default.

- If you create a selection on a layer and then add a mask, the mask will automatically show the selected area and hide everything else.

- If you add a layer mask to a layer with no selection in place, the mask will show everything on the layer.

- On the layer mask itself, white is used to show or reveal layer contents, while black is used to hide parts of the layer. Gray is used as a blending tool because it acts as a trigger for levels of transparency.

- Edits can be made to a layer mask with the Brush tool, Pencil tool, Fill command (from the Edit menu), or Gradient tool.

- When working with layer masks, you'll need to be aware not only of which layer you're editing, but also of whether you're editing the layer content or the layer mask.

- You can see and edit just the mask in grayscale mode. You can also disable the mask to see all of the layer content.

- A layer mask can be deleted. At the time of deletion, you'll have to choose whether to click the Apply button, which applies the mask to the layer before deleting the mask (it's safest to do this if you've saved a copy of the layer with the mask intact), or the Delete button (if you want to start anew).

CUT-AND-PASTE COLLAGE

While a student at the University of California, Irvine, Jonathan Cairns created *Filthy*, a digital collage from appropriated materials **(FIGURE 8.2)**. The comic panels, pixelated photo of Lonelygirl15 (search for her on YouTube if you don't know the reference), and scans or screenshots of news articles juxtaposed in the background represent digital and analog sources of information and entertainment for the bull-headed, hybrid figures wandering in the foreground.

FIGURE 8.2 Jonathan Cairns, *Filthy*, 2006. Digital collage, 24 by 30 inches.

WHAT YOU'LL NEED

Download the following source materials to complete the exercises in this chapter:

✔ The **chapter08-workfiles.zip** file which contains four photographs in the **chapter08-start** folder: an image of a hand I created for this exercise, a stock image of an ant, and other images from online sources.

You can download the photographs from the companion website or use the source materials. In these exercises, you'll learn how to see image relationships through juxtaposition.

WHAT YOU'LL MAKE

In the exercises in this chapter, you'll create a cut-and-paste style collage in which the edges of the images are visible, solid lines **(FIGURE 8.3)**. A sample of the finished project (**chapter08.psd**) is also provided in the download file, in the folder **chapter08-results**.

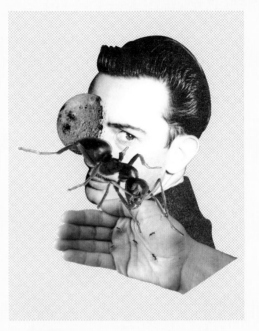

FIGURE 8.3 The final collage created in the Chapter 8 exercises.

Did I mention that the Pen tool can be hard to teach to new users? Well, this chapter contains a double-whammy. Layer masks are also difficult for those new to Photoshop. Remember, you have to start somewhere. It's okay to mess up while working on these exercises: That's the point of practice. When it's time to implement these ideas in your own work, however, you'll be ready to combine the precision of the Pen tool with the intelligence of the layer mask. I've included extra online video material to support this chapter, because it can be much easier to understand these processes by watching rather than reading.

 EXERCISE 1

SET UP THE COLLAGE WORKSPACE

The final collage will fit a workspace of 5.5 by 7 inches at 300 dots per inch (DPI), so keep this final target in mind while viewing the largest image component. Coincidentally, the first image you'll place in the document, the photograph of Salvador Dalí, is the largest. You'll use a cutout around his bust as a visual anchor for other juxtaposed images.

1. Open Photoshop, and create a new document (File > New) with the following settings: Select the Print category tab, then set up the document to be 5.5 inches wide by 7 inches in height, 300 pixels/inch, RGB color mode. Choose White in the Background Contents area, and click Create.

You can download the portrait of Dalí from www.loc.gov/pictures/item/2004662765.

2. Download the large TIFF image of Salvador Dalí from the Library of Congress (LOC) website (**FIGURE 8.4**), or open it from the **chapter08-start** folder. If you're working with the original download from the LOC website, rename the file **dali.tif** and place it in a folder on your Desktop named **chapter08** before opening it in Photoshop.

3. Crop the photo so that only Dalí's head is in the frame (**FIGURE 8.5**). This will give you a more accurate understanding of the size of the part of the file that you'll use in the collage.

REMINDER Did you forget how to use the Crop tool? See Chapter 4, Exercise 5.

4. View the document's resolution by choosing Image > Image Size to open the Image Size dialog box. Notice that the image was saved at 400 DPI. *Safely* (meaning, do not add pixels to the document) change the resolution to 300 DPI. Make sure that the Resample Image box is *not* checked before you make this change (**FIGURE 8.6**).

FIGURE 8.4 Download the largest available file from the Library of Congress website.

FIGURE 8.5 The Dalí image is cropped to include only his head.

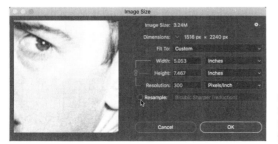

FIGURE 8.6 Turn off the Resample Image option (clear its checkbox) in the Image Size dialog box to redistribute pixels.

FIGURE 8.7 You'll see selection edges around the Dalí image as a result of choosing Select > All. When the image is selected, copy it before clicking the tab of the new document where you'll paste the selection.

5. Dalí's head is nearly as large as the new document, so you now can be assured that the image will be large enough to meet your specifications. Click OK to exit the Image Size dialog box if you haven't done so already. Press **Command-A/Ctrl-A** to select all of the image on the active layer. Press **Command-C/Ctrl-C** to copy the selection. Click the tab of the untitled (new) document (**FIGURE 8.7**). Press **Command-V/Ctrl-V** to paste the image of Dalí into the empty document. Rename the layer **dali**. Choose File > Save As and save the working collage document as **chaptero8.psd**.

6. Close **dali.tif**. You don't need to save changes you made to the document.

ⓔⓍⓔⓇⓒⒾⓢⒺ 2   TRACE AN IMAGE CONTOUR WITH THE PEN TOOL

In this exercise, you'll trace the contour of Dalí's head and shoulders with the Pen tool by placing anchor points in key locations on the perimeter of the shape. The anchor points should be set in places where the path of the line changes or is about to change. The Pen tool will make a path, not a selection. Your goal is to create a closed path outlining Dalí's bust. In this exercise, you will make a loose outline, which you will modify and refine in Exercise 3. A closed path is a complete shape—the starting and ending anchor points are the same. Ultimately, you'll save the path in the Paths panel.

SCREENCAST 8-1 TRACING WITH THE PEN TOOL

Most students find the Pen tool hard to learn without seeing a demonstration. I've created a video demonstrating this exercise on the *Foundations of Digital Art and Design* Vimeo playlist (see the companion website for a link).

All screencasts are available on the companion website, www.digitalart-design.com or on the Vimeo playlist, bit.ly/foundations-demos.

1. Continue to work in the Photography Workspace. (Choose Window > Workspace > Photography if another workspace is active.) Select the Pen tool from the Tools panel (FIGURE 8.8).

2. You can start anywhere to begin creating your path. I clicked the Pen tool once on the dent in Dalí's hair to begin my path (FIGURE 8.9).

3. Release the mouse. My second anchor point is just over the first curve of his hair. If you click once past that curve, you'll notice that the path created by two clicks is a straight line (FIGURE 8.10). Because you want the path to curve at this point, press **Command-Z/Ctrl-Z** to undo the last step. Instead of a single click, position the mouse in the same location, but this time press and hold the mouse button while dragging mostly to the right but also slightly downward (FIGURE 8.11). You'll see the curve begin to form. Drag until the curve traces the contour of his hairline.

ZOOM IN When you're creating a path or a selection or making any type of image manipulation, you really want to see what you're doing in a close view.

REMINDER You must start and end the path on the same anchor point to close the path.

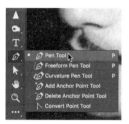

FIGURE 8.8 The Pen tool grouped with other related tools.

FIGURE 8.9 Begin a path with the Pen tool, and notice the anchor points that are created on the image.

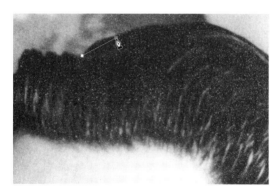

FIGURE 8.10 A straight path is created by two clicks with the Pen tool.

FIGURE 8.11 Notice the resulting Bezier handles on either side of the anchor point. These let you control the curve. While drawing the path, you can ignore the handles. After the path has been made, you may want to use the Direct Selection tool to modify anchor point positions or Bezier handles.

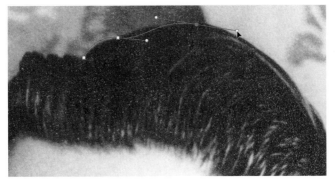

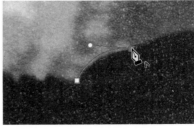

FIGURE 8.13 Option-click/Alt-click an anchor to delete a Bezier handle. This enables you to change the direction of the path.

FIGURE 8.12 Drag the Bezier handle to alter the shape of the curve.

4. The next place you want to click is toward the top back of Dalí's head. I've purposefully pressed the mouse button and dragged to try to make the path fit my contour in the way that I watch new students do this (FIGURE 8.12). Notice that the last part of the path starts to meet my needs, while the first part deviates from my intentions. When you create a curve, the next anchor point will be drawn in the direction of the previous curve. In this case, the direction of the previous curve is essentially the opposite of the direction that my path should be taking. Again, press **Command-Z/ Ctrl-Z** to undo this error. You need to make one crucial move before drawing this path in the next step.

5. Because the curve changes the direction of the path, and because the contour does not follow what the Pen tool is set to do, tell the anchor point to remove the Bezier handle directing the curve. Accomplish this by pressing the Option/Alt key while clicking the anchor point (FIGURE 8.13). Now one of the handles is missing, but as you plot your next anchor point, you'll notice that you can control the curve to fit the needs of your path.

6. Now plot the point you tried in Step 4 at the top of Dalí's head. Drag slightly downward so the path matches the contour of his head (FIGURE 8.14). The curve of the path aligns beautifully with the shape of his head.

FIGURE 8.14 Drag the Bezier handle to match the path to the contour of the image.

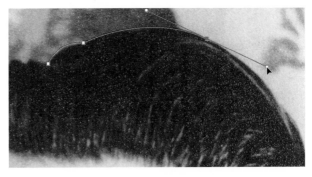

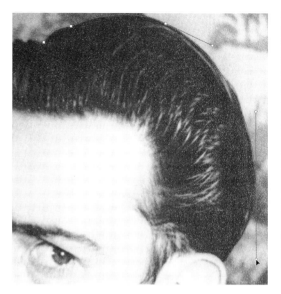

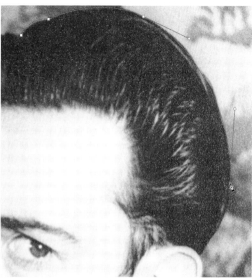

FIGURE 8.15 Fit anchor points to modify the path. It should match the contour of the image.

FIGURE 8.16 Remove a Bezier handle to change the direction of the path.

7. Zoom out slightly, if necessary, and plot the next anchor. I placed the cursor and dragged downward near the lower-bottom of Dalí's head to fit my path around the shape (FIGURE 8.15). My anchor point is purposefully above the area where the curve changes again to move back inward.

8. Option-click/Alt-click the anchor point, again, to remove one of the Bezier handles and allow the path to change directions (FIGURE 8.16).

9. Your next click will be just above his ear. Keep working in this fashion around the perimeter of Dalí's head. If you're not sure when to Option-click/Alt-click the anchor point, you can always try to make the next move and see if the path is following the contour. If it doesn't, press **Command-Z/Ctrl-Z** (Undo) and delete a Bezier handle. It's okay to work in a way that includes an element of experimentation and best-guessing until you understand the tools. When you get to the bottom part of the bust, you can make a large, sweeping curve that excludes the furry element near his jacket (FIGURE 8.17).

10. You must complete or "close" the path by making your last click meet up with your first anchor point. Notice that the Pen tool displays a circle icon near the bottom of the tool to indicate that the click you're about to make will close the path (FIGURE 8.18).

PEN TOOL If the path is not closed, you won't be able to convert the path to a selection (which is, in this case, the purpose of creating the path).

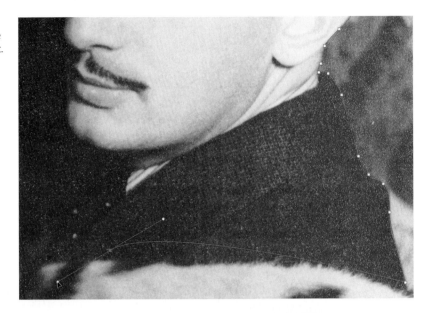

11. The Paths panel is grouped with the Layers panel. Click the tab of the
    Paths panel to open it, then save the path in the Paths panel by double-
    clicking the **Work Path.** Name the path **dali-head,** and then save the file
    by pressing **Command-S/Ctrl-S** (FIGURE 8.19). Now the path is saved with
    the file.

FIGURE 8.19 Double-click the
work path to name and save it.

MODIFY PATHS

EXERCISE 3

The path that you create with the Pen tool doesn't need to be perfect after your first effort at tracing the contour. You'll almost always have to make modifications to the path once it's closed. In this exercise, you'll modify the path so it fits the contour of Dalí's bust. I deliberately run into pitfalls in the next several steps to demonstrate how to make modifications to a path. Your process may not follow these steps exactly, but you should be able to learn how to modify your path by viewing this series of steps.

1. Zoom in to about 200% by pressing **Command-+/Ctrl-+**. Inspect your path; you can start anywhere. I'll begin in the same area where I started plotting my anchor points. I'm looking for any place where the path doesn't fit the contour of my shape.

2. Choose the Direct Selection tool from the Tools panel (**FIGURE 8.20**). This is the same tool you used in Illustrator to modify the paths created in Chapter 3. The first modification I'll make is in a place on the back of Dalí's head where the path includes a little bit of the background. I'll simply drag the path and move it inward so the contour of the path is on the outline of his dark hair (**FIGURE 8.21**).

3. I've noticed that my path is also slightly askew near Dalí's ear. In this situation, the curve doesn't match the contour. I can control this by modifying the Bezier handle. First, I'll click the anchor point with the Direct Selection tool to show its Bezier handles. Then, I'll drag one of the handles to see how that modifies the curve (**FIGURE 8.22**). Click anywhere outside the path to deactivate it when the modification is complete.

If you use the Direct Selection tool to move the path in one area, be mindful of how the rest of the path may change. Sometimes this isn't the best solution, because the change in one location disrupts the path everywhere else. Keep reading: One of the next steps might be a better solution for your situation.

FIGURE 8.20 You can use the Direct Selection tool to modify paths and anchor points.

 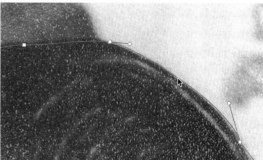

FIGURE 8.21 Drag the path with the Direct Selection tool to move it closer to the contour of the image.

FIGURE 8.22 Drag Bezier handles to modify curves for the best fit around image edges.

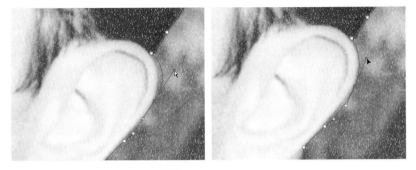

FIGURE 8.23 Move anchor points and modify Bezier handles around the contour of the image.

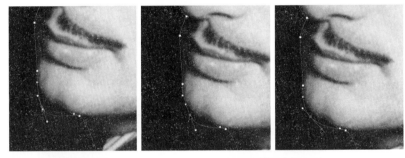

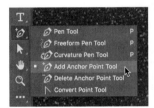

FIGURE 8.24 Use the Add Anchor Point tool to create new anchor points on a path.

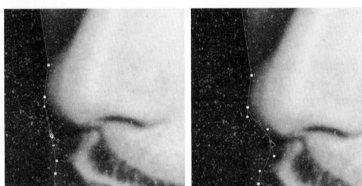

FIGURE 8.25 I added an additional anchor point near the curve of Dalí's nose, then I used the Direct Selection tool to modify the anchor point and its Bezier handles, changing the shape of the path to fit the curve beneath the nose.

4. In some cases, you may need to move the anchor point and modify the Bezier handle (**FIGURE 8.23**).

5. You also might need to add an anchor point and then modify it. To add an anchor point, click the path directly with the Add Anchor Point tool (**FIGURE 8.24**). Then, use the Direct Selection tool to make modifications (**FIGURE 8.25**).

6. Finally, you may need to convert an anchor point from one that indicates a straight, angular connection of lines to one that supports a curve. The Convert Point tool (FIGURE 8.26) is used for this purpose. With it, you can click any anchor point to change it from anchoring a straight line to anchoring a curve. In my path, there is a section of hair waves that are repeatedly drawn with curves. Somehow, one of my last dips took on a hard angle. I used the Convert Anchor Point tool to change that anchor point from straight to curvy and to modify the end of my path (FIGURE 8.27). You may need to adjust it so it is closer to the contour of the hairline with the Direct Selection tool.

7. I'm still not happy with that last hair area. I noticed an extra anchor point. Too many anchor points will make your path bumpy or inconsistent. When using the Pen tool, the dictum "less is more" couldn't be more appropriate. I used the Delete Anchor Point tool (FIGURE 8.28) to eliminate one of the anchor points and then the Direct Selection tool to reposition the path (FIGURE 8.29).

8. Press **Command-S/Ctrl-S** to save your work.

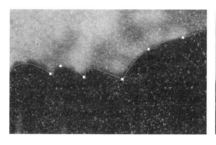
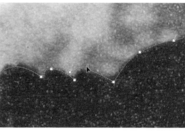

FIGURE 8.26 Use the Convert Point tool to change an anchor from a curve to a straight edge (or vice versa).

FIGURE 8.27 Convert anchor points to support a hard angle, rather than a curve.

FIGURE 8.28 Use the Delete Anchor Point tool to simplify a path by eliminating anchors.

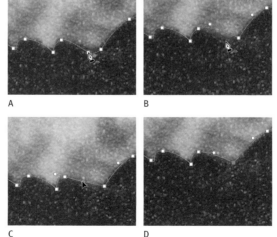

A

B

C

D

FIGURE 8.29 Clockwise from top left: **A.** Click an unwanted anchor point with the Delete Anchor Point tool. **B.** The resulting path has one less anchor point. **C.** Drag a Bezier handle to modify a curve. **D.** The resulting path outlines the contour of the image.

EXERCISE 4 CONVERT A PATH TO A SELECTION TO A LAYER MASK

This exercise may seem short, but it can be extremely helpful. You'll need to memorize these steps to convert a path to a pixel-based mask. Now that the path is saved in the Paths panel (Exercise 2, Step 11) and you've modified it to best reflect the contour of your image (Exercise 3), it can easily be transformed into a selection. You'll use the selection to create a layer mask, hiding the background imagery surrounding Dalí's bust.

1. In the Paths panel, activate the path by clicking it once (the path will appear blue); then click the Load Path As A Selection icon (FIGURE 8.30).

FIGURE 8.30 Load a path as a selection from the Paths panel, and notice the marching ants around the selection edges in your document.

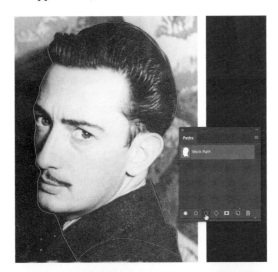

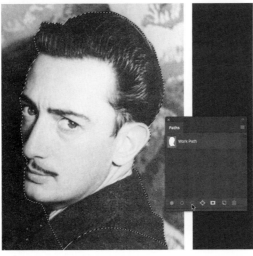

2. Look at the Layers panel. Only one layer, **dali**, should be active. (Click it once if it somehow became inactive.) Click the Add Layer Mask icon at the bottom of the Layers panel (**FIGURE 8.31**). The marching ants surrounding your selection are translated on the layer mask as a black-and-white representation of the areas hidden (not selected) and shown (selected). Press **Command-S/Ctrl-S** to save your work.

LAYER MASKS: TO SELECT OR NOT TO SELECT

You can add a layer mask to an image layer at any time. For instance, you can:

- Begin with a path, convert it to a selection, and then add the mask (a perfect way to work when you want a crisp edge around the image area).
- Make a basic selection with the Lasso tool or one of the Marquee tools and then add a mask.
- Skip selecting entirely and just add a layer mask to edit with black, white, or gray using brushes or fills.

3. Inspect the **dali** layer. The layer has two icons. On the far left is the layer thumbnail. I like to think of this as the "content icon" because you can see the actual content of the layer represented by its icon. Click once on this to make it active; you'll see four white corners surrounding the layer thumbnail (**FIGURE 8.32**). When the layer thumbnail is active, any action will modify the layer itself. For instance, painting with black paint on the image while the layer thumbnail is active literally adds black paint to the image (**FIGURE 8.33**). (If you followed my drawing activity in Figure 8.33, press **Command-Z/Ctrl-Z** to undo the brushwork.)

4. Continue to inspect the **dali** layer. To the right of the layer thumbnail is the layer mask thumbnail. The icon is a black-and-white representation showing which parts of the layer are hidden (the black background areas)

and which parts are on display (the white bust). Click once on this icon to activate it. Again, you'll see four white corners surrounding the layer mask thumbnail (**FIGURE 8.34**). When the layer mask thumbnail is active, you'll be modifying the mask, not the content. This is typically achieved with white, black, or shades of gray using the Brush, Pencil, or Gradient tools. You can also select an area and fill it with white, black, or gray on the mask. If I painted with black paint on the image while the layer mask thumbnail was active, I would be adding black paint to the mask. This is different than adding color to the pixels of the bitmap image. Here, I'm telling the mask where to hide pixels. Black indicates hidden pixels, so my same mustache-inspired swoop of black renders part of Dalí's face transparent as I add it to the layer mask (**FIGURE 8.35**). (If you followed my drawing activity in Figure 8.35, press **Command-Z/Ctrl-Z** to undo the brushwork.)

FIGURE 8.32 The layer thumbnail of the **dali** layer is active.

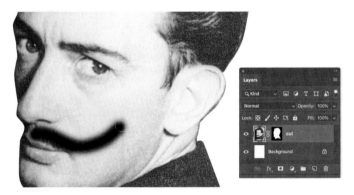

FIGURE 8.33 The active part of the layer will be modified. In this case, black paint is applied to the content of the layer, not the mask. So a black line is drawn on the layer. Notice how the line is visible only in sections of the image where the mask is white.

FIGURE 8.34 The layer mask is active, and its thumbnail is highlighted.

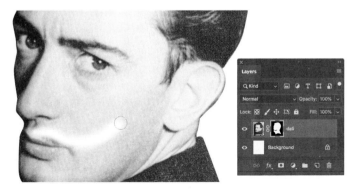

FIGURE 8.35 The active part of the layer is modified as a result of the black line drawn on the layer mask. Pixels in the area of the image are hidden where the line was drawn, which means that the white layer beneath it is visible in that area. The black line is visible on the layer mask (for now, notice it in the thumbnail).

SCALE, ADJUST, AND ORGANIZE

By default, a layer mask is linked to its layer thumbnail. This means that when you move or scale the contents of the layer, the mask will reposition or scale accordingly. In this exercise, you'll make minor modifications to the layer content. Be sure that the layer thumbnail is active before you begin.

1. Click the **dali** layer content thumbnail.

2. Press **Command-R/Ctrl-R** to show the rulers; then drag a guide from the left ruler to about one-third of the distance across the document space.

3. Press **Command-T/Ctrl-T** (or choose Edit > Free Transform) to decrease the scale of Dalí's bust. Drag the top-left transformation box downward and to the right until Dalí's nose is in line with the guide you created (**FIGURE 8.36**). Press the Return key to commit the transformation. Select the Move tool and hold down the Shift key to constrain the movement to a 90-degree angle while you adjust the vertical position of the **dali** layer so that the top of his hair is about an inch from the top of the document.

4. Add a Hue/Saturation adjustment layer, then select Colorize to create a monotone wash on the bust of Dalí. Adjust the Hue to set the color in the range of cyan (**FIGURE 8.37**).

You can see a video demonstrating how to use the Rectangular Marquee selection tool to measure the space precisely when numbers aren't your best friend on the *Foundations of Digital Art and Design* Vimeo playlist (linked from the companion website).

WATCH OUT! In prior versions of Adobe Photoshop, the rule was to always press the Shift key while scaling an image to prevent it from resizing disproportionally. New to Adobe Photoshop 2019 is a Free Transform command that automatically scales proportionally. This is great for new learners, but throws experienced users for a curve. If you press Shift while scaling or transforming an image the proportions will *not* be constrained.

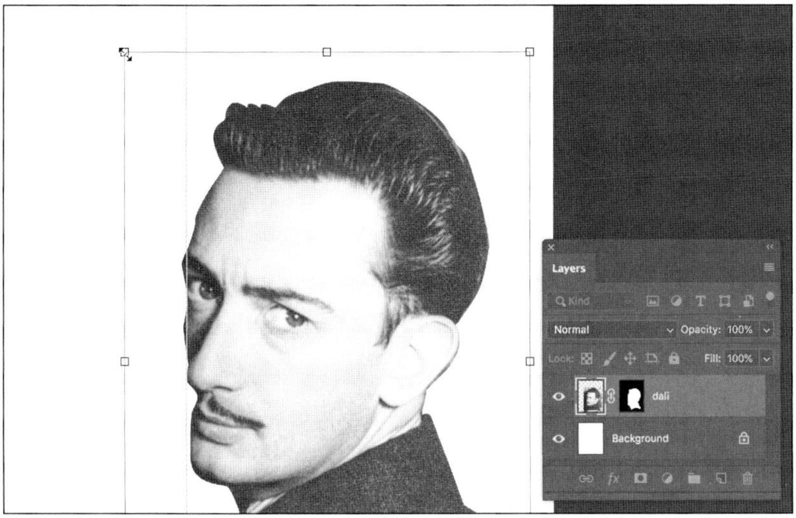

FIGURE 8.36 When the Layer Content and Mask icons are linked in the Layers panel, they will be transformed together. In this image, Dalí's torso and the mask used to control its hidden parts are scaled down and repositioned.

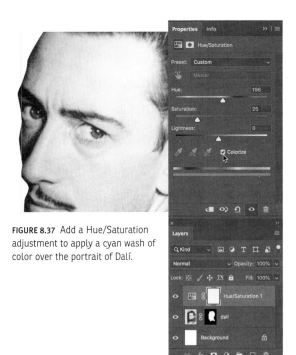

FIGURE 8.37 Add a Hue/Saturation adjustment to apply a cyan wash of color over the portrait of Dalí.

FIGURE 8.38 Select layers to organize, and then choose New Group From Layers from the Layers panel menu.

5. Finally, organize the Layers panel by grouping the two top layers. The adjustment layer should already be active, so Shift-click the **dali** layer to add it to your layer selection. Click the hard-to-see and unlabeled panel menu icon at the top right of the Layers panel to see a list of Layers panel commands. Choose New Group From Layers (**FIGURE 8.38**). Name the group *dali*, and click OK. The two layers are now organized into a single group. You can click the sideways arrow to expand or collapse layers contained in the *dali* group. Collapse the *dali* group before proceeding to Exercise 6. Press **Command-S/Ctrl-S** to save your work.

 EXERCISE 6 COPY A LAYER TO AN OPEN DOCUMENT

Starting with the release of Photoshop CS4 (2008), new documents open in tabs rather than in separate windows. Copying a layer from one open document to another is not terribly intuitive with this feature. You'll accomplish that task in this exercise.

1. Open **hand.psd**, an image I created for use in this collage. (It's saved in the **chapter08-start** folder on the companion website.) Notice that the document contains a layer group named *hand*. In it is a layer containing a photo of a hand and a Levels adjustment layer.

2. Collapse the layer group, and click the folder so the entire group is active. Select the Move tool from the Tools panel. Press and hold anywhere within the image of the hand in the application window (not in the Layers panel), and drag the pointer over the tab of our composite document, **chaptero8.psd** (FIGURE 8.39). The **chaptero8.psd** file will come to the foreground of the open documents.

3. Continue to hold the mouse button down and drag down from the tab into the Dalí image document (FIGURE 8.40). Release the mouse. If it didn't work for you on the first attempt, try it again. (It took me three or four tries the first time I learned to do this with tabbed documents.)

FIGURE 8.39 Copy a layer or layer group to an open file: Activate the layer or layer group, position the Move tool in the application window (anywhere on the image), and then drag the image to the tab of the opened document. Keep the mouse button depressed as you move on to the second step (Figure 8.40).

FIGURE 8.40 Move the pointer from the open tab down into the application window and release the mouse. View the Layers panel—the layer or layer group will join the stacking order.

FIGURE 8.41 The hand juxtaposed in front of Dalí's face. Notice how the hand is on top of the face in the stacking order of the layers.

ACCESSING FREE TRANSFORM You can access Free Transform without using keyboard shortcuts or the Edit menu by selecting Show Transform Tools in the Options bar for the Move tool. I do not activate Show Transform Tools because the tools get in the way of my ability to see details throughout my work process. For me it's easier to press **Command-T/Ctrl-T** when I need to access Free Transform. Everybody develops their own working processes. You should experiment—maybe you will like seeing the Transform Tools as you work.

FREE TRANSFORM You can rotate and scale an image with the Free Transform command. To rotate, position your pointer just outside one of the four corner points and then drag.

IMAGE CREDIT Earth's Moon captured by the Apollo 16 metric camera in 1972 is available at nssdc.gsfc.nasa.gov/imgcat/html/object_page/a16_m_3021.html.

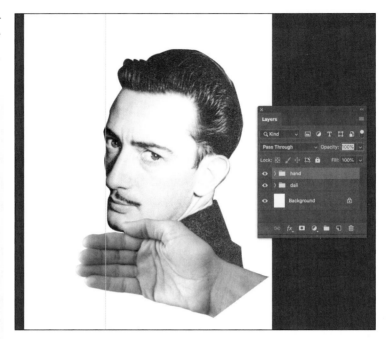

4. With the entire *hand* group active, use the Move tool to position the hand in the composite so the thumb is near Dalí's chin. Then, press **Command-T/Ctrl-T** to access Free Transform. Rotate the hand by dragging just outside one of the four corner points to about –38° (the rotation value is displayed in the Options bar), and press the **Return/Enter** key to commit to the transformation. Set the hand in place so the thumb barely touches Dalí's chin (**FIGURE 8.41**). Save your work. You can close the **hand.psd** document now that it's part of the composite image, **chapter08.psd**.

 THE MAGIC WAND

Once in a while, the Magic Wand tool can produce desired results nearly effortlessly. When you click part of an image with the Magic Wand tool, it selects pixels near the location you clicked as determined by color. It *attempts* to select like-colored pixels. From experience, I know that it's not always successful. You'll soon understand when you'll be able to work magically with the wand and when you'll have to spend time with the Pen tool. You can adjust this tool like all others using the Options bar.

1. Download the moon image from the companion site or the National Space Science Data Center. (Use the high-resolution TIFF, and rename the file **moon.tif**.) Open the **moon.tif** document in Photoshop.

2. With the **moon.tif** document open in Photoshop, press **Command-A/Ctrl-A** to select the entire image area and then press **Command-C/Ctrl-C** to copy the image. Click the **chapter08.psd** tab to activate the collage composition. Press **Command-V/Ctrl-V** to paste the moon from its home document to the collage. You can close **moon.tif** when you see the moon pasted into the Dalí collage image.

It's very common to go through the **Command-A/Ctrl-A, Command-C/Ctrl-C**, tab, **Command-V/Ctrl-V** steps and see nothing pasted into a new document. If this happens to you, check which layer was active in the starting document. Usually, the problem is that you started on an empty layer or an adjustment layer and, therefore, copied no pixel data.

NASA IMAGES IN THE PUBLIC DOMAIN

Photographs taken by astronauts, photographers, or mechanical cameras for NASA are part of the public domain, because they were commissioned by the U.S. government. An excellent database of images is located at nasaimages.org, and, of course, you can browse nasa.gov. I found the moon photograph by doing a Google image search for the word "moon," knowing that I wanted to click through to a page that looked like it might be hosted by NASA or the U.S. government. Another option is NASA on the Commons, a Flickr photostream that's easy to search and includes public domain photographs.

3. Rename the new layer **moon**. Select the Magic Wand tool from the Tools panel (**FIGURE 8.42**). In the Options bar, set the Tolerance level to 18 (meaning, select like-colored pixels within a range of 18 levels brighter or darker). Select the Anti-Alias and Contiguous options to make the edges of the pixel selection crisp and to create a selection based on image areas that touch one another. Make sure that the Sample All Layers box is not checked, as you want to sample and select only pixels on the moon layer. Click once anywhere in the black image space surrounding the moon. You'll see a selection around the contour of the moon and into its crevices on the right side (**FIGURE 8.43**).

WATCH OUT! Did the Magic Wand tool select something entirely different than what you expected? Make sure that the moon layer is active before selecting the moon image! You'll always have to watch out for activating the layer that you intend to work on.

FIGURE 8.42 The Magic Wand tool is used to select like pixels in a bitmap image.

FIGURE 8.43 The selection edges around the moon's contour and a view of the Magic Wand options.

4. Add a layer mask to the **moon** layer (FIGURE 8.44). Surprise! The result is the opposite of what you wanted. If you selected the area that you wanted to remove and then added a mask, don't worry. The good news is that it's simple to invert your layer mask. Make sure the layer mask is active, and then choose Image > Adjustments > Invert. Or press **Command-I/Ctrl-I**, a good keyboard shortcut to know if you, like me, will repeatedly find yourself flip-flopping the selected area (FIGURE 8.45).

5. Click the layer thumbnail to make the content of the layer active. Position, scale, and rotate the moon so it seems to be popping out of where Dalí's eye should be. Use the Move tool followed by Edit > Free Transform again, as you did in Exercise 6. Press **Return/Enter** to confirm the transformation.

6. Clean the layer mask (see the sidebar).

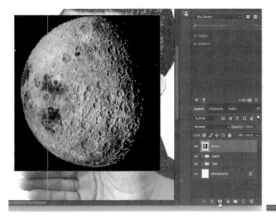

FIGURE 8.44 When you add a layer mask, the selected pixels will be visible. In this case, the selected pixels are the parts that you intend to hide.

FIGURE 8.45 When the colors on the layer mask are inverted, the hidden pixels become visible, and the visible pixels become hidden.

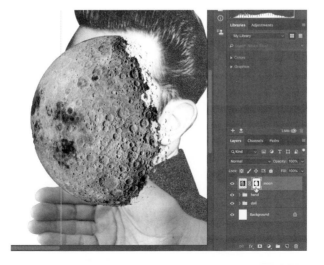

CLEAN UP THE MOON: HOW TO FINE-TUNE A LAYER MASK

Did you notice a thin, gray line creating a rectangle around the edges of where the moon background once was? The initial selection must not have included all of the black background. You'll need to modify the layer mask to eliminate the unwanted line from the collage. This basic technique is useful for removing unwanted artifacts from a layer mask.

1. Click the moon layer mask thumbnail to activate it.

2. Select the Brush tool from the Tools panel. In the Options bar, make sure that the Opacity and Flow are set at 100% and the Mode is Normal.

3. Make sure that black is loaded into the Foreground color chip. (You'll use black paint to hide this part of the layer.)

   SWAP COLORS Press the letter **X** on the keyboard to swap the foreground and background colors (black and white) as you are working on the mask.

4. Reduce or increase the size of the brush so it just covers the width of the line by tapping the **Left Bracket** ([) or **Right Bracket** (]) key, respectively.

5. Click just one time at one of the four corners of the black line (the starting point for one of the lines if you think of them as four separate lines). Don't drag **(FIGURE 8.46)**.

6. Reposition the mouse to the end of the first line. Press the Shift key and click once **(FIGURE 8.47)**. The drawing and painting tools will create a straight line if you click once; then move the mouse, press Shift, and click again (as in most Adobe applications).

7. Repeat steps 5 and 6 to hide the remaining three black lines.

FIGURE 8.46 Click once on the beginning of a line with black paint on the layer mask.

FIGURE 8.47 Reposition the mouse and Shift-click to draw a straight line on the mask, eliminating unwanted visible lines on the layer.

EXERCISE 8 SELECT, COPY, PASTE, REPEAT

Repetition is the best way to learn new techniques in Photoshop. Most of the steps in this exercise will be similar to those you've experienced in previous exercises. When images are juxtaposed to create a collage, repetition and contrast are two forces that help the viewer understand the visual message. In the final collage file (mine is saved as **chapter08-results.psd**), the large, dominant ant contrasts in size with the repeated smaller ants crawling on the palm of the hand (a memorable scene in *Un Chien Andalou*, a Surrealist film directed by Dalí and Luis Buñuel). The large ant also makes contrast in direction with the vertical plane anchored by Dalí's bust. Another way of stating this is that the large ant is a dynamic visual force, while the bust of Dalí is static. The yellow color wash that you will add to the images of the hand and moon in the course of this exercise will add a recurring color element to the composition.

1. In Photoshop, open the ant image from the **chapter08-start** folder.

2. Choose Select > All, then copy and paste the ant image to the **chapter08. psd** collage file (see Exercise 7, Step 2). Close **ant.jpg**.

3. Name the new layer **ant**, and attempt to select the white background surrounding the ant with the Quick Selection tool. This tool is grouped with the Magic Wand. It behaves similarly but allows you to draw on the areas you want to select, similar to holding Shift with the Magic Wand tool to add to its selection. You'll find that increasing the Brush size to about 32 will be helpful. Drag around the negative space surrounding the ant. You will make a selection that fits the contour of the ant and includes parts of its legs (FIGURE 8.48).

FIGURE 8.48 Draw a "quick" selection with the Quick Selection tool. The options for this tool include a brush size and a choice about what is sampled (the current layer or all layers). You can see my selection includes what I desired (the background) and parts I did not want to select (the legs).

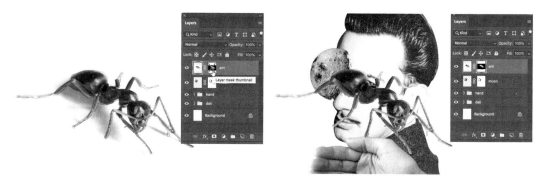

FIGURE 8.49 Paint the legs back into the mask while viewing them with the mask deactivated (left). On the right side you can see the results of the mask.

4. Click the Add Layer Mask icon on the **ant** layer. Invert the mask (**Command-I/Ctrl-I**). Clean the layer mask on the **ant** layer. You may need to brush in a leg or parts of legs using white paint. (Remember that white paint will make those layer parts visible.) For this portion of the exercise, I used white paint on a small brush in the layer mask while the mask was deactivated. I pressed the Shift key while I clicked the mask to deactivate and activate it while editing. I also hid the other layers by clicking the eyeball icon next to them for a clear view of those tiny ant legs (**FIGURE 8.49**).

5. Make the layer thumbnail active. Consult the final resulting image (Figure 8.3), then move, scale, and rotate the ant using the Free Transform command (**Command-T/Ctrl-T**).

6. Add a yellow color wash to the hand and moon images, starting with the hand. You can use a Hue/Saturation adjustment layer, or you can do this in the Blue channel of a Levels adjustment layer (because blue is the complement of yellow). Because the *hand* layer group already includes a Levels adjustment, I modified the midtone blue levels (**FIGURE 8.50**).

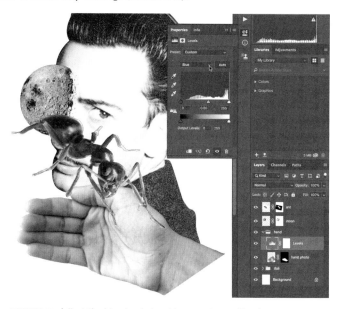

FIGURE 8.50 Adjust the blue levels to add a monotone yellow hue.

FIGURE 8.51 Create a clipping layer between the **Levels** and **hand photo** layers.

7. Add an adjustment of your choice to apply a yellow color wash to the moon image. I repeated a Levels adjustment and modified the midtones in the blue channel.

CLIPPING LAYERS

Option-clicking/Alt-clicking between layers will clip the top layer to the layer beneath it. You can use this to keep an adjustment layer tied directly to layers positioned beneath it. You can also clip layers to create a mask. Option-click/Alt-click between layers a second time to separate the clipping group.

8. Did you notice that as you add adjustments above each layer, they affect the whole document? The image of Dalí became much less cyan because these adjustments for yellow (or away from blue) were made to the **hand** and **moon** layers. Coincidentally, those two layers appear above the **dali** layer in the stacking order of the Layers panel. In this step, you'll *clip* the adjustment layer to the one layer it should affect. Press the Option/Alt key while clicking between the adjustment layer and the image layer beneath it; then repeat this on the second pair of adjustment and image layers (**FIGURE 8.51**).

9. Organize your Layers panel with a new layer group, *moon*, to contain the moon and its adjustment layer.

10. Finally, duplicate the **ant** layer, scale and rotate it, and then duplicate the smaller ant and repeat to create the ants in the palm of the hand. I made the copies of the small ant by Command-Option-dragging/Ctrl-Alt-dragging it.

11. Create a copy of the **hand photo** layer and name it **hand w shadows**. Add a small shadow beneath each ant using the Burn tool (set to Midtones, 10%) to make them appear more connected to the hand (**FIGURE 8.52**). "Floating" images are often easily grounded with a small shadow. When you're done, organize the duplicate ant layers into their own layer group. Clip a Black & White adjustment layer to the group. Save your results in PSD format. You can view my process in the *Screencast 8-2: Duplicate, Transform, Burn, Organize, and Adjust—Ants in the Hand* video.

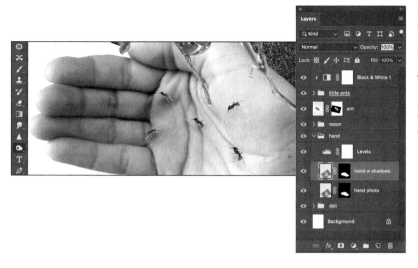

FIGURE 8.52 Duplicate the **ant** layer, resize and rotate it using Free Transform, then add a small shadow beneath the ant to the **hand w shadows** layer. You can repeat until the hand is covered with ants or declare victory after adding just a few.

SCREENCAST 8-2 DUPLICATE, TRANSFORM, BURN, ORGANIZE, AND ADJUST—ANTS IN THE HAND

Readers who enjoy experimentation will likely be able to transform and place the ants without much guidance. However, in this video demonstration I complete Step 9 of Exercise 8 for those who want to see my step-by-step process.

All screencasts are available on the companion website, www.digitalart-design.com or on the Vimeo playlist, bit.ly/foundations-demos.

 LAB CHALLENGE

Create a Dada-style collage in which the edges of the contours are visible to suggest the conceptual tension between the juxtaposition of visual elements. This requires a tension between at least two separate ideas. Use layer masks, selection tools, and adjustment layers when necessary—and don't forget to organize the Layers panel as you work.

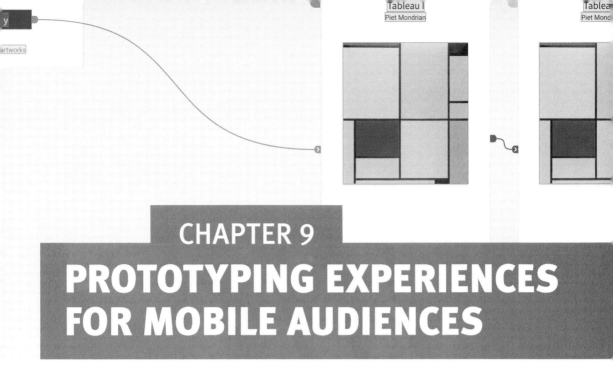

CHAPTER 9
PROTOTYPING EXPERIENCES FOR MOBILE AUDIENCES

THE EXERCISES IN this chapter will demonstrate how to prototype a basic experience on a digital device. You'll start by viewing a paper and pencil user flow diagram to map interaction ideas before creating a prototype in Adobe XD that you can test and share on your mobile device.

Prototypes model an exploration of how an idea might be expressed. All designers create prototypes, although they may not use that specific word: Fashion designers create garment prototypes to explore how an article of clothing might feel, fold, and fit; automotive designers better understand car proportions using full-scale clay models; interaction designers simulate screens to explore how software might be used. Prototypes help designers explore interaction scenarios using simulated artifacts. For example, the artist collective SWEAT created the interaction prototype that appears in **FIGURE 9.1** before developing the game *Migraciones* (**FIGURE 9.2**).

This chapter is co-authored by Cassini Nazir and xtine burrough, colleagues at the University of Texas at Dallas.

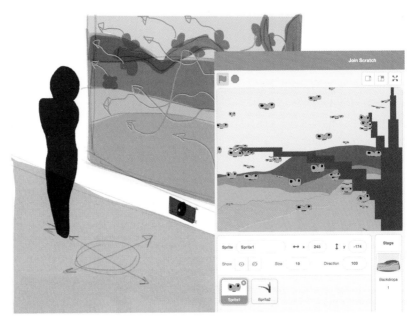

FIGURE 9.1 *Migraciones* sketch and prototype by SWEAT (Esteban Fajardo, Chris GauthierDickey, Rafael Fajardo), 2017. Hand drawn interaction sketch (left) created using the Paper app (available from WeTransfer) in 2017; and, rapid prototype screenshot (right) created in Scratch 2.0 in early 2018. Image courtesy of the artists.

FIGURE 9.2 *Migraciones* in-engine screenshot by SWEAT (Esteban Fajardo, Chris GauthierDickey, Rafael Fajardo), 2018. Screenshot taken within final executable version of *Migraciones* developed in Unity3D mid-2018. Image courtesy of the artists. This socially-conscious game is situated in an art gallery, where the gallery audience becomes the "gamer."

A common misconception is that prototypes focus on only the look and feel of an artifact. Stephanie Houde and Charles Hill note that prototypes may also explore implementation, how a thing might be created (using code or components), as well as the role the artifact might play in a person's life or how it might change a person's role [1]. A prototype that explores all three aspects is an *integration* prototype (FIGURE 9.3).

Anything can be a prototype—even old bicycle parts. When Sam Farber's wife's arthritis resulted in her having difficulty gripping a metal potato peeler, he wondered, "What if this tool could be made more comfortable?" Designers Davin Stowell and Daniel Formosa recognized the grip size and material were wrong for repetitive tasks: The grip was too small, and the metal too painful against the hand. The earliest prototype combined a metal potato peeler with the rubber handlebar grip from a bicycle [2]. Refining this early prototype over time ultimately led to the OXO Good Grips peeler in use today (FIGURE 9.4).

Just as important to the creation of prototypes are the conversations prototypes can provoke. Prototypes begin a process of iterative exploration and refinement, informed by conversations around it. Along the way, you gain insights with each new conversation and each new prototype about how your artifact could be improved.

In the exercises in this chapter, you won't prototype physical objects like a potato peeler, but you will prepare an interactive design—a concept for a color matching game.

To produce the final composition, you'll learn to use Adobe XD and review many of the skills you've learned in previous chapters, such as interactions between colors and creating vector shapes; and begin working with type, which you'll learn more about in the next section.

REFERENCE [1] Stephanie Houde and Charles Hill, "What Do Prototypes Prototype?" In *Handbook of Human-Computer Interaction (2nd Ed.)*, M. Helander, T. Landauer, and P. Prabhu (eds.). Amsterdam: Elsevier Science B. V, 1997.

REFERENCE [2] Early prototypes of Smart Design, Inc.'s potato peeler are in Cooper Hewitt's collection, Accession number 2011-50-20. The earliest prototype combined a metal potato peeler with a rubber bicycle handlebar grip, as you can see at cprhw.tt/o/2EiRX. Also, Sam Farber describes the exploration process in Gary Hustwit's documentary *Objectified* (2009).

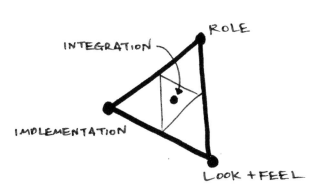

FIGURE 9.3 Cassini Nazir's hand-drawn representation of Stephanie Houde's model represents dimensions of a prototype.

FIGURE 9.4 The co-authors of this chapter, Cassini and xtine, both have Good Grips peelers in their kitchens. What's in your kitchen?

SCREEN RESOLUTION

LINK PaintCode's page, "The Ultimate Guide to iPhone Resolutions," is helpful to understand relationships among points, pixels, and physical screen size. You can find it at paintcodeapp.com/news/ultimate-guide-to-iphone-resolutions.

LINK *Paintings and Painters: An Art Game* (1977–78) designed by Jim Hoekema for Charles and Ray Eames, may be the first prototype of an interactive art game system ever built. Although the tools and mediums have changed and multiplied since Hoekema's first design, the basic development and thinking around prototypes is much the same. See Hoekema's IXDA18 talk at vimeo.com/255580131.

Chapter 5, *Resolution and Value*, briefly touched on screen resolution. However, for this chapter you'll create a design with a screen purpose in mind: an application (*app*) for mobile devices. Adobe XD allows you to design and prototype experiences for web and mobile devices.

One challenge of designing for mobile devices is that you never know the resolution of the end user's *viewport*—the specific screen area in which the user experiences networked digital content. Because a design will have to be legible at various screen resolutions, vector images are preferred in application development. You will learn to create vector graphics to alleviate concern for bitmapped pixilation or blurriness for viewers using high-resolution devices.

GETTING STARTED WITH XD

For these exercises, you'll use text and simple vector shapes to simulate buttons in a prototype for a game inspired by Jim Hoekema's *Art Game* (see the link nearby). Yours will be an interactive matching game that asks the player to identify colors in works of art.

Adobe XD enables you to create or edit vector shapes (lines, circles, and squares) as well as more complicated shapes (such as Bezier curves and path combinations)—just like those you created in Illustrator for exercises in Chapter 3.

WHAT YOU'LL NEED

Download the following source materials to complete the exercises in this chapter:

✔ The file **chapter09-workfiles.zip** which includes **chapter09-start.xd**.

WHAT YOU'LL MAKE

In the exercises in this chapter, you'll create a simple color-matching game that samples colors from famous works of art (**FIGURE 9.5**). You'll learn to create app screens as well as transitions and buttons to connect them.

FIGURE 9.5 Your Adobe XD file will be inspired by a hand-drawn diagram Cassini made (Figure 9.6). In the following exercises you will create a prototype for a color matching game.

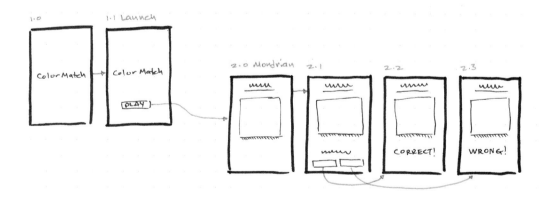 EXERCISE 1 · ARTICULATE THE DESIGN CHALLENGE

In these exercises, you'll develop a high-fidelity, high-resolution prototype that simulates a color-matching game. *Fidelity* refers to how close what you're making looks to the final design. *Resolution* refers to the amount of detail (such as text and images). A low-fidelity prototype is usually completed quickly, using paper and pen, and helps you explore your ideas early in your design process. High-fidelity prototypes are refinements of your early ideas and take more time to develop. They are made with digital applications, like XD.

While you're completing these exercises for educational purposes, you should be learning to articulate visual solutions when developing a design that demonstrates a process. There are many ways to approach the mindful and material activities associated with design. These exercises use a process developed at Stanford University called *Design Thinking*. It has five phases: empathize, define, ideate, prototype, and test. For the following exercises, you will complete the last two phases: prototype and test. This prototype is loosely based on Jim Hoekema's *Art Game*, completed while working for Charles and Ray Eames.

Because an app is often expressed on multiple screens, it is useful to create a *user flow diagram* to explain how those screens are connected. In the diagram, numbers and names are applied to each screen (FIGURE 9.6). When you are finished prototyping the app, your XD artboards will look similar to the user flow diagram.

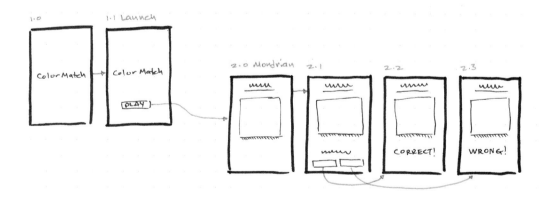

FIGURE 9.6 The resulting file for the exercises in Chapter 9 will include six artboards as seen in this user flow diagram—one for each demo step of the user experience.

Refer to these steps while you're working through Exercises 2–5. The diagram in Figure 9.6 represents the interaction design goals.

Demo step 1: The user opens an app and is presented with a launch screen that orients them to the app. Digital apps often display a loading screen to the user while loading media assets for the app in the background.

Demo step 2: The user taps a button bearing a label, such as Play or Begin, to enter the game.

Demo step 3: The game presents a painting and two paint chips. The user is asked to correctly select a paint chip showing the color in the painting.

Demo step 4: The user selects either the correct or incorrect answer.

Demo step 5: The user is presented with a feedback screen based on the value of the answer selected in step 4.

EXERCISE 2 SET UP ARTBOARDS

Just like in Adobe Illustrator, the *artboard* in XD is the work space for your prototype. It simulates the physical screen size of the device you will be using.

1. Open the **chapter09-start.xd** file. It contains basic artboards for an iPhone 6/7/8 Plus screen. You can adjust the size or attributes of an artboard by double-clicking it. These artboards were created at the right size for the device we had on-hand (an iPhone 6), but the option to include Responsive Resize was not turned on for the artboard **1.1 Launch Page**. Turning on Responsive Resize automatically rescales groups of objects in the layout, while preserving placement and scale, to match the user's device size. Because your design should be flexible enough to accommodate any device, you will activate this option. Choose the Select tool from the Toolbar, and double-click the artboard. In the Property Inspector at the right side of the application workspace, click the Responsive Resize switch to turn it on **(FIGURE 9.7)**.

FIGURE 9.7 Turn on Responsive Resize to activate XD's automatic resizing function.

2. Click away from the artboard to deselect it. When you create a new file in XD, the application defaults to Design mode (**FIGURE 9.8**). Design mode allows you to create the screens you will develop for the app by creating and modifying artboards. There are two artboards in the **chapter09-start** file, each of which corresponds to one screen in the app: **1.1 Launch Page** and **2.2 Mondrian Match**.

In Exercise 5 you will switch to Prototype mode to test the app you have created.

3. Duplicate the first artboard to create an additional screen that includes all of its components. Click the title **1.1 Launch Page** to select that artboard. You'll know you've selected it when the title changes to blue and a blue selection box appears around the entire artboard. Press **Command-C/Ctrl-C** to copy the artboard and **Command-V/Ctrl-V** to paste it. You should see a duplicate launch screen beside the original (**FIGURE 9.9**).

4. Rename the first two artboards so they match the user flow diagram in Figure 9.6. Double-click the title of the first artboard and enter "1.0" in its title field. Retitle the second artboard "1.1 Launch" (**FIGURE 9.10**).

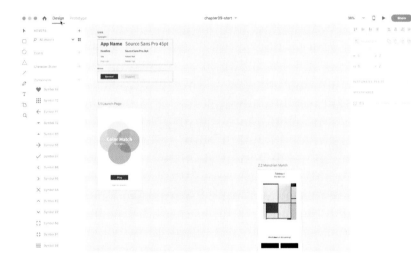

FIGURE 9.8 Edit screens in Design mode, and edit interactions in Prototype mode. Symbols included in this file are shown in the Asset panel, expanded of the left side of the application.

FIGURE 9.9 (LEFT) The duplicate artboard appears next to the original, and the title is amended with a sequential number.

FIGURE 9.10 (RIGHT) After renaming the first two artboards.

5. Zoom in to modify artboard **1.0** (press **Command-+/Ctrl-+**). Delete the two buttons (Play and About the artworks) at the bottom of the layout— marquee over them, and press the **Delete/Backspace** key (**FIGURE 9.11**).

6. Zoom out (**Command- –(minus)/Ctrl- –**) and move in the application frame to view artboard **2.2 Mondrian Match**. Dragging on the trackpad moves your view in the application; you can also press the **spacebar** to activate the Hand tool. Copy artboard **2.2 Mondrian Match**, and paste it three times. These three duplicates will show different *states* in your app. States communicate the status of a component or interactive element.

7. Rename these four second-level artboards so they match the titles of the screens in the user flow diagram: **2.0 Mondrian**, **2.1**, **2.2**, and **2.3** (**FIGURE 9.12**).

FIGURE 9.11 Change the first artboard (left) to a title screen with no buttons on it (right).

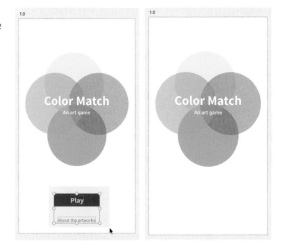

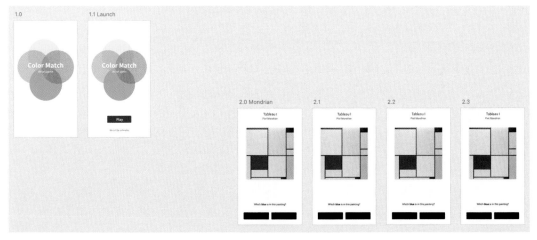

FIGURE 9.12 Create three copies and rename them to match the user flow diagram.

USER INTERFACE (UI) KITS

You'll notice that there are items outside of the artboards, such as buttons, typography, and system icons. These common components comprise a User Interface (UI) Kit. A UI Kit is a comprehensive list of components that you can use to create an app screen.

XD allows you to easily download kits for commonly used devices (such as phones, tablets, and watches). Simply choose File > Get UI Kits.

You can download kits for Apple iOS, Google Material, Microsoft Windows, and other operating systems. When using these kits, it is helpful to consult the Human Interface Guidelines (or HIG) for the particular device you have chosen. The HIG explains good practices, conventions, and recommendations. Using elements from the HIG provides a consistent experience across apps.

Although you won't use one of these UI Kits for exercises in this chapter, you should know that you can easily download a kit for any device or operating system you choose to prototype **(FIGURE 9.13)**.

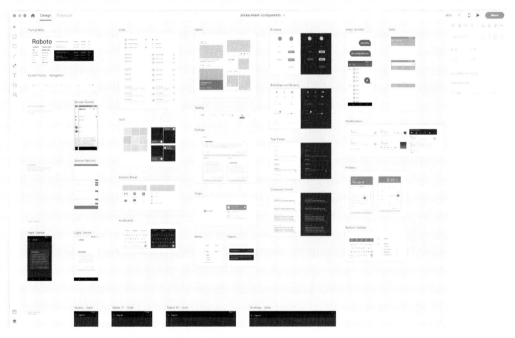

FIGURE 9.13 User interface kits are available for various operating systems.

LINK View the Apple Human Interface Guidelines at developer.apple.com/design. The Google HIG is called Material Design and can be found at material.io. Designers have been creating these systems for years. Modern HIGs echo messages from industrial designer Henry Dreyfuss' 1955 book *Designing for People*.

EXERCISE 3   ADDITIONAL VISUAL DESIGN

If you downloaded a UI Kit, you'll need to return to the **chapter09-start.xd** file. Do this by choosing Window > chapter9-start.xd.

Consult the color match game user flow diagram (Figure 9.6) as you work on these exercises. In this exercise you will be prototyping the four screens needed to demonstrate steps 2.0 through 2.3. In XD you will create the transitions and design the artboards representing various screens.

1. The artboard **2.0 Mondrian** will transition to artboard **2.1**. Because these two screens will always be experienced as a sequence, their visual layout should be similar. Only the title and image of the painting should be seen in **2.0 Mondrian**, so delete the buttons and the line of text just above them without editing the position of the other design elements like you did for artboard **1.0** in Exercise 2, Step 5.

2. Change the color of the two black buttons on artboard **2.1**. The left button will be the correct color seen in the painting, and the right button will be the incorrect color. Press **V** to make sure the Select tool is loaded. Click the black button on the left to select it. In the Appearance section of the Property Inspector on the right, the Fill is set to black. Click the Eyedropper tool to the right of Fill (**FIGURE 9.14**), and then click a blue area in the painting to fill the selected shape with a sample of color from the painting (**FIGURE 9.15**). The left button is a blue represented in the painting (in this case, #282D77), so it is the correct answer in the game.

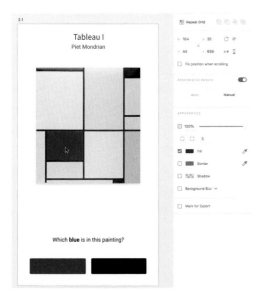

FIGURE 9.14 Load the Eyedropper to sample a color from the painting.

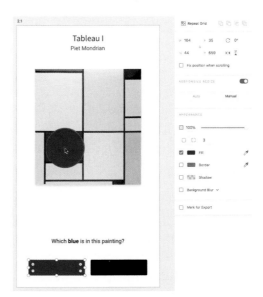

FIGURE 9.15 Click in the blue area to fill the left rectangle with the correct answer, which is a shade of blue found in the painting. Your shade of blue may be different depending on where you click to sample.

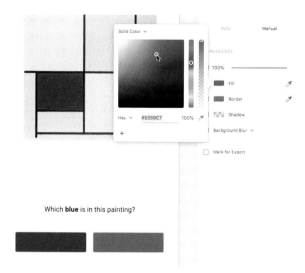

FIGURE 9.16 Select a color related to the shade of blue in the painting for the button that will be the wrong choice.

Which **blue** is in this painting?

3. Select the black button on the right and edit its fill. Because you'll make this button the incorrect color you could leave it black, but you may want to make the game more challenging. In the Appearance section of the Property Inspector, click the black rectangle next to Fill. The color picker opens. Click the Eyedropper tool inside the color picker and sample the left button to load its color. Back in the color picker, drag the pointer upward across the large square color spectrum to lighten the color. The game difficulty can adjusted by making the colors extremely different (#3D3FAC) for an easier challenge or similar (#2F3489) to create a more difficult challenge. Because this is the first question in the game, make it easy for the user **(FIGURE 9.16)**. Click anywhere off of the artboard to close the color picker.

When using any Adobe application, you should always have your screen at or near full brightness. You won't notice the color differences on your screen if it is in low-brightness mode.

4. Edit artboard **2.2** to match the user flow diagram. Select the two black buttons at the bottom of the screen, and press the **Delete/Backspace** key.

5. Select the text object that says, "Which blue is in this painting?" Remember that the textbox should stay in the same position on this artboard as it appears on the others to retain consistency throughout the prototype. In the Text area of the Property Inspector, click the Left Align button. Double-click the text object to modify the type. Enter the text, "Correct. Mondrian is one of the 20th century's most recognizable artists, influencing architecture, industrial design, and the graphic arts." Set the word "Correct" in bold using the Font Weight menu in the Text area of the Property Inspector, and use a line break (press **Return/Enter**) to set it on its own line. You'll need to lengthen the text object by dragging the handle in the middle of the bottom edge of the text object down **(FIGURE 9.17)**.

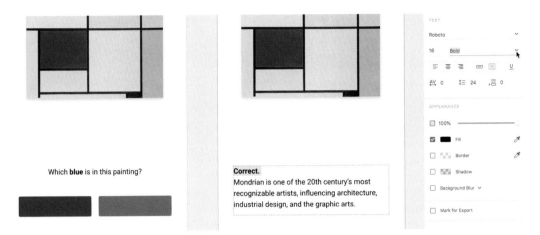

FIGURE 9.17 Edit the text in the text object for the correct answer. Use the Font Weight menu to set "Correct" in bold. The *baseline* is an invisible line upon which type sits. Notice the baseline of the word "Correct" in artboard **2.2** creates continuity by sharing its alignment with the baseline of the question posed in artboard **2.1**.

FIGURE 9.18 Artboard **2.3** is modified to provide feedback that the incorrect answer was selected.

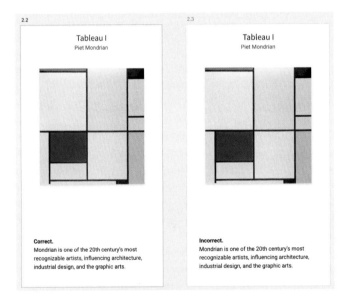

6. Edit artboard **2.3**. Load the Select tool. Delete the text object and buttons in the lower half of the artboard. Copy the "Correct" text object from artboard **2.2**. Click artboard **2.3** to select it, and press **Command-V/Ctrl-V** to paste the text object. It will paste in the same relative location. Change the text from "Correct" to "Incorrect" **(FIGURE 9.18)**. You have prepared all of the artboards required for this prototype. In the next exercise, you will add connections between each artboard.

EXERCISE 4 — CONNECT THE PROTOTYPE SCREEN

Now that the visual designs for all of your screens are complete, you will connect the screens using transitions and buttons. *Transitions* create automatic connections—they are usually time-based. *Buttons* are triggers initiated by the user that connect screens in the user flow diagram.

1. Switch to Prototype mode by clicking Prototype on the Application toolbar (**FIGURE 9.19**). The workspace changes—in Prototype mode you have only two tools in the left Toolbar. You may need to zoom out to see all six artboards (or Press **Command-0/Ctrl-0** to use the Zoom To Fit All command).

2. So far, your artboards are disconnected. You'll create an Automatic transition from artboard **1.0** to **1.1 Launch** by using a time trigger. Click artboard **1.0**. A blue tag appears on the side of the artboard with a white arrow (**FIGURE 9.20**). Drag the arrow to the artboard you'd like to connect it to, in this case **1.1 Launch** (**FIGURE 9.21**). In the pop-up window that appears choose Time from the Trigger menu. Set the delay to 1 second, and choose Auto-Animate from the Action menu (**FIGURE 9.22**).

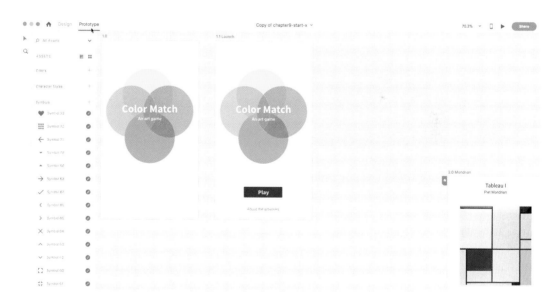

FIGURE 9.19 Switch your working mode from Design to Prototype.

FIGURE 9.20 The blue tag holding the white arrow initially appeared to the left side of artboard **1.0**.

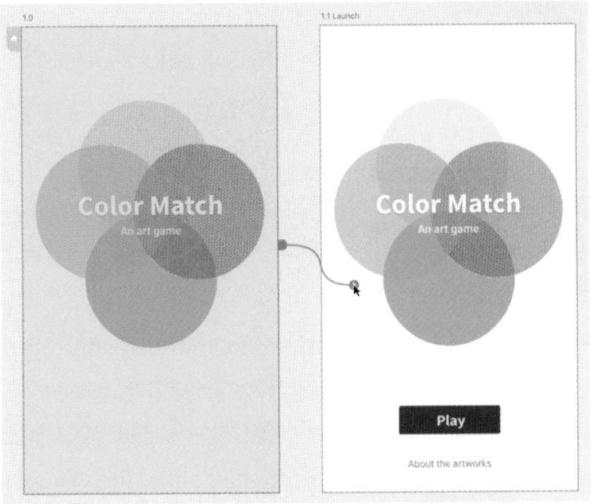

FIGURE 9.21 Connect the arrow to artboard **1.1 Launch**.

FIGURE 9.22 Set the Trigger and Action options.

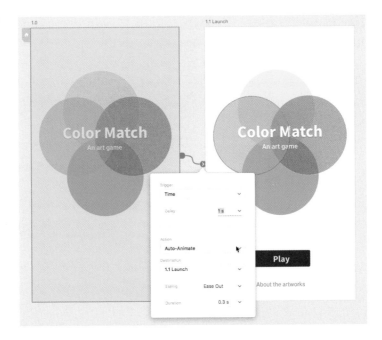

3. Click outside of the artboard to set the transition. Select artboard **1.0**, then click the Play button at the top right of the XD interface (next to the blue Share button) **(FIGURE 9.23)**. You'll see a preview of the currently selected artboard as a simulated screen that transitions automatically to **1.1 Launch** **(FIGURE 9.24)**.

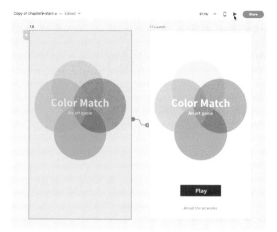

4. Close the simulation. Click the arrow to access the transition settings (**FIGURE 9.25**), and then adjust the easing, duration, and delay settings in the dialog that appears. Preview your work again. Change the duration to 3 seconds. Does the transition seem too fast, too slow, or just right? Modify the timing until you feel it is right.

5. Select the Play button graphic on artboard **1.1 Launch**, and drag the blue arrow to **2.0 Mondrian** (aren't you glad we named these artboards?). Set the trigger to Tap and the Action to Transition with a Dissolve animation (**FIGURE 9.26**).

6. Select the **2.0 Mondrian** artboard and drag the blue tab on the right side of the artboard to **2.1**. Set the Trigger to Time with a 2 second delay (enter "2" into the Delay field) similar to the transition created in Step 2. Set the Action to Auto-Animate.

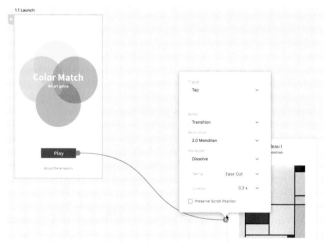

FIGURE 9.25 Click the arrow between artboards to access the transition settings.

FIGURE 9.26 The tap trigger is used to change a graphic to a functioning button between artboards in your prototype.

7. On artboard **2.1,** select the first button (the correct color) and drag the arrow to its appropriate artboard according to the user flow diagram (**2.2**). Set the Trigger to Tap and the Action to Auto-Animate.

8. Select the second button (the incorrect color) on artboard **2.1,** and drag it to its appropriate artboard according to the user flow diagram (**2.3**). Set the Trigger to Tap and the Action to Auto-Animate (**FIGURE 9.27**).

9. You can easily view all of the connections you have created by selecting everything on all of the artboards in the document—press **Command-A/ Ctrl-A** (**FIGURE 9.28**).

10. Test the prototype by clicking the Play button in the Application toolbar, and fix any errors.

FIGURE 9.27 The triggers are set between the two buttons on artboard **2.1** and the appropriate artboards (**2.2** and **2.3**) according to the user flow diagram.

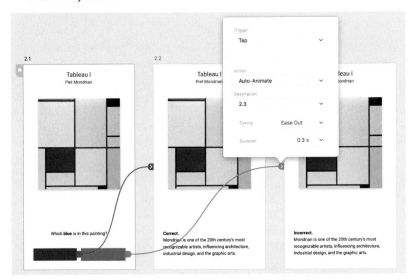

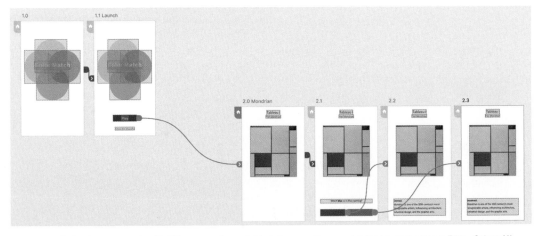

FIGURE 9.28 A simple way to make all of the connections visible is to press **Command-A/Ctrl-A** or to choose Edit > Select All.

EXERCISE 5 TEST AND SHARE

Prototypes can demonstrate a design process and generate intelligent conversations around interfaces. You've built a simple prototype of a game. Now that your first iteration of the prototype is complete, share it on your mobile device.

1. Download the Adobe XD app to your phone from the Google Play or Apple App Store. Launch the app, and login with your Adobe account credentials. Tap the Live Preview button at the bottom of your device's screen (its icon depicts a phone display superimposed on a desktop display). XD will prompt you to connect your device using a USB cable.

2. Once connected, open XD on your computer and click an artboard. It will load (and appear) on your phone. Once the prototype is loaded on your phone you can share it with friends or peers to see how they interact with it.

3. Always test your prototype. For example, as you begin sharing with others, you may come across someone who can't distinguish the color blue (FIGURE 9.29). They may still be able to complete the game because they are distinguishing the level of brightness, not the hue. Testing often gives you results you couldn't predict.

Someone may ask you why the "About the artworks" button on artboard **1.1 Launch** doesn't activate anything (or they may say, "It's broken!"). XD allows you to quickly edit and refine your app to improve the overall user experience.

LINK Kyle Soucy's "Sins of a UX Researcher" identifies pitfalls that you should avoid as you share your prototype with others. Review the 15 "sins" at www.slideshare.net/usableinterface/sins-of-a-ux-researcher-24107286.

FIGURE 9.29 At left, the original prototype artboard **2.1**. To its right, simulated screens for tritanopia (blue-yellow-color vision deficiency), protanopia (red-green color vision deficiency), and total color vision deficiency.

 **LAB CHALLENGE**

Add an artboard for the "About the artworks" button. Then, select another artwork and create a second "level" for the Color Match game. You'll need to create a Next button on artboards **2.2** and **2.3**. When you've created the screens, make sure to test and share to get feedback.

FIGURE S4.1 A Pueblo petroglyph (a rock carving, as opposed to a rock painting which would be referred to as a *pictograph*) in Boca Negra Canyon at Petroglyph National Monument in New Mexico. It was likely carved by ancestors of today's Pueblo Indians. Puebloans had lived in the Rio Grande Valley since before 500 CE.

SECTION 4
TYPOGRAPHY

TYPOGRAPHY IS the visual design of language. It's an essential component of any media presentation that includes words. As mentioned in the introduction, readers and students of this book are enrolled in a wide variety of academic programs. The communications department where I used to teach doesn't require students to complete a course in typography. The School of Art, Technology, and Emerging Communication where I teach now just added a required typography course to its Design and Production degree plan.

So this is what I tell all my students: *Take at least one typography class.* Go to a community college, sit in on a university class for no credit, do whatever you have to do to take at least one course in type. Without a knowledge of typography, you'll be left with a basic visual vocabulary for images but not for the design of words.

There are many resources for learning typography. My favorite books include Ellen Lupton's *Thinking with Type*, which is accompanied by an outstanding website full of tools for students and educators alike; John Kane's *A Type Primer;* Erik Spiekermann's *Stop Stealing Sheep & Find Out How Type Works;* and Emil Ruder's *Typographie: A Manual of Design.*

Imagine a day in your life where you never see a printed word (on a screen, on paper, on the highway, on a billboard, or on informational signage). Life as we know it would be drastically different and wholly uninformed without the written word. Surely, we would rely on pictographs, petroglyphs (FIGURE S4.1), or design some other means of communicating ideas, but isn't it convenient that in the English language we have to consider only 26 letterforms? This section focuses on the intelligent consideration of the design of letterforms with regard to how they appear when printed or on the screen, how the display of text is best planned for the human eye, and how type relates to other design elements.

LETTERFORMS

Letterforms are designed by typographers who manipulate the shapes of common glyphs (letterforms, numbers, and other communicative symbols). Typographers place a special emphasis on the relationships between thin and thick lines, positive and negative space, the space that a glyph occupies, and more. Although you won't be designing new letters in the exercises in this section, you'll begin to notice the differences among typefaces. Each font has its own personality. Your choice of a typeface for a project should be informed by its style and the message you intend to communicate in your project. Toward this end, you'll learn some basic anatomical definitions and historical classifications that will help you make informed decisions.

LINK See the Library of Congress's interactive Gutenberg Bible exhibit at www.loc.gov/exhibits/bibles/the-gutenberg-bible.html#obj0.

The movable type developed by the German blacksmith Johannes Gutenberg revolutionized European cultures in the 15th century (FIGURE S4.2). Ideas could be transmitted via printed matter with a new ease, much as the invention of the Internet transformed communication in the latter part of the 20th century. The way in which type is disseminated, however, has changed in the last 500 years. Glyphs were once physical objects, carved into metal or wood, and then inked and pressed onto paper, vellum, or other materials. Printers in the predigital era faced the same design issues (such as alignment and spacing) that you'll tackle with digital tools. Just as Photoshop's Burn and Dodge tools are direct descendants of darkroom techniques (discussed in Chapter 7), the leading and kerning you'll learn about in this section are descendants of movable type.

FIGURE S4.2 Johannes Gutenberg (and his craftsmen), Gutenberg Bible opened to the beginning of the Gospel of Luke, 1454 or 1455. Courtesy of the Library of Congress [LC-USZ62-110333]. From the Library of Congress website: "The Gutenberg Bible is composed of 1,282 pages. Each page measures 17 x 12 inches. The type is set in two columns, forty-two lines each, from which it has become known as the 'forty-two-line Bible,' or 'B42.'" Today's viewers have greater difficulty reading this text because the style of the typeface—Blackletter— is uncommon in body copy.

FIGURE S4.3 A diagram showing selected elements of a letterform. Serifs are rendered in magenta. For a more robust directory, visit the Letter Anatomy page on Ellen Lupton's *Thinking with Type* website at thinkingwithtype.com/contents/letter/#Anatomy.

WHAT'S IN A LETTER?

A traditional typography course would cover the many parts of a letter in depth. I've limited the following list of definitions to those you'll need for a basic conversation about type in a work of design or digital art. **FIGURE S4.3** showcases a letter's baseline, x-height, cap height, serif, ascender, and descender. The *baseline* is the invisible line that a letter, word, or sentence sits on: It's the implied line that keeps typography moving in one direction. The *x-height* is the distance from the baseline to the top part of a lowercase letter in any font, while the *cap height* is the distance from the baseline to the top of an uppercase letter. Because typefaces can have enormous or tiny x-heights, the size of this part of the letterform influences the amount of space the letter takes up in a composition and the viewer's perception of the size of the type. The *serif* is a small detail that hangs off the end of some of the strokes defining a letterform. *Ascenders* and *descenders* are parts of the letter that escape above the x-height or below the baseline, respectively.

CLASSIFICATIONS OF TYPE

John Kane identifies classes of type on a historic timeline in his book *A Type Primer* in **TABLE 10.1**. Although developed as a new classification of type, italic is now a common style addition to typeface families (**FIGURE S4.4**). Kane suggests that square serifs, for instance, were a response to the advertising industry's need for bold, heavy, commercial type (**FIGURE S4.5**).

Martin Majoor (designer of the Scala typeface, among others) coined the *Nexus Principle* [1], whereby multiple typefaces including both sans serif and serif letters are created based on one form.

REFERENCE [1] Read more about Majoor's Nexus Principle at: www.martinmajoor.com/4.2_nexus_article_overview_majoor.html.

You can activate and use Nexus with the Adobe Fonts feature of your Adobe Creative Cloud account. You will find Nexus is available in these styles: Mix, Sans, Serif, and Typewriter.

Although it's not a good idea to set too much body copy in italic, you will notice the shortened line length when letterforms are slanted with decreased kerning.

Although it's not a good idea to set too much body copy in italic, you will notice the shortened line length when letterforms are slanted with decreased kerning.

FIGURE S4.4 Italic is now a common type style or variation. The same sentence appears here in Caslon 10/12 point (read as "10 over 12 points," meaning the size of the font is 10 points and the leading, or space between the lines, is 12 points). The top sentence is rendered in italic, and the bottom is in Roman style. Notice how the italic style occupies less space on the page than the regular variation of the same typeface.

FIGURE S4.5 *An American Time Capsule: Three Centuries of Broadsides and Other Printed Ephemera*, the fourth of six advertisements of Boston Printing, 1860. Library of Congress, Rare Book and Special Collections Division. In this advertisement: bold, commercial type includes serifs, sans serifs, slabs, and more!

HISTORIC TIMELINE OF CLASSES OF TYPE

CLASS/DATE	EXAMPLE	
Blackletter 1450	X	Designed to emulate handwriting styles of monks and scribes in northern Europe.
Oldstyle 1475	X	Oldstyle was "based upon the lowercase forms used by Italian humanist scholars for book copying (themselves based upon the ninth-century Caroline miniscule)" [2].
Italic 1500	X	Although developed as a new classification of type, italic is now a common style addition to typeface families.
Script 1550	X	Meant to emulate engravings and still used today in casual and formal typographic messages.
Transitional 1750	X	Revision of Oldstyle to further define the contrast between thick and thin strokes.
Modern 1775	X	Extreme contrast is achieved in Modern typefaces such as Bodoni and Didot.
Square Serif 1825	X	Includes a new modification specifically to the serif, which appears blockish and heavy (sometimes referred to as *Egyptian* or *slab*).
Sans Serif Developed in 1816 by William Caslon but not used widely until the 1900s.	X	The serif was eliminated completely so the letterforms appear even more geometric. Variations on the sans serif form include humanist, geometric, and calligraphic forms.

TABLE 10.1

SERIF VS. SANS SERIF

It's important for digital artists and designers to be able to distinguish the difference between serif and sans serif typefaces (**FIGURE S4.6**). Legibility is one of a typographer's key concerns, and the differences between these two typeface styles can greatly influence the legibility of the text in particular situations. A serif typeface is easier to read in the body copy (paragraph text, for instance) of printed documents, such as newspapers, magazines, pamphlets, and brochures. The serifs offer contrast between the paper and ink that aids reading in this situation, where light is reflected from the paper to the reader's eye.

REFERENCE [2] John Kane, *A Type Primer*, New York: Pearson, 2002, 47.

Help!	**Help!**
Help!	**Help!**
Help!	Help!
Help!	Help!
Help!	Help!

FIGURE S4.6 In the left column, the word "Help!" is set in several *serif* typefaces: Adobe Caslon Bold, Adobe Garamond Bold, FF Scala Bold, Goudy Old Style Bold, and Didot Bold. On the right side, the *sans serif* typefaces used are Helvetica Black, Akzidenz Grotesk Extra Bold, Franklin Gothic Medium, News Gothic Bold, and Univers 65 Bold.

EXAMPLES OF SERIF AND SANS SERIF TYPEFACES

Serif typefaces include Caslon, Sabon, Garamond, Palatino, Baskerville, Bodoni, and more. On the web, you might commonly see Open Serif, Georgia or Times New Roman, among others.

Sans serif typefaces include Akzidenz Grotesk, Helvetica, Gill Sans, Franklin Gothic, Futura, Univers, and more. On the web, you might commonly see Open Sans, Roboto, Verdana or Arial, among others.

Sans serif typefaces are easier to read in body copy that appears on a screen, such as websites, mobile apps, and videos. Because light is being projected from the screen to the reader's eye, the tiny serifs at the edges of the letterform become an annoyance that hinders legibility, while the crisp edges of the sans serif form are simpler to perceive. In 2019, The League of Imaginary Scientists created an interactive work in response to climate change. It included a text made of tiny ice cubes. When installed in the gallery, the ice-text looked like a sans serif typeface made of pixels (**FIGURE S4.7**). Once you begin noticing typefaces in the material world, you will find them everywhere.

FIGURE S4.7 *The Waiting-for-the-Rain Machine*, The League of Imaginary Scientists, exhibited at A Ship in the Woods, 2019.

REFERENCE [3] You can see the movie trailer on director Gary Hustwit's website, www.hustwit.com/helvetica.

One of the most impactful and controversial fonts is Helvetica. The 2007 movie named for the font, *Helvetica*, includes interviews with an international group of typographers and graphic artists who, for the most part, have strong opinions about the typeface Helvetica [3]. This ubiquitous font, designed by Max Miedinger in 1957, has been used in commercial advertising, corporate logos, information graphics, and so on for more than 50 years. Some designers view this modern, geometric typeface as a stifling indicator of a homogenous corporate culture. Others find beauty in the letterform's chameleon-like flexibility. This particular font and Gary Hustwit's movie provide an opportunity for reflection on the physical and symbolic differences between Roman typefaces (old style, transitional, and modern) and sans serif letterforms.

TYPE AND IMAGE

Philip Meggs's 1989 book *Type and Image* remains one of my favorite resources for articulating the relationship between two visual elements that could be read as graphic and abstract, dominant and symbolic, or signs and pictures. Meggs quotes French critic and philosopher Roland Barthes in an observation of the way in which the word became subservient to the image as society's pace quickened in the 20th century, "Formerly, the image illustrated the text (made it clearer); today the text loads the image, burdening it with a culture, a moral, an imagination" [4]. Typography can be rendered as an image form (see the Google Doodle note in this section). Text can alter the meaning of an image or direct the viewer toward an interpretation. As type and image are juxtaposed, their relationship dictates a layer of meaning to the viewer. Conventionally, type is isolated from images (for instance, in the way this book is designed). Juxtaposing text and image in surprising ways can result in a powerful message. Meggs suggests, "Frequent use is made of type that surprints or overprints an image and type that reverses or drops out from the image…to create strong visual hierarchy and effective communication" [5]. In the exercises in this chapter, you'll overprint big, bold text on the collage you created in Chapter 8. The type will become a new graphic element in the composition, and its vector format will contrast with the photographic texture of the collage.

REFERENCE [4] Philip B. Meggs, *Type and Image: The Language of Graphic Design* (New York: Van Nostrand Reinhold, 1989), 41.

REFERENCE [5] Meggs, 45.

In Chapter 10, you'll add type to the collage you created by completing the Chapter 8 exercises for Luis Buñuel and Salvador Dalí's film *Un Chien Andalou.*

Google Doodles are short animations that transform the Google type-based logoform into a themed motion graphic. View the whole collection at www.google.com/doodles.

CONTRAST AND HIERARCHY ON THE GRID

Typefaces are designed in sets known as *families,* which include a variety of styles and point sizes. A display font may have a limited family (or none at all), while a typeface revised and redesigned for different type factories will include a lush set of varieties (**FIGURE S4.8**). Although you may need only one version of a typeface for a headline (where you might use a display font), it's important to choose a large family for variations made in body copy. Using a single type family for the body copy in a layout will help keep the composition unified. However, using multiple varieties of that family will let you create typographic contrast. These two elements, unity and contrast, are used to direct the reader's gaze as she scans a layout. To organize the layout, a simple (invisible) grid is established, and type is limited to alignment along its horizontal or vertical guides. Contrast is introduced through the usage of multiple guides. Hierarchy is established through contrast and the perception of

In Chapter 11, *The Grid*, you'll use a grid to organize a typographic layout. You'll create contrast and hierarchy through space, size, and typographic varieties.

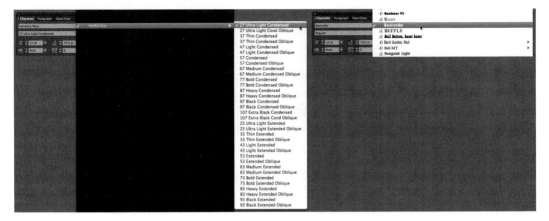

FIGURE S4.8 The lengthy list in the center shows variations for the typeface Helvetica Neue. The display typefaces listed on the right include few or no variations.

isolation or a shift in the ratio between negative and positive space. Different parts of the text (headings, body copy, image captions, and so on) play different roles in the composition—each corresponds to a different level of hierarchy and should be treated visually as such.

WHICH APPLICATION SHOULD I USE?

In Chapter 12, *Continuity*, you'll develop a multimedia project using Adobe Premiere Pro. Because the final video file is meant to be viewed on the screen, you'll use a sans serif typeface.

REFERENCE [6] xtine burrough, "Create A PDF Portfolio Using Adobe Illustrator," October, 2010, www.peachpit.com/articles/article.aspx?p=1636981. Although the article is slightly out of date, it demonstrates the process in a format that is easy to follow.

For typography work, Adobe Illustrator, which you're already familiar with, and Adobe InDesign both have advantages. Since 2013, the demand for multimedia production and screen-based media has increased, and the role of the digital production artist includes working on these types of jobs. Printed media projects with multiple pages or surfaces for creative expression and communication are created by graphic designers who may create works for the screen but also specialize in working with paper. Illustrator has all the tools you need to produce posters, identity materials (business cards, letterhead, logo designs), and other one-page items. Covered briefly in bonus chapter 14, *Pagination and Printing*, InDesign has additional tools and panels useful for controlling the design of multipage layouts.

I recommend that students create a straightforward PDF of their portfolios for email correspondence with human resources staff or internship supervisors. You can easily accomplish this using multiple artboards in Illustrator. I've documented the process in an article on Peachpit.com [6], for anyone who doesn't want (or have the time) to learn a new application.

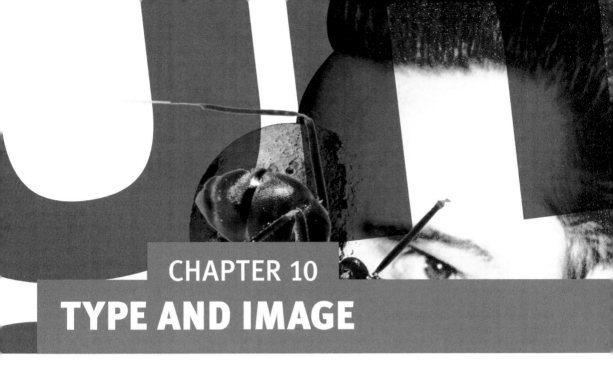

CHAPTER 10
TYPE AND IMAGE

THE EXERCISES IN this chapter will provide technical and aesthetic lessons in the juxtaposition of type and image. In these exercises, you'll finalize the *Un Chien Andalou* poster that you started as a collage in Chapter 8, *Select, Copy, Paste, Collage*. You'll also place your Adobe Photoshop collage file into Adobe Illustrator to set the type and create a PDF document for viewing or printing.

CONTRAST AND RHYTHM

Contrast and rhythm are essential principles to keep in mind when designing with type. In Gestalten TV's interview with Erik Spiekermann, the Berlin-based typographer compared type design to musical composition. The silence between notes in music is equivalent to the positive and negative spatial relationships in typographic design (FIGURE 10.1). Spiekermann says,

REFERENCE [1] See the complete interview with Erik Spiekermann, "Putting Back the Face into Typeface" on Vimeo at vimeo.com/19429698

> Type is all about rhythm and space. It's actually not about form very much. You look at the rhythm and the contrast of the word...Every word has a rhythm. It's like looking at a park or a building. You don't see the details, you see all of it...What we read is the contrast between thick and thin, light and dark, square and round. And the rhythm is the rhythm of words, of spaces between words, spaces between characters. Just as in music, that makes it exciting. If it was just the notes without any meter or timing, every tune would sound the same. So my role is to put rhythm into [the layout] [1].

REFERENCE [2] See video documentation of Empty Words by Jürg Lehni and Alex Rich (2008) at vimeo.com/16379809.

To demonstrate rhythm and space in typographic design, *Empty Words* by Jürg Lehni and Alex Rich (FIGURE 10.2) is an installation of mechanized typography using a standard CNC plotter, a rotated LCD display, an Apple TV, and a software interface [2]. The resulting drilled posters display text written by participants. Letters are formed of repetitive circles, drilled at a uniform speed. Drilled holes in the paper create contrast between presence and absence (of the paper or the letterform, depending on how you think of it). The effect is reminiscent of 0s and 1s or the on and off nature of digital technologies. The similarity of the letterforms and the speed with which they're created contribute to the rhythm of the work.

FIGURE 10.1 An example of Erik Spiekermann's work from his Gestalten TV interview.

FIGURE 10.2 Top: Jürg Lehni and Alex Rich, *Things to Say*, Kunst Halle Sankt Gallen, 2009. Furniture by Martino Gamper. Bottom: Jürg Lehni and Alex Rich, *Empty Words*, 2008.

FIGURE 10.3 Sagmeister & Walsh for Aizone: an advertising campaign for a luxury department store in the Middle East. The legibility of this composition relies on the stark contrast between the typography and the body in value (black and white) and movement (horizontal type across a vertical body). Rhythm unifies the message because the size of the type is nearly as large as the body on the page. The organic flow of the hand-drawn letterforms feels as personal and intimate as the naked form.

SAGMEISTER TEAM FOR AIZONE Creative Director: Stefan Sagmeister; Art Director/Designer: Jessica Walsh; Photographer: Henry Hargreaves; Body Painter: Anastasia Durasova; Creative Retoucher: Erik Johansson; Hair Stylist: Gregory Alan; Producer: Ben Nabors, Group Therapy; Production Designers: John Furgason, Andy Eklund.

REFERENCE [3] Philip Meggs, *Type and Image: The Language of Graphic Design* (New York: Van Nostrand Reinhold, 1989), 56.

When an image is introduced into the graphic equation, it's important to establish contrast and rhythm between the image and the type. But when text is overprinted or superimposed on an image, contrast must be extreme. Legibility relies on contrast, which can be adjusted as a relationship between two or more elements in terms of size, hue, value, shape/form, amount of negative space, and so on (FIGURE 10.3). In the following exercises, you'll mesh typography with the collage created in Chapter 8.

Philip Meggs writes, "*Simultaneity* means fusing unlike forms so that they exist or occur at the same time. Borrowing a visual technique from their contemporaries, the cubist painters in Paris, futurist artists also used it to mean fusing more than one view of an object into one image" [3]. The following exercise relies on this notion of simultaneity for the viewer to understand the fusion of the type and image in the visual communication. Specifically, you'll create a single block of large type, left aligned on a single margin, and superimposed over the organic composition defined by the collage. The rectangular shape of the type and its crisp, vector shapes contrast with the photographic, irregular shapes in the image. You'll repeat the image of the moon (covering Dalí's eye) as a substitution for the letter "o" in the word "*Andalou.*"

TEXT BOXES

In Adobe applications such as Illustrator and Photoshop, you can use the Type tool in two main ways to set type on the page. You can click with it one time anywhere on the page and create a single, long line of type. This is a great way to add a headline or display type to the page. Alternatively, you can drag with the tool to create a text box. (In Adobe InDesign, this action creates a text frame.) This establishes the width of a column of text. The type you add conforms to the size of the box (which can always be modified). When you know you're setting body copy, columns of text, or text that should appear on multiple lines to fit a certain space, plan to create a text box or text frame with the Type tool. In the following exercises, you'll create a single text box. In the next chapter, you'll explore both methods of working with the Type tool.

TEXT ADJUSTMENTS: KERNING AND LEADING

Once you place copy in a text box, you'll likely need to modify its formatting. You can set such character elements as the typeface, size, variation or style, and more, as well as such paragraph elements as alignment, indents, and hyphenation. These are all decisions you'll make based on an informed view of the typography with which you're working. The *informed nature* of your view is what you'll be crafting throughout all the exercises in this section. There are many pieces of the typographic puzzle to keep in mind at once, so you'll learn small, central elements of typographic design in each chapter.

Three typographic spacing issues specific to a block of text include *kerning*, or the horizontal space between the letters in a single word; *tracking* (sometimes called *letter spacing*), or the evenly distributed horizontal space between let-ters in a line of type; and *leading*, or the vertical space (or distance) between each line of text. You will explore all of these throughout Chapters 10, 11, and 12. In the following exercises, you will modify the kerning of the large text in order to adjust the contrast and repetition of the typeface as it relates to the image beneath it.

The keyboard shortcuts for adjusting kerning, tracking, and leading are easier to use than the Adobe panels, and they're simple to remember: press the Option/Alt key in combination with one of the arrow keys: Left, Right, Up, or Down. If you're adjusting kerning, as you will in the following exercises, place your Type tool insertion point between two letters (that is, nothing is selected) and then press **Option-Left Arrow/Alt-Left Arrow** (to tighten the space between the letters) or **Option-Right Arrow/Alt-Right Arrow** (to separate the letters). You can adjust tracking by selecting a line of type and using the same keyboard shortcuts, and you can adjust leading by selecting one or more lines of type and using the same shortcuts (substituting the Up Arrow and Down Arrow keys).

In the following exercise, you'll pay particular attention to contrast and the repetition of space between letters. When there's too much space between letters, the reader will notice the negative space (likely the white space) and lose focus on the letterforms (the positive space). If there's not enough space between letters, the shapes seem to run together, and the viewer has a hard time differentiating letters, resulting in poor legibility **(FIGURE 10.4)**. Because the type will be on top of the image in the following exercises, tight kerning between letterforms will help the viewer see and read the block of type as one, legible, unavoidable visual group. However, you'll be sensitive to creating large enough rhythmic gaps between the letters for the viewer to be able to discern the words "*Un Chien Andalou*."

Finally, to make this even more difficult, true, even spacing between the letters (that is, if you literally measure the space between the letters and make them all exactly the same) will not result in an optically harmonic typographic layout (that is, it won't look good!) **(FIGURE 10.5)**. There are some situations where you'll pull two letters closer together (for instance, watch for this between slim and round letters such as the letters "l" and "o" or "o" and "u") or push them farther apart (such as an "A" and "n" where the uppercase "A" requires more space, even though the overall amount of white space between the letters seems full).

FIGURE 10.4 In the composition on the left, the overprinted type is kerned (in the case of the line containing only two letters) or tracked too tightly. Letters nearly run into each other, resulting in poor legibility. The composition on the right displays equally poor legibility for the opposite reason: the kerning is too loose. The gaps between the letters draw too much attention to the negative space.

Un Un
Chien Chien
Andalou Andalou

Un Un
Chien Chien
Andalou Andalou

FIGURE 10.5 The type on the left is tracked with precisely the same amount of space between each letterform. Notice the uneven spacing between the resulting text block, especially between, for instance, the "A" and "n" or "L" and "o" in *Andalou.* The type on the right is kerned to create optical harmony.

WHAT YOU'LL NEED

Download the following source materials to complete the exercises in this chapter:

✔ The **chapter10-workfiles.zip** file which includes **chapter10-start.psd**. If this file looks familiar, it is because it's a copy of the **chapter08-results.psd** file. You will build upon what you learned and created in Chapter 8.

Place or copy this file into a folder on your hard drive named **chapter10**. You'll save a new Illustrator file there in the first exercise.

You'll benefit from the ability to see the relationship between positive and negative space in letterforms.

WHAT YOU'LL MAKE

In the exercises in this chapter, you'll finalize a type and image collage based on the Surrealist film *Un Chien Andalou* by juxtaposing its name on top of the collage you created in the Chapter 8 exercises where the "o" in "*Andalou*" is replaced with the photo of the moon (**FIGURE 10.6**). You'll be working with both Photoshop and Illustrator, toggling between the applications to separate parts of the image for the final layout composition. Overprinted, extra-large, sans serif typography is a modern treatment traced to Swiss International typographic styles, which you will explore further in the next chapter.

FIGURE 10.6 The resulting file after completing Chapter 10 exercises.

EXERCISE 1

DEFINE A COLOR MODE, THEN PLACE AND RELINK AN IMAGE

In their traditional four-color printing presses, commercial printers use four inks—cyan, magenta, yellow, and black (abbreviated as CMYK)—so images destined for print are often created in CMYK color mode. Consumer inkjet printers, however, are designed to be compatible with files made for the screen in RGB color mode. If you try to print a CMYK-mode document on such a consumer printer, you'll inadvertently create a conflict: You'll set the document to the print profile only to have to alter the color mode once the new document is created. Setting the file to match the color mode of your printer is one of the many ways you can attempt to synchronize the colors on the screen and those in the resulting prints.

If you need to change the color mode after you have created a new document, you can choose an option from the File > Document Color Mode submenu.

1. Create a new file in Adobe Illustrator by pressing **Command-N/Ctrl-N** or by choosing File > New. In the New Document dialog box, click the Print category and modify the settings to create a 7 by 9-inch document showing units as inches. Notice that the print profile automatically assumes that you'll be creating a document in CMYK color mode. Click Advanced Options to display the settings, choose RGB Color from the Color Mode menu, then click Create **(FIGURE 10.7)**.

FIGURE 10.7 Illustrator document settings include changing the color mode to RGB.

2. Choose File > Place, and select the file **chapter10-start.psd** from the **chapter10-start** folder. Do not turn on the Link option, because you want to embed the image in the Illustrator document. Click the loaded cursor on the artboard to place the image on it. Save the file as **chapter10-results.ai**.

Notice that in the final file (**FIGURE 10.6**), the large ant on a diagonal baseline appears in front of the type. You're about to add typography on top of this image. However, the ant will appear beneath the type if you leave it *flattened* into the collage. In the next steps you will save a new ant-less version of the file and then replace the **chapter10-start.psd** file embedded in the Illustrator document.

3. Toggle to Photoshop, or launch it if it is not open, then open **chapter10-start.psd**.

4. In the Layers panel, click the eyeball icons of two layers to hide them: **ant** and **Background**. You should see a grid in the background of the collage, indicating transparent areas.

5. Choose File > Save As, and name the file **chapter10-no-ant.psd**. Be sure to save the file to the **chapter10** folder or wherever you're saving your Chapter 10 work files. I saved mine in the **chapter10-results** folder.

6. Toggle back to Illustrator. Choose the Selection tool, and click the placed image once. Choose Window > Links to show the Links panel. From the panel menu in the top-right corner of the Links panel, choose Relink (**FIGURE 10.8**).

KEY COMMAND When working in multiple applications, press Command-Tab/Alt-Tab to switch quickly among them.

In Step 5, you could have saved on top of the **chapter10.psd** file because you didn't delete the ant, you simply hid it. I've found that new students are easily confused when the file name doesn't indicate a change, so I made an extra/duplicate file.

FIGURE 10.8 Relinking image files simplifies the design process, as the newly linked file is substituted for the current image, while maintaining the same position.

7. Select the **chapter10-no-ant.psd** file, and click Place. In the Photoshop Import Options dialog box that opens next, choose Flatten Layers To A Single Image. The new version of the file replaced the file that displayed the large ant (**FIGURE 10.9**).

 ## ADD A TEXT BOX

In this exercise, you'll superimpose a text box on the collage image. Letters are typically designed to be well-spaced for small sizes (between 8 and 16 points). However, once the type is enlarged, you'll notice that

FIGURE 10.9 The collage of Dalí, the moon, and the hand now appears without the large ant.

the spacing between the letterforms becomes disharmonious. You'll kern the large letters in this exercise. When you add other graphic elements to the design, you may end up repositioning or modifying the type. Remember to keep an eye on the spacing between *all* design elements in the document (not only the kerning) during the entire design process. You may need to revisit your kerning efforts toward the end of these exercises.

1. In the Illustrator Layers panel, rename Layer 1 to **collage** and then lock the **collage** layer. Add a new layer named **type**.

2. Select the Type tool (**FIGURE 10.10**), and draw a large box on top of the collage image. By default, Illustrator provides dummy text to fill the box. While it remains highlighted, replace it with the title of the movie: *Un Chien Andalou.*

3. While the text box is still active, press **Command-A/Ctrl-A** to select all of the type in the text box. Because the Type tool is active, the Control panel shows options for it. Click Character on the Control panel to expand the Character panel. Set the typeface properties for the active text as seen in **FIGURE 10.11.** I used Verdana Bold because I can trust that most, if not all, readers will have Verdana installed on their computers. If you use a different typeface, your settings will likely be different than mine. If I were to create this in a lab where I knew which typefaces were installed, I might select a geometric typeface, such as Futura, or a grotesque typeface (one of the older sans serif typefaces), such as Franklin Gothic, instead.

FIGURE 10.10 The red outline shows the box drawn with the Type tool. The text is entered on the **type** layer.

FIGURE 10.11 (ABOVE) Click Character in the Control panel to expand the typographic options. I like to highlight the Font Size field and press **Shift-Up Arrow** or **Shift-Down Arrow** to increase or decrease the size of the text by ten points at a time until it approximately fits the text box.

FIGURE 10.12 (LEFT) The type should be set to 90 points. Expand or collapse the type box to fit the words on the number of lines you desire.

4. Use the Selection tool to modify the size of the text box by dragging any of the anchor points surrounding the box (**FIGURE 10.12**). Notice that the type inside the box remains aligned on its baseline while conforming to fit the shape of the box by pushing letters that no longer fit down to new lines or by fitting more letters on a longer line-length. In other words, the integrity of the letterform is upheld while the space within which the type is set changes. Resize the text box so it fits the 90-point word "*Andalou*" on a single line.

RESIZE AND KERN DISPLAY TYPE

EXERCISE 3

FONT SIZE KEYBOARD SHORTCUTS You can press **Shift-Up Arrow** or **Shift-Down Arrow** to increase or reduce the Font Size value by 10 points. Press **Up Arrow** or **Down Arrow** alone (no Shift key) to increase or reduce the Font Size value by a single point.

In these exercises, the only type that exists in the final document is large display type (that is, any type that's larger than body copy). All of the type is set in one text box. However, you'll modify each of the three words separately using the Type tool.

1. Deselect the text box by clicking outside of it with the Selection tool. Click the Type tool in the Tools panel to select it. It's very easy to accidentally make a new text box or line of text with the Type tool when you're trying to select existing type. So be attentive to your document in this step. Place the Make New Type pointer (**FIGURE 10.13**) near enough to the letter "U" in "*Un*" to change it to the Select Type pointer (**FIGURE 10.14**). Then drag over the first word (**FIGURE 10.15**).

2. I want this first word to be so large that it covers most of the collage image beneath it. Because it's only two letters long, it will be the largest word in the three lines of type. With the first word selected, any changes I make in the Character panel will affect only that word. You can type in a new size (which would likely be a guessing game to repeat until you see the size you like), or you can use the keyboard shortcuts (my personal preference). Highlight the Font Size field and press **Shift-Up Arrow** (increasing the Font Size value by 10 points) until the text covers the collage—in my case, the result was 260 points (**FIGURE 10.16**). I find it easier to watch my design while pressing keys, which lets me evaluate the results while modifying

FIGURE 10.13 A view of the Type tool pointer when you're about to create new type—move the pointer closer to the text if this is not your intention.

FIGURE 10.14 A view of the Type tool pointer when you are about to edit preexisting type.

FIGURE 10.15 Highlight "*Un*," the first word in the document.

FIGURE 10.16 Increase type size in the Font Size field while analyzing your adjustments on the artboard.

the settings simultaneously. Did you notice how these two letters crept far apart as they increased in size? You'll have to adjust the kerning in the next steps.

3. Modify the spacing of the letters in the word "Un" by adjusting the kerning. Place the Type tool pointer between the letters "U" and "n" and click. You'll see a flashing insertion point (FIGURE 10.17). Press **Option-Left Arrow/ Alt-Left Arrow.** Each time you press this key command, the kerning tightens. Repeat the key command until the letters are close enough together to read as though they relate to one another, but not so close that they're overlapping or difficult to read (FIGURE 10.18).

FIGURE 10.17 Position the Type tool pointer between the "U" and "n" and click once to place the insertion point. To modify the kerning, press **Option-Left Arrow/Alt-Left Arrow** to narrow the spacing until the letters are easy to read.

FIGURE 10.18 There is less space between the letters "U" and "n." The result of kerning these letters is that the two letters appear to have a tighter relationship with one another and are easy to read together as one unit.

VIEW THE CHARACTER PANEL

You can leave the Character panel open by pressing **Command-T/Ctrl-T** or by choosing Window > Type > Character. If you leave this panel open while you're kerning, you'll see the results in its Set The Kerning Between Two Characters field. (FIGURE 10.19).

FIGURE 10.19 Display the Character panel from the Type submenu in the Window menu.

FIGURE 10.20 Tighten the space between the letters "h" and "i" and between "i" and "e" by pressing **Option-Left Arrow/Alt-Left Arrow**.

FIGURE 10.21 View the work at 100% or actual size to review the spacing between letters.

4. Repeat Steps 2 and 3 for the next line of type, "*Chien.*" I ended up with a Font Size value of 130 points, and I kerned the letters "h" and "i," as well as "i" and "e," a bit tighter than the letters "C" and "h" (**FIGURE 10.20**) and "e" and "n."

5. Expand the text box if the last line is hidden. Increase the type size of "Andalou" to 100 points, and adjust the kerning so that the space appears optically even between the letterforms. Remember that this means some letters will in fact be closer to one another while some will have more distance between them—optical harmony is not equivalent to mechanical sameness.

6. View your work at 100% to see how the positive and negative spaces between the letterforms read (**FIGURE 10.21**).

KERNTYPE

For additional practice and help with kerning letters, play Mark MacKay's interactive game, *KERNTYPE* (**FIGURE 10.22**), at type.method.ac.

FIGURE 10.22
Warning: This game is highly addictive. I was relieved to score 100%, although you can see that my adjustments deviated just slightly from the answer

7. I'm about to rotate the text box, but before I do something like this I always create a copy of the text box and leave it positioned off the artboard. Use the Selection tool with the Option/Alt key to drag a duplicate of the text box to any position outside the artboard. Leave it there and pay no attention to it for the rest of the exercises. Consider this step a good habit rather than an action necessary to complete the exercise.

FIGURE 10.23 The text is rotated counter to the image elements in the collage to create contrast. You can also see part of my copy of the text box on the artboard.

8. Select the Rotate tool by clicking it in the Tools panel. You'll have to use this tool to rotate a text box. Select the text box on the artboard by using this shortcut to access the Selection tool temporarily: Press the Command/Ctrl key and click the text box to select it. Release the Command/Ctrl key, and you're back to the Rotate tool. Drag one of the anchor points surrounding the text box to the left, slightly, to rotate the type (FIGURE 10.23).

9. While the text box is still selected, set its opacity to 60% in the Appearance area of the Properties panel (FIGURE 10.24). The black type on top of the collage made the type more dominant than necessary for a simultaneous reading of the type and image juxtaposition. Reducing the transparency doesn't hinder legibility because this type is so large, and it aids the visibility of the underlying collage image.

FIGURE 10.24 The type is 60% opaque, resulting in 40% transparency. You might also notice details from the Character panel are visible beneath the Appearance area.

FIGURE 10.25 When there's too much leading, you'll notice the white spaces between the lines of type and legibility suffers. Select all of the text and adjust the leading with **Option-Up Arrow/Alt-Up Arrow** to tighten the space, or **Option-Down Arrow/Alt-Down Arrow** to add more space.

FIGURE 10.26 The type is more legible when the leading is adjusted to decrease the space between the lines.

10. The amount of vertical space between the lines of type is preventing the block of text from being easily read as one unit. I notice the spaces between the lines of text more so than the lines of text themselves. Decrease the leading to fix this typographic issue. Choose the Type tool, then select all the text, and press **Option-Up Arrow/Alt-Up Arrow** to tighten the leading. You can start by repeating that key command a bunch of times; I pressed **Option-Up Arrow** 11 times to begin (**FIGURE 10.25**). Eventually, you'll have to adjust the single line for "*Chien*" and the single line for "*Andalou*" separately (**FIGURE 10.26**).

You'll learn about the Gestalt *Law of Continuity* in the next chapter.

11. Finally, tweak the left alignment of the first letters in each of the three words. Define the left edge of the text block so you have something to align to. Select the Line tool from the Tools panel. Drag with it to draw a thin blue line extending down the layout at the edge of the letter "U" to show the misalignment with the other two words. Press **Command-5/Ctrl-5** or choose View > Guides > Make Guides to transform the line into a diagonal guide (**FIGURE 10.27**).

FIGURE 10.27 Draw a line to use as a diagonal guide, then press **Command-5/Ctrl-5**.

FIGURE 10.28 Set each of the words so it is the first word on a new line (using the **Return/Enter** key to set a paragraph break). Then add one space before each letter on the second and third lines so that you will be able to kern them "back" to fit along the implied line put into motion by the large "U." Don't worry if letters in longer words grow outside of the text box until after you have adjusted the kerning.

FIGURE 10.29 The first letter in each word is aligned with the implied line set by the edge of the large letter "U."

12. You'll use kerning to adjust the horizontal position of the start of each line of text. At the moment, "*Chien*" and "*Andalou*" are at the beginning of lines just because that's how the text happened to wrap in the limited space available. To align the first letter of each word, "*Chien*" and "*Andalou*," you'll have to add a line break between them and precede the first word with an empty space so you can kern between the word and the space holder at the left margin. Place the insertion point just before each word and press the **Return/Enter** key; then press the **spacebar** to add one space (FIGURE 10.28). Press **Option-Left Arrow/Alt-Left Arrow** as many times as needed to bring the first letter in each word back into alignment with the implied line of continuation suggested by guide following the edge of the letter "U" (FIGURE 10.29).

EXERCISE 4 REPLACE TYPE WITH AN IMAGE

Adding typography to the composition has created contrast between the sharp vector contours of the type and the photographic texture of the collage. In this exercise, you'll add the large ant on top of the type, creating yet another spatial relationship between the type and the image. You'll also replace the "o" in "*Andalou*" with the photograph of the moon. For these two additions, you'll want to isolate the two images (the ant and the moon) in their own Photoshop documents.

1. Toggle back to Photoshop, and open **chaptero8-no-ant.psd**. Make the **ant** layer visible. Click the layer thumbnail of the **ant** layer to activate it; then press **Command-A/Ctrl-A** to select all, **Command-C/Ctrl-C** to copy the layer, **Command-N/Ctrl-N** to make a new Photoshop document (make sure Clipboard is selected in the New Document dialog box), and the **Return/Enter** key to accept the new document settings.

MOVING LAYERS Use the Move tool to move the **ant** layer from the application window to the open tab for the new document; then bring the tool into the application window of the new document before releasing the mouse. (See Chapter 8, Exercise 6, Step 2 for more details and images documenting this process.)

2. Move the **ant** layer from the **chaptero8-no-ant.psd** document to the new document. Did you press **Command-V/Ctrl-V** to paste the ant into the new document? If so, you'll find that the ant photograph is pasted, but the paste command didn't attach the layer mask to the pasted photograph. Press **Command-Z/Ctrl-Z**. Go back to the **chaptero8-no-ant.psd** file, deselect the selection of the ant (**Command-D/Ctrl-D**), and move the layer from this document to the new one using the Move tool. When you copied the ant layer, you were copying the dimensions required for the new document to contain the layer.

3. Option-click/Alt-click the mask thumbnail on the **ant** layer to clean it—all parts of the background should be black. Use the Brush tool with black paint to fill in any white gaps **(FIGURE 10.30)**. Option-click/Alt-click the mask thumbnail to return to the normal view.

FIGURE 10.30 Paint with black paint on the layer mask to hide parts of the image background around the ant. Option-click/Alt-click the layer mask to return the layer to its normal viewing state.

4. Drag the Background layer to the Trash icon at the bottom of the Layers panel to delete it. Now the ant should appear on transparency, indicated by the default Photoshop white-and-gray grid.

5. Choose File > Save As (**Command-Shift-S/Ctrl-Shift-S**) to save the new document as **ant.psd** in your **chapter10** folder. It's a Photoshop file that you'll place in Illustrator.

6. Repeat Steps 1 through 5 to create a document with the **moon** layer group (be sure to copy and paste the layer and its adjustment into a new document and then clean the mask), and save the new document as **moon.psd** in your **chapter10** folder.

CROP If you want to go the extra mile, you can also crop the transparent space from the **moon.psd** document before saving it.

7. Return to Adobe Illustrator. Create a new layer named **top images** in the Layers panel. Choose File > Place, and select **ant.psd.** Move the ant onto the image. I liked the relationship between its two back right legs as a V-shape surrounding Dalí's eye (which also placed its front right feeler into a position that points to a smaller ant) (**FIGURE 10.31**).

8. Place **moon.psd** onto the image, and position it over the "o" in "*Andalou.*" Add a drop shadow to the moon image by choosing Effect > [Illustrator Effects] Stylize > Drop Shadow. I left most of the default settings in place, but changed the opacity to 55%. Select the Preview option to see your results before committing to the shadow effect (**FIGURE 10.32**).

FIGURE 10.31 The ant is placed over the text. A view of the Layers panel shows the stacking order.

FIGURE 10.32 Choose Effect > [Illustrator Effects] Stylize > Drop Shadow to integrate the moon into the typography and other collage elements by casting its shadow onto them.

9. Although the moon will print over the letter "o," it's a good idea to remove the letter. This means that you need to delete the letter from the text box and then kern the "u" into position. Select the Type tool, then click on the line of type away from the moon—for instance, position your pointer between the letters "d" and "a." Once the insertion point is on the line of type, use the **Right Arrow** key to move the insertion point so it is just after the "o". Press **Delete/Backspace** to remove the "o." Naturally, the "u" will move to take its place, behind the moon. Press the **spacebar** twice. Finally, press **Option-Left Arrow/Alt-Left Arrow** twice to tighten the kerning between the "u" and the spaces after the letter "l" (FIGURE 10.33).

FIGURE 10.33 Remove the letter "o" behind the image of the moon and kern the letter "u" into place.

EXERCISE 5 — ADD VECTOR SHAPES TO FRAME THE COMPOSITION

Now that you've added more graphics on top of the typography, you'll continue to make contrast between the bitmap and vector images. The frames you'll create in this exercise are simple rectangles with a slight shape modification using the Direct Selection tool.

1. To begin making the frame, select the Rectangle tool and set black as the fill color with no assigned stroke. Drag out a simple rectangle that roughly matches the width of the top left ascender of the letter "U" in the word "*Un*." Use the size of the width in this part of the letter as the approximate size of the height of the frame to make a relationship between the frame and the typography. Once you've determined the width, rotate the shape 90 degrees. Stretch it to the width of the composition to build the top part of the frame (FIGURE 10.34).

FIGURE 10.34 Base the width of the rectangle used to make the top frame on the width of a letterform. Rotate the rectangle 90 degrees, move it into position, and stretch it to create the top part of the frame.

2. Choose the Direct Selection tool, and deselect the rectangle. Then, select just the bottom-right anchor point and press **Shift-Up Arrow** about four times to move this anchor point toward the top-right anchor (**FIGURE 10.35**). The static rectangular shape is transformed into a dynamic form, mimicking the dynamic structure of the composition.

3. Move the top portion of the frame into position over the top of the letter "U" in "*Un*." Copy and paste the shape to create the left edge of the frame. Rotate the new shape to the left to align it with the implied line made by the typography. Position the new shape, and lengthen it to fit the left side if you need to (**FIGURE 10.36**).

4. Select the Eyedropper tool (**FIGURE 10.37**). Make sure the Fill color chip is in the foreground of the Tools panel. Command-click/Ctrl-click the shape that makes the top frame to temporarily transform the Eyedropper tool to the Selection tool and select it. Click the ant's head to fill the top portion of the frame with a red hue (**FIGURE 10.38**) to create a repetition of hue in the layout.

FIGURE 10.35 Use the Direct Selection tool to move an anchor point and modify the shape of the frame.

FIGURE 10.37 The Eyedropper tool in the Tools panel.

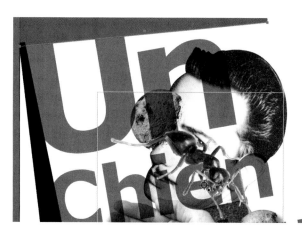

FIGURE 10.36 The left part of the frame is adjusted to fit the composition.

FIGURE 10.38 The red hue in the top frame shape is based on a color sampled from the ant.

FIGURE 10.39 Click the Copy button in the Reflect dialog box to create a duplicate of the selected paths reflected across an axis.

FIGURE 10.40 A view of the composition with the frame moved closer into its final position. My work falls off of the artboard. I will make revisions in the next exercise.

5. Select the two frame edges and group them: Press **Command-G/Ctrl-G.** While the group is selected, double-click on the Reflect tool. (It hides beneath the Rotate tool in the Tools panel.) In the Reflect dialog box, click the Vertical button and click the Copy (not the OK) button (FIGURE 10.39).

6. While the new frame edges are still selected, double-click the Reflect tool again. This time reflect the new group of shapes across the Horizontal axis. Click the OK (not Copy) button. Nudge the frame roughly into position with the Selection tool (FIGURE 10.40).

 FINAL DESIGN ADJUSTMENTS

This exercise is a simple series of final adjustments. The frame is off-center—mine is off the artboard, and the type could better fit the alignment of the frame edge now that they are both in place. The line at the bottom of the hand makes a tense contrast and brings the eye to nothing in the compositional space, so you will adjust the bottom red frame to cover it.

1. You may need to revise the frames. When I started to edit them I realized that I did not create a new layer for them. Begin by moving the frame shapes to a new **frame** layer. Select the two groups of shapes, press **Command-X/Ctrl-X** to cut them. Make a new layer. Press **Command-Shift-V/Ctrl-Shift-V** or choose Edit > Paste in Place. Name the new layer **frames**. Make sure the **frames** layer is at the top of the stacking order in the Layers panel.

2. Choose the Direct Selection tool and Shift-click the two anchor points on the right side of the top red frame shape to modify them simultaneously. While they're selected, nudge the two anchors to the right until they just barely touch the black frame. When they touch, press **Shift-Left Arrow** twice to create negative space on this part of the frame. Repeat the same process with the top two anchor points on the black frame at the left side of the artboard, using the **Down Arrow** key (FIGURE 10.41).

3. To create a break in repetition, flip the right frame so it tapers from the bottom to the top. Select the shape, then double-click the Reflect tool. Select the Horizontal Axis button and click OK. Double-click the Reflect tool once again, but this time select Vertical and click OK.

4. Revise the bottom frame to make it a rectangle that fills the bottom portion of the page. You can use this large rectangular shape as an area that the hand will appear to grow out of in the next step (thus, you can hide the bottom edge of the hand, which distracts the eye in this composition, in this overlapping shape). Press **Command-Shift-Right Bracket/Ctrl-Shift-Right Bracket** to move this new rectangle to the foreground, or to the front of the composition's layer stacking order (FIGURE 10.42).

5. Note that the **collage** layer in the Layers panel remains locked from Exercise 2 Step 1. Unlock it, select it, then rotate and move it until the hand appears to grow out of the red rectangle at the bottom of the document (FIGURE 10.43).

FIGURE 10.41 Anchor points on the top and left frame elements are nudged into place with the Direct Selection tool and the arrow keys.

FIGURE 10.42 Revise the bottom frame so it becomes a large rectangle and move it to the foreground of the compositional space.

FIGURE 10.43 Revise the collage so the hand is repositioned to hide its bottom edge.

6. These next two adjustments are minor: Ungroup the frames if they are still grouped. Move the left and top frame slightly so they touch the left edge of the artboard. Next, move the textbox containing the movie title to the left and down so the letters are slightly obscured by the left frames and the "A" in "*Andalou*" is growing out of the red rectangle at the bottom of the page (**FIGURE 10.44**).

7. Reposition the moon image so it is better integrated with the typography.

8. Finally, move the right frame to its own layer and put it in the bottom of the stacking order (below the **collage** layer). Set the shape to 35% Opacity in the Properties panel. Adjust this frame so it extends from the red rectangle to the top of the page (**FIGURE 10.45**). The arm should seem to grow out of the bottom red frame. Depending on how your collage relates to the frames, you may also need to unlock the collage layer and make further adjustments. You can match Figure 10.45 or design this composition to fit your aesthetic judgment. Don't forget to press **Command-S/Ctrl-S** to save the file.

FIGURE 10.44 Revise the edges of the frame on the left side and the type so that it is repositioned in alignment with the left side and bottom of the composition space. Notice how the "A" in "*Andalou*" grows from the bottom rectangle.

FIGURE 10.45 The right frame contrasts the other frame elements with its lower opacity and stronger line movement to the top of the page.

You can create clipping masks in Adobe Illustrator to hide or show design elements. In Exercise 6, you hid the lower edge of the hand by placing a red rectangular shape on top of it. This works in this instance, but sometimes you need to apply a clipping mask on the hand so that you do not need to always rely on another design element. Clipping masks fall outside the scope of this chapter, so I've demonstrated this technique in this chapter's screencast.

All screencasts are available on the companion website, www.digitalart-design.com or on the Vimeo playlist, bit.ly/foundations-demos.

 LAB CHALLENGE

Create a type and image relationship in which the image is used to replace a word or letterform or to extend the typographic letterform (FIGURE 10.46). Use Photoshop to edit the image or images and Illustrator to set the typography.

FIGURE 10.46 Oded Ezer, *Helvetica Live!* poster, 2004. The *Helvetica Live!* poster presents formal intersections between the famous Helvetica letters and various object silhouettes. Consciously ignoring logical context, Ezer was influenced by Dadaist methods and contemporary virtual hybridizations of animals and human beings. Copyright Oded Ezer.

Grids and Geometry

CHAPTER 11

THE GRID

THE EXERCISES IN this chapter will provide technical lessons and aesthetic exercises in using a grid to align a typographic layout. Following the Swiss International Style of typographic composition, the final layout includes hierarchies of type that readers can consume with an economy of eye movements. You'll continue to use tools learned throughout chapters in this section, with an emphasis on Adobe Illustrator's type tools. In the next chapter, you'll revisit continuity in typography by way of a multimedia presentation that you will make in Adobe Premiere Pro. Your knowledge and familiarity with Adobe tools and panels will assist you in learning a new application.

The grid is essentially a tool that helps artists and designers organize and align a composition. As a utilitarian device, the grid has been used in urban planning since the Indus Valley civilization (present-day Pakistan) and ancient Rome. The simple organization of vertical and horizontal lines is also used in sketching electrical circuit diagrams. Engineering draftsman Harry Beck revitalized cartography with his grid-based 1931 redesign of the London Underground map, which used only 45- and 90-degree angles [1].

REFERENCE [1] The Real Underground Morphing Map (seen in Figure 11.1) is best demonstrated at www.fourthway.co.uk/realunderground. (Note: to view this site you must have the Adobe Flash Player plug-in installed.)

LINK You may also enjoy Michael Bierut's article "Mr. Vignelli's Map" at designobserver.com/feature/mr-vignellis-map/2647.

REFERENCE [2] John Pavlus, "London Tube Map Sparks Furor Over What "Design" Means," August 4, 2011, *Fast Company*. www.fastcompany.com/1664692/london-tube-map-sparks-furor-over-what-design-means.

REFERENCE [3] Ellen Lupton and J. Abbott Miller, eds., *The ABCs of the Bauhaus and Design Theory* (Princeton Architectural Press, 1991), 28.

Max Wertheimer, Kurt Koffka, and Wolfgang Köhler founded Gestalt psychology. Many students of art theory and visual communication today refer to writings by Wertheimer and his student, Rudolf Arnheim.

His version became a beloved work of design, although there was one major rivalry between form and function: Because the map displayed equal space between stations, it in no way reflected the actual London landscape (FIGURE 11.1). Erik Spiekermann notes that the map is not a *map* at all, but rather a diagram [2]. This story of how the grid can abstract reality is a reminder of its cold and schematic nature. While the grid is an essential device for organization, it's also devoid of the complexities and nuances inherent in the human condition. So the grid and its emphasis in the Swiss International Style have come to connote design that is efficient, organized, and legible, but also unfeeling, non-emotive, and machine-oriented.

Ellen Lupton and J. Abbott Miller explain the grid as a "structural form pervading Bauhaus art and design, [that] articulates space according to a pattern of oppositions" [3]. The obvious oppositions are the vertical and horizontal structures inherent to a grid, which you'll create with guides. Positive and negative space, implied lines of never-ending continuity and abrupt spatial impositions, rhythms formed by repetition and then challenged by a lack of repetition, and geometric and organic forms are all possible dyads when placed in a relationship on a grid.

GESTALT

The Bauhaus school was in operation from 1919 to 1933. Coincidentally, new Gestalt (the German word for "shape") psychological studies in perception were developed in Berlin from the 1920s to the 1940s. The primary concept of Gestalt is the commonly stated truism, "The whole is greater than the sum of its parts." Indeed, readers, viewers, and users will classify and organize whole structures (layouts, grids, symbols, forms, and so on) before recognizing the minor parts used to compose them. This regular, simple, symmetric, and orderly way of perceiving is known as the *Law of Prägnanz*, one of the eight Gestalt laws.

Understanding the Gestalt properties and laws will help you anticipate how your viewer will experience the visual works you create. Because these properties and laws relate to the split between the whole and its parts, understanding Gestalt will fine-tune your ability to create visual unity. When relating design elements to one another (and the page or viewing space) on the grid, you should intentionally orchestrate visual unity and its opposite, discontinuity.

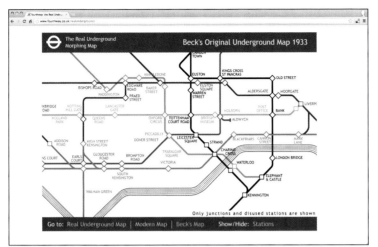

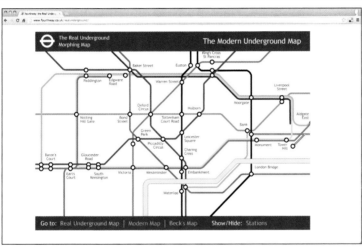

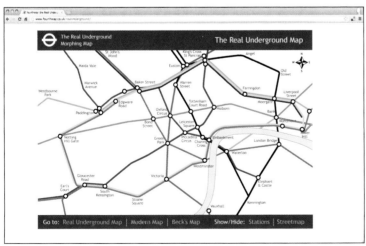

FIGURE 11.1 The map of London's Underground, based on Harry Beck's electrical grid-inspired design, contrasts with London's actual landscape.

EIGHT GESTALT LAWS YOU CAN'T LIVE WITHOUT

The Wikipedia page for Gestalt Psychology is an excellent resource as it has brief descriptions and images for each law and property (en.wikipedia.org/wiki/Gestalt_psychology). Here's a quick list of laws you can draw on when creating visual unity:

1. Proximity: Elements near one another are united.

2. Similarity: Elements like one another (in shape, color, or value, or so on) are united.

3. Closure: Elements missing minor visual details will be united into a functioning form in the mind of the viewer. (For example, even if you never see a cartoon character's toenail, you still assume the character has feet and toes.)

4. Symmetry: Elements balanced on or around a center point are united.

5. Common Fate: Elements moving in the same direction are united.

6. Continuity: Elements aligned on an implied guide are united.

7. Good Gestalt: Elements that are repetitive, simple, and orderly are united. This is sometimes referred to as the *Law of Prägnanz*.

8. Past Experience: Elements encountered in the past will affect how new, similar elements are perceived and united.

REFERENCE [4] Ellen Lupton, *Thinking with Type* (Princeton, NJ: Princeton Architectural Press, 2004), 115.

Ellen Lupton reiterates the importance of negative space in *Thinking with Type*, writing, "Designers focus much of their energy on margins, edges, and empty spaces, elements that oscillate between present and absent, visible and invisible" [4]. As mentioned in Chapter 1, *The Dot, the Path, and the Pixel*, the Gestalt property of multistability indicates that the relationship between the visible and invisible is unpredictable. While developing the grid for exercises in this chapter, be attentive to margins, edges, and empty spaces.

SWISS INTERNATIONAL STYLE

REFERENCE [5] Lupton, 8.

In *Thinking with Type*, Lupton writes, "Swiss designers in the 1940s and 1950s created design's first total methodology by rationalizing the grid. Their work, which introduced programmatic thinking to a field governed by taste and convention, remains profoundly relevant to the systematic thinking required when designing for multimedia" [5]. This emphasis on systematic logic directly correlates the motives of mid-20th century Swiss designers with those of today's digital artists. As this is a foundational text, it focuses on the language and tools common to typography with the grid-based Swiss International Style as a guide. The style that has become associated with Swiss designers emerged in Russia, Germany, and the Netherlands in the 1920s. It was made famous by works and texts that urged a novel approach to typography, such as Jan Tschichold's *The New Typography* (1928) and Josef Müller-Brockmann's *Grid Systems in Graphic Design* (1961). As Diogo Terror writes for *Smashing Magazine*, "Keen attention to detail, precision, craft skills, system of education and technical training, a high standard of printing as well as a clear refined and inventive lettering and typography laid out a foundation for a new movement that has been exported worldwide in [the] 1960s to become an international style" [6].

Lessons from the Swiss International Style include seemingly simple tenets that are much more difficult to execute on your first try than they are to memorize. (I've noticed many students who can memorize and produce this list on a quiz, but struggle to demonstrate the aesthetic principles in their homework.) What follows is a modified version of Tschichold's principles, outlined in *The New Typography*. A typographic layout should contain:

- Imbalanced asymmetry
- Active negative space
- Minimal use of illustrations or decorations
- Color for the purpose of navigation
- Extreme groupings of contrasting elements

In this chapter, the typographic layout will be simple. You'll work with just two guides that you'll understand as implied lines demonstrating the Gestalt *Law of Continuity*.

SENTENCES AND PARAGRAPHS

When assembling type into sentences and paragraphs, there are a number of design issues to consider, including alignment, line length, and spacing. Each of these relate to legibility in as much as they relate to the overall composition. There are basic principles of legibility, of which most people are unaware. So if you show your work to others and it includes typography, you may have to educate your audience.

LINE LENGTH AND SACCADIC MOVEMENTS

English readers move their eyes from left to right across the page or screen, following the length of the line. This is a simple truth. New to you might be the *saccadic* movements that the eyes follow when reading or seeing in general. The eyes don't focus in one location. Instead, they move back and forth rapidly. When reading, the eyes move "in little hops—called 'saccades'—and

REFERENCE [6] See www.smashingmagazine. com/2009/07/17/lessons-from-swiss-style-graphic-design.

LINK Explore the exhibition *The New Typography* (December 23, 2009–July 25, 2010) at the Museum of Modern Art at www.moma. org/visit/calendar/ exhibitions/1015, and be sure to click the "View the exhibition checklist" link.

LINK Explore the Swiss Poster Collection in the Carnegie Mellon University Libraries at luna.library. cmu.edu/luna/servlet/ CMUccm~3~3.

Lorem ipsum dolor sit amet, consectetur adipiscing elit. Phasellus blandit, dui ut vehicula lacinia, diam dolor accumsan dolor, id auctor nulla libero et risus. In ut eros ut nibh ultricies rhoncus. Proin iaculis venenatis justo sed eleifend. In hac habitasse platea dictumst. Ut ut nunc sed odio lacinia consequat. Morbi ipsum justo, suscipit non consectetur eu, varius in nisi. Mauris interdum bibendum congue. Pellentesque euismod, eros sed auctor porta, eros sem elementum ipsum, vel semper tellus purus in lorem. Duis ac nulla nec neque tristique tincidunt id quis leo. Cras bibendum mattis orci at rhoncus. Nulla magna mauris, ornare eget convallis eget, commodo vel urna. Vestibulum in facilisis lorem. Integer sollicitudin, eros non adipiscing posuere, orci velit dignissim dui, id tempus ligula risus non augue.

Nulla facilisi. Cras id nisl lectus, at pretium odio. Nulla ornare enim non velit ornare ultrices. Integer vel arcu eros. Morbi fermentum dictum augue et ultrices. Cum sociis natoque penatibus et magnis dis parturient montes, nascetur ridiculus mus. Maecenas id porta urna. Donec porta mi congue tortor pellentesque vel condimentum purus suscipit.

Lorem ipsum dolor sit amet, consectetur adipiscing elit. Phasellus blandit, dui ut vehicula lacinia, diam dolor accumsan dolor, id auctor nulla libero et risus. In ut eros ut nibh ultricies rhoncus. Proin iaculis venenatis justo sed eleifend. In hac habitasse platea dictumst. Ut ut nunc sed odio lacinia consequat. Morbi ipsum justo, suscipit non consectetur eu, varius in nisi. Mauris interdum bibendum congue. Pellentesque euismod, eros sed auctor porta, eros sem elementum ipsum, vel semper tellus purus in lorem. Duis ac nulla nec neque tristique tincidunt id quis leo. Cras bibendum mattis orci at rhoncus. Nulla magna mauris, ornare eget convallis eget, commodo vel urna. Vestibulum in facilisis lorem. Integer sollicitudin, eros non adipiscing posuere, orci velit dignissim dui, id tempus ligula risus non augue.

Nulla facilisi. Cras id nisl lectus, at pretium odio. Nulla ornare enim non velit ornare ultrices. Integer vel arcu eros. Morbi fermentum dictum augue et ultrices. Cum sociis natoque penatibus et magnis dis parturient montes, nascetur ridiculus mus. Maecenas id porta urna. Donec porta mi congue tortor pellentesque vel condimentum purus suscipit.

FIGURE 11.2 These two views of *Lorem ipsum* placeholder text show the contrast between the easy reading of a suitable line length (right) and the difficulty in staying with a long line length (above).

REFERENCE [7] Peter Orton, PhD. "Computer Text Line Lengths Affect Reading and Learning," IBM Center for Advanced Learning. edlab.tc.columbia.edu/files/eye-tracking%20article.pdf.

come to brief stops, about 250 milliseconds each—called 'fixations'"[7]. It's during this fixation time that the eyes see and read multiple words. Then the gaze regresses into a backward movement before hopping forward again. At the end of the line, the eyes sweep back to the beginning of the next line of type and proceed again.

Once you know how the eye moves during reading, you can design typography for the best possible reading conditions (**FIGURE 11.2**). Most readers will be able to read a line length of nearly five inches before having to cycle through a regressive phase. In *The Elements of Typographic Style*, Robert Bringhurst suggests that the line length for body copy be limited to 45 to 75 characters or 3 to 5 inches. This is a wide range that's meant to allow for multiple columns on a page (where you would use a shorter length). In *Typographie*, Emil Ruder suggests an optimal length of 50 to 60 characters (including spaces). Others offer an equation of 1.5 to 2.5 times the size of a lowercase alphabet set in whichever typeface and size you're using.

ALIGNMENT: LEFT, RIGHT, CENTERED, JUSTIFIED

Alignment is not just the button you press to align a paragraph to the left, center, right, or in a justified block (**FIGURE 11.3**). Alignment can also be used within a typographic design to signify hierarchy. Indentations or negative spaces can be combined with an invisible line of continuation to help readers make associations between blocks of text through their alignment. You'll see how to arrange for this in the following exercises.

FIGURE 11.3 In this layout of a 1902 edition of the *Washington Times*, several varieties of alignment are used to create contrast and hierarchy in a unified grid across seven columns.

SPACING: KERNING AND LEADING

Contrast and rhythm are essential design principles that affect how the viewer understands a typographic layout. Rhythm is understood through regular repetitions and interruptions. Contrast is understood through differences once similarities have been established. The rhythm of text can be controlled by two types of spacing:

- The space between letters: *kerning* between individual letters or *tracking* (letter spacing) across whole sentences, paragraphs, or documents

- The space between lines of type: *leading* (line spacing)

You'll learn more about how to adjust these basic typographic elements throughout the exercises in this section (**FIGURES** 11.4 and 11.5). Contrast also occurs within blocks of text as the type relates to the page. Squint your eyes and view all three paragraphs in Figures 11.4 and 11.5. The gray value that you see in your squinted view of the text block is created by the combination of text and whiteness on the page. The top paragraph reads as a dark gray, the middle paragraph translates to a medium gray, and the bottom paragraph is light gray. The text is easiest to read when the gray is close to a medium or medium-dark value.

Lorem ipsum dolor sit amet, consectetur adipiscing elit. Phasellus blandit, dui ut vehicula lacinia, diam dolor accumsan dolor, id auctor nulla libero et risus. In ut eros ut nibh ultricies rhoncus.

Lorem ipsum dolor sit amet, consectetur adipiscing elit. Phasellus blandit, dui ut vehicula lacinia, diam dolor accumsan dolor, id auctor nulla libero et risus. In ut eros ut nibh ultricies rhoncus.

Lorem ipsum dolor sit amet, consectetur adipiscing elit. Phasellus blandit, dui ut vehicula lacinia, diam dolor accumsan dolor, id auctor nulla libero et risus. In ut eros ut nibh ultricies rhoncus.

Lorem ipsum dolor sit amet, consectetur adipiscing elit. Phasellus blandit, dui ut vehicula lacinia, diam dolor accumsan dolor, id auctor nulla libero et risus. In ut eros ut nibh ultricies rhoncus.

Lorem ipsum dolor sit amet, consectetur adipiscing elit. Phasellus blandit, dui ut vehicula lacinia, diam dolor accumsan dolor, id auctor nulla libero et risus. In ut eros ut nibh ultricies rhoncus.

Lorem ipsum dolor sit amet, consectetur adipiscing elit. Phasellus blandit, dui ut vehicula lacinia, diam dolor accumsan dolor, id auctor nulla libero et risus. In ut eros ut nibh ultricies rhoncus.

FIGURE 11.4 The tracking in the top paragraph is tight; notice the setting of −40 in the Character panel. The middle paragraph is unadjusted. The bottom paragraph tracking is set to +40 in the Character panel. The type is set loosely, with too much space between the letters.

FIGURE 11.5 The leading in the top paragraph is tight; notice the setting of 11.2 in the Character panel. Also notice that the type size is 11 points. This combination of point size and leading is articulated as 11/11.2. The middle paragraph is unaltered at 11/13.2. The bottom paragraph is light because of the increased leading of 11/17.2.

WIDOWS AND ORPHANS

Typographically speaking, widows and orphans break the rhythm of a block of text (**FIGURE 11.6**). *The Chicago Manual of Style* defines an *orphan* as a line that appears at the bottom of a page or column and a *widow* as a dangling word or sentence fragment (the last sentence or word in a paragraph) that appears at the start of a new column. There's no universal agreement about these definitions (and which is which), but both are to be avoided. If you notice dangling text, adjust the leading, type box (or line length), margins, or letter spacing (for the whole block), or force a paragraph break.

Lorem ipsum dolor sit amet, consectetur adipiscing elit. Morbi est est, posuere sit amet congue sit amet, eleifend sit amet nunc. Cum sociis natoque penatibus et magnis dis parturient montes, nascetur ridiculus mus. Fusce dolor justo, vulputate eu fermentum nec, bibendum ut mauris. Sed feugiat lobortis mauris, ut porttitor tortor egestas a. Vestibulum ante ipsum primis in faucibus orci luctus et ultrices posuere cubilia Curae; Donec ac justo sit amet enim egestas tristique vitae sollicitudin elit. Mauris sit amet sem at lacus lacinia sollicitudin. Sed sit amet fringilla arcu. Lorem ipsum dolor sit amet, consectetur adipiscing elit. Etiam eu orci sit amet dolor pellentesque dictum vel sit amet lorem. In hac habitasse platea dictumst. Nam dolor massa, pretium nec vehicula at, sodales non erat. Mauris magna arcu, ultrices at pharetra et, rhoncus vel nisi. Praesent ultricies sodales sem vel mollis. Curabitur turpis sapien, pretium at luctus sit amet, fermentum et

lorem.
Vestibulum ut sollicitudin dui. Donec porta est odio. Aliquam neque libero, adipiscing eget eleifend vitae, sagittis id libero. Suspendisse potenti. Mauris tristique dapibus nibh ac pretium. Curabitur vestibulum vestibulum massa, imperdiet pulvinar quam scelerisque in. Maecenas ac magna lacus, vitae molestie quam. Aliquam erat volutpat. Quisque sodales dictum erat ac mattis. Vivamus a ante egestas leo laoreet ornare eu nec turpis. Nam hendrerit magna quis lectus pharetra sit amet sollicitudin nulla porta. In dolor tortor, pellentesque a rhoncus vitae, ultrices vel enim. Phasellus tempor posuere laoreet. Aenean ultricies elit vel quam bibendum ut sodales felis placerat. Vestibulum ante ipsum primis in faucibus orci luctus et ultrices posuere cubilia Curae.

Lorem ipsum dolor sit amet, consectetur adipiscing elit. Morbi est est, posuere sit amet congue sit amet, eleifend sit amet nunc. Cum sociis natoque penatibus et magnis dis parturient montes, nascetur ridiculus mus. Fusce dolor justo, vulputate eu fermentum nec, bibendum ut mauris. Sed feugiat lobortis mauris, ut porttitor tortor egestas a. Vestibulum ante ipsum primis in faucibus orci luctus et ultrices posuere cubilia Curae; Donec ac justo sit amet enim egestas tristique vitae sollicitudin elit. Mauris sit amet sem at lacus lacinia sollicitudin. Sed sit amet fringilla arcu. Lorem ipsum dolor sit amet, consectetur adipiscing elit. Etiam eu orci sit amet dolor pellentesque dictum vel sit amet lorem. In hac habitasse platea dictumst. Nam dolor massa, pretium nec vehicula at, sodales non erat. Mauris magna arcu, ultrices at pharetra et, rhoncus vel nisi. Praesent ultricies sodales sem vel mollis. Curabitur turpis sapien, pretium at luctus sit amet, fermentum et lorem.

Vestibulum ut sollicitudin dui. Donec porta est odio. Aliquam neque libero, adipiscing eget eleifend vitae, sagittis id libero. Suspendisse potenti. Mauris tristique dapibus nibh ac pretium. Curabitur vestibulum vestibulum massa, imperdiet pulvinar quam scelerisque in. Maecenas ac magna lacus, vitae molestie quam. Aliquam erat volutpat. Quisque sodales dictum erat ac mattis. Vivamus a ante egestas leo laoreet ornare eu nec turpis. Nam hendrerit magna quis lectus pharetra sit amet sollicitudin nulla porta. In dolor tortor, pellentesque a rhoncus vitae, ultrices vel enim. Phasellus tempor posuere laoreet. Aenean ultricies elit vel quam bibendum ut sodales felis placerat. Vestibulum ante ipsum primis in faucibus orci luctus et ultrices posuere cubilia Curae.

FIGURE 11.6 The word *"lorem"* is both a widow and an orphan in this example: it dangles at the top of the first paragraph in the right column (top) and at the bottom of the last paragraph in the left column (bottom).

WHAT YOU'LL NEED

It's not necessary to download image files to complete the exercises in this chapter, but you will need some text to place in your layout.

✔ I generated a poem using such words as "grid," "organized," "geometry," and "boring" (some people think this style lacks emotion or excitement) on the Make a Poem generator at runokone.com (www.runokone.com/makeapoem). You can use my text, available in **chapter11-workfiles.zip** on the companion website, or generate your own poem.

✔ You will activate Aktiv Grotesk Ex, a typeface available in Adobe Fonts, so be prepared to use your AdobeID login credentials.

You'll benefit from seeing how the grid aids alignment in a typographic layout design. The *Law of Continuity* will be obvious when the guides are visible and still evident when guides are invisible.

WHAT YOU'LL MAKE

In the exercises in this chapter, you'll create an Illustrator file with cyan and magenta shapes used as virtual leading or measuring blocks to make the spatial relationships in the composition visible. You will also create a PDF document with trim marks set for a 10 by 16 print containing a typographic layout to be printed on tabloid (11 by 17 inch) paper (FIGURE 11.7).

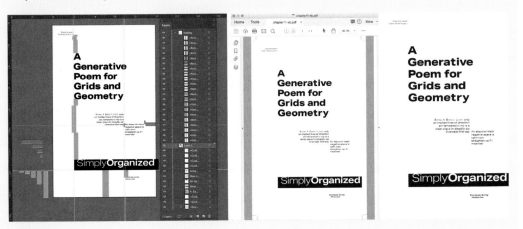

FIGURE 11.7 The resulting native and PDF files created in this chapter's exercises. Negative spaces mathematically relate to one another as a result of using a set of "measuring blocks." You can see my measuring blocks (the magenta and cyan rectangles) and layers in the native document on the left. I hid the cyan and magenta rectangles (stored on a separate layer named *leading*) used to measure space on the artboard when I saved the file as a PDF with trim marks (middle). The right image is a view of the PDF cropped from the trim marks set in the file.

EXERCISE 1

ALTERNATIVE PAPER SIZES

Begin by creating a new file in Illustrator. In many situations, the paper you'll be printing on is not the same size as the document you're designing. Create a 10 by 16 inch document in preparation for printing on tabloid paper with trim marks in place. To do this, set the document at the alternative size.

You'll select the paper size later during the printing process. Trim marks (which you'll add in Exercise 7) will help you cut the paper to the specified working size.

1. Open Illustrator, and choose File > New or press **Command-N/Ctrl-N** to start a new document.

2. In the New Document dialog box, click the Print preset category and choose Inches from the units menu. Enter a Width value of 10 inches and a Height value of 16 inches, and click Create.

3. Choose File > Save or press **Command-S/Ctrl-S** to save your new document, and name it **chapter11.ai**.

GUIDES AND THE GRID

While you may sometimes know exactly where to place guides, most of the time you'll set guides intuitively, based on relationships among other design elements on the page. I'll demonstrate my intuitive working process for establishing guides on the page in this exercise. Then you'll sort out the relationship between the measurements of the black rectangle and the page.

In this exercise, you'll create hierarchy on the page by contrast through scale and an active use of negative space. The largest element on the page is the negative space, but the largest *foreground* element is a black rectangle overlaid with the white text "SimplyOrganized." View the final image file (Figure 11.7) for a visual reference as you are working, and use your eye to judge approximately where these two items should be placed on the artboard you created in Exercise 1. You'll fix their placement later.

1. Set the Illustrator workspace to Layout.

2. Create a black rectangle with no stroke value that extends most of the way across the page.

3. Click once with the Type tool, and add the text "SimplyOrganized." Set the color of the text to white and the size to 60 points. You'll load a sans serif typeface from Adobe Fonts next.

4. As part of your Creative Cloud account, Adobe Fonts offers thousands of fonts you can activate to use within Adobe applications for no extra charge. Select the text, then click the Character menu on the Control panel. At the top of the menu, click Find More, and then click the Filter Typefaces By Classification icon. In the panel that appears, click Sans Serif in the Classification section and Heavy Weight in the Properties section

PRINTING It's not time to print yet, but if you would print this document it would have to be on a paper size of 10 by 16 inches or larger. Because 10 by 16 inches is not a standard U.S. paper size, you would print this document on tabloid-size (11 by 17 inches) paper and trim it to size. Check your printer to see if this is possible. If it isn't, you may need to visit a consumer printing shop, such as FedEx Office or Staples, or a lab or service through a school, university, or library. Before printing, you should find out if the color mode should be RGB or CMYK and adjust the file by choosing an option from the File > Document Color Mode submenu.

REMINDER When you're creating just one line of type, like a headline, click once with the Type tool and enter the text. Reserve dragging with the Type tool to create a text box for longer lines of copy.

(FIGURE 11.8). Then, click the Activate icon (a cloud that gains an arrow when the typeface is downloading) next to the typeface Aktiv Grotesk Ex. Click OK to activate the font. It is now loaded to your Creative Cloud account, and you can use it immediately.

KERNING REMINDER See Chapter 10, Exercise 3, Step 3 for a demonstration of kerning.

5. Set the text "Simply" in Aktiv Grotesk Ex Light and "Organized" in Bold (FIGURE 11.9). Don't forget to adjust the kerning on such a large block of type.

6. Select the black rectangle, and view its Height value in the Transform panel, which appears on the right side of the application window because you chose the Layout workspace. The height of the rectangle I drew was close to one inch, and I prefer layouts with measurements that are easy to relate to (numbers that are easily divisible). I modified the value by entering "1 in" in the Height box, and I noticed that by default the Width and Height fields were linked. I pressed **Command-Z (Ctrl-Z)** to undo my modification, unchecked the link icon, and re-entered "1 in" in the Height field (FIGURE 11.10). My rectangle is one inch tall.

FIGURE 11.8 Find a new typeface to use from Adobe Fonts by filtering for a sans serif typeface available at a heavy weight.

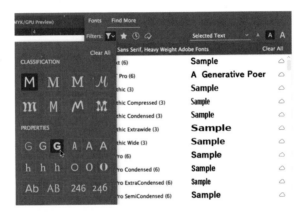

FIGURE 11.9 A single line of white text set on a black rectangle in Aktiv Grotesk Ex.

FIGURE 11.10 Use the Transform panel to adjust the Height value of the rectangle. Be sure to unlink the Width and Height fields by deselecting the link icon.

FIGURE 11.11 Careful observation of the geometric relationships between the objects added to the page and the proportions of the page itself (as measured by the rulers) allows you to place guides that will govern the position of other elements on the page. The result is a pair of horizontal and vertical guides set at the intersection of the bottom-left corner of the rectangle.

7. Show the rulers if they're not already visible (press **Command-R/Ctrl-R**), and then drag a vertical guide from the left ruler to the left edge of the black rectangle. Don't release the mouse because you are using the guide to observe your measurements. When I did this, I could see that my rectangle landed just a tad past two inches on the horizontal ruler. Place the guide at two inches to make the numeric relationships between elements conform to simple numbers or fractions. Do the same with a horizontal guide at the bottom of the black rectangle. Mine landed at 13.5 inches. Working in whole numbers or easy fractions (eighths, fourths, thirds, or halves) makes transforming and scaling elements a bit easier when I want them to relate to one another and the page geometrically. Move the black rectangle so it aligns with the new guides; you will nudge the type into place in Exercise 4 (**FIGURE 11.11**).

EXERCISE 3 CREATE YOUR OWN "VIRTUAL LEADING" SPACERS

This simple, first element on the page will relate to every other item in the composition. To make this point clear, you'll create a series of rectangles in cyan (heights) and magenta (widths) to show how the final elements on the page will stack up. This may seem abstract right now, but you'll see in Exercise 5 how you can use these measuring blocks as stand ins for chunks of negative space in your composition. This is a digital analogy to the concept of "leading" in analog typesetting—blocks of lead were literally inserted into the layout to preserve negative space.

1. Zoom in to the bottom of the page and create a rectangle whose height exactly fills the space between the bottom of the artboard and the bottom edge of the black rectangle. (Hint: you already know this will be 2.5 inches based on where you placed the guides in Exercise 2, Step 7; however, a guide can easily be just a hair off so this way you'll have an accurate visual aide.) The width of the new rectangle is not important (**FIGURE 11.12**).

FIGURE 11.12 Create a new rectangle to represent the height of the space from the bottom of the artboard to the bottom edge of the black rectangle.

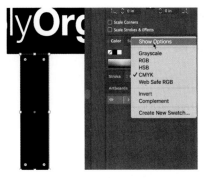
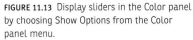

FIGURE 11.13 Display sliders in the Color panel by choosing Show Options from the Color panel menu.

FIGURE 11.14 Change the color of the rectangle to 100% cyan with sliders in the Color panel. Be sure to move the black slider to 0%.

2. Set the Stroke value of the rectangle to None, and fill it with cyan using the Color panel. If you do not see the color sliders, choose Show Options from the panel menu **(FIGURE 11.13)**. Use 100% cyan and 0% of magenta, yellow, and black **(FIGURE 11.14)**.

3. Move the cyan rectangle off the artboard, and align its top with the guide that marks a distance of 13.5 inches from the top. This will help to remind you that this rectangle serves as a spacer for vertical distance. Double-click the Scale tool in the Tools panel (located adjacent to the Rotate tool, and nested with the Reshape and Shear tools). In the Scale dialog box, select the Non-Uniform Scale option. Enter 100% for the Horizontal value and 50% for the Vertical value, then click the Copy button to make a copy that's half as tall as the original **(FIGURE 11.15)**.

FIGURE 11.15 Create a copy of the cyan rectangle at half of its size using the Scale dialog box.

4. The copy will be created in front of the original. Use the Selection tool to move it to the left or right of the original and align its top to the same guide as the original cyan rectangle **(FIGURE 11.16)**.

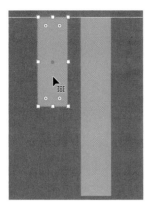
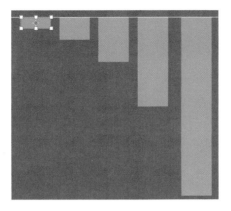

FIGURE 11.16 The scaled copy is half the size of the original. Position it using the guide at 13.5 inches.

FIGURE 11.17 Five scaled copies of the cyan rectangles are positioned next to each other, and aligned along the same guide.

5. Select the second rectangle, and repeat the scaling and alignment in Steps 2 and 3 three more times (**FIGURE 11.17**), resulting in five blocks that are successively halved in height. (See the sidebar *Get Efficient with Keyboard Shortcuts* for a fast way to accomplish the three copies.) You'll make use of these shapes to measure height values in the negative space within the composition after you've added more elements to the positive space in the next exercises.

GET EFFICIENT WITH KEYBOARD SHORTCUTS

You can complete the three additional copies using the key commands in Step 3 by staying with the Scale tool, rather than alternating between the Scale and Selection tools. Once you've made the copy, press the **Command/Ctrl** key to access the Selection tool and keep the Command/Ctrl key pressed as you move the rectangle into position. Release the key, and you're back to the Scale tool. Press the **Return/Enter** key to enter the Scale dialog (without double-clicking the tool). Go ahead and click the Copy button because the settings are already established from your prior use of the tool. Press and hold the Command/Ctrl key to move the next rectangle, release the key, press Return/Enter, click the Copy button, and repeat.

6. Repeat Steps 1, 2, and 3 to create magenta rectangles in a variety of related widths. Start with a magenta rectangle that exactly fills the space between the left edge of the page and the vertical guide (aligned with the black rectangle at approximately two inches from the left edge of the page). Be sure to set the color of the rectangle to 100% magenta and 0% cyan, yellow, and black (**FIGURE 11.18**). Move it off the artboard, then create four additional rectangles, each with half of the previous rectangle's width—this means you will leave the vertical scale at 100% and set the horizontal scale to 50% (**FIGURE 11.19**).

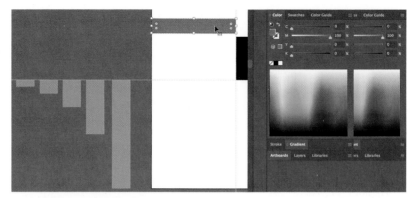

FIGURE 11.18 Create the first magenta rectangle to measure the width of the space between the left margin and the first vertical guide.

FIGURE 11.19 Magenta rectangles demonstrate a variety of proportional widths.

EXERCISE 4 USING YOUR VIRTUAL LEADING

You created and modified text in Chapter 10, Exercise 2. In this chapter, there are two text boxes that will contain a complete poem. You can use the poem I created or make your own now. You'll also adjust the leading and set some of the type using a font variation. Kerning will not be an issue in this situation because the body copy is traditionally of a small enough size that the typeface remains well-kerned.

1. In recent versions of Illustrator, new text boxes are automatically filled with placeholder type. Create a new text box by dragging anywhere on the artboard with the Type tool. You'll correct the positioning of the box later. "*Lorem ipsum*" placeholder text fills the box.

2. The type settings from the last time you used the tool are active, so this copy appears in large, bold type. Enter the title of the poem, "A Generative Poem for Grids and Geometry." You will use variations of Aktiv Grotesk Ex throughout these exercises. Change the style to XBold, and leave the font size at 60 points (FIGURE 11.20).

3. Align the poem title on the vertical guide, and tighten the leading. You can see that I pressed **Option-Up Arrow** (**Alt-Up Arrow**) with the text selected until my Character panel showed the type as 60 point type at 66 point leading (often written in shorthand as 60/66) (FIGURE 11.21).

4. Now that the title is positioned horizontally, use your virtual leading spacers to position it vertically. Copy the largest blue rectangle onto the artboard, and place it above the "SimplyOrganized" text block. Make a second copy of the same shape, and place it directly on top of the first. In my composition, the next shape will have to be smaller—copy one of the smaller spacer blocks from outside of the artboard to this part of the composition. Usually you will have to reposition text blocks to organize them so they maintain the measurements you are creating in the composition.

5. Adjust the text block vertically until the bottom of the last line just touches the third cyan spacer block. (FIGURE 11.22).

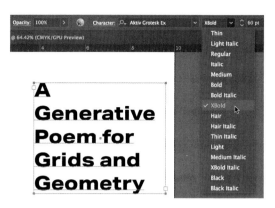

FIGURE 11.20 Choose a different style of the original font for the title of the poem.

FIGURE 11.21 Tighten the leading for the title.

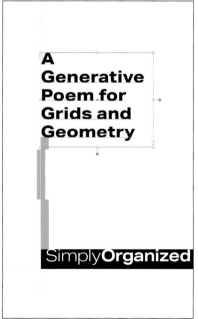

FIGURE 11.22 Virtual leading helps to measure the space between the black rectangle and the title copy. I moved each of the cyan shapes slightly to the left or right so the individual shapes are easily seen.

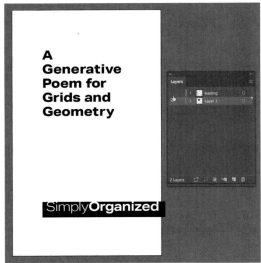

FIGURE 11.23 (ABOVE) Measure the margin space for "SimplyOrganized" using the second smallest magenta measuring block.

FIGURE 11.24 (RIGHT) Move the virtual leading to its own layer, so you can easily make it visible and invisible with one click. Kern the large type once the clutter is cleared from the artboard.

6. With this virtual leading on the page, take a close look at the text, "SimplyOrganized." I had intuitively placed this text box with a small amount of margin into the left edge of the black box. Now I will use the second-smallest magenta (width) measuring block to precisely set the text in a margin space that relates to other negative spaces on the page (FIGURE 11.23). Review the typography as you will make further adjustments concerning this type in the next exercise: "Simply" should be set in Aktiv Grotesk Ex Light and "Organized" in Aktiv Grotesk Ex Bold, with no space between the words, in 60 points.

7. Clean up the document and prepare for the next steps, which will include adding more virtual leading and type. Place all of the virtual leading spacers on their own layer named **leading** (don't forget about Edit > Paste In Place). Make the layer invisible (click the eyeball icon), and deactivate guides (press **Command-; (semicolon)/Ctrl-;**) so you have an unfettered view of the type on the page. Kern the large type if it needs adjusting (FIGURE 11.24).

 ## PLACING ANOTHER GUIDE ON THE GRID

Refer to Figure 11.7, as you are setting the remaining typography. The third and fourth text boxes you will place on the artboard contain most of the content of the poem. These text boxes are aligned on the artboard along a second guide. In fact, the bold italic text "Somebody Boring Always you" is also aligned on this guide, which results in two text blocks aligned on one side of the guide and one on the other. This uneven distribution of weight helps move the viewer's eye through the composition. This second guide is a major contributor to the information flow on the page. It establishes a line of continuation (referring to the Gestalt *Law of Continuity*) or an implied line within the compositional layout. By aligning these three items on the same guide, you're helping the reader to group the elements together. Because the guide is so essential to the layout, you'll want to ensure that its placement is logical within the system of your page. You'll continue to use the measuring blocks, or virtual leading, created in Exercise 3 to accomplish this task.

1. If the guides you created are invisible, press **Command-;/Ctrl-;** to show them. Zoom in, and drag a vertical guide from the ruler on the left side of the artboard to the right edge of the letter "y" in the word "Geometry" (FIGURE 11.25).

KEYBOARD SHORTCUT
You can unlock locked guides by pressing **Command-Option-;/Ctrl-Alt-;**.

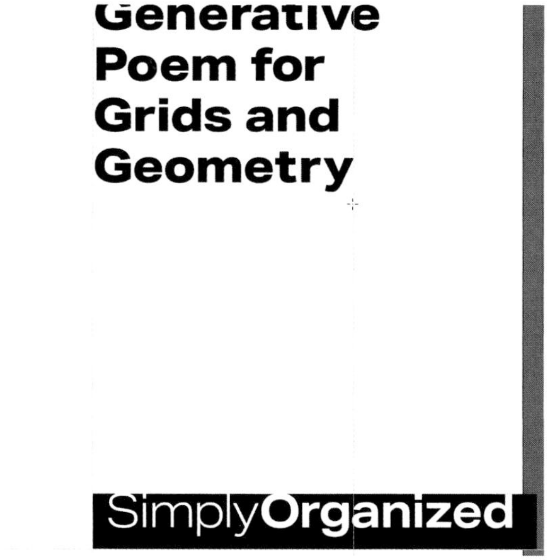

2. Readjust kerning or positioning now that this second guide has been placed. I put my cursor before the letter "S" in "Simply" and pressed **Option-Right Arrow/Alt-Right Arrow** to make the line of text ever so slightly move to the right. In other words, I kerned the entire line over by one click to allow for the "a" in "Organized" to be alongside but not intercepted by the second vertical guide. I tightened the kerning on "Generative," but the "e" is now even more obviously intercepted by the guide (FIGURE 11.26). I feel more comfortable with this position. When the guides just barely cut off a shape (a letterform is a shape), the resulting relationship appears accidental.

FIGURE 11.25 When I placed this guide I noticed it barely intersects the "a" in "Organized" and the "e" in "Generative." I will adjust the kerning in the next step to account for this.

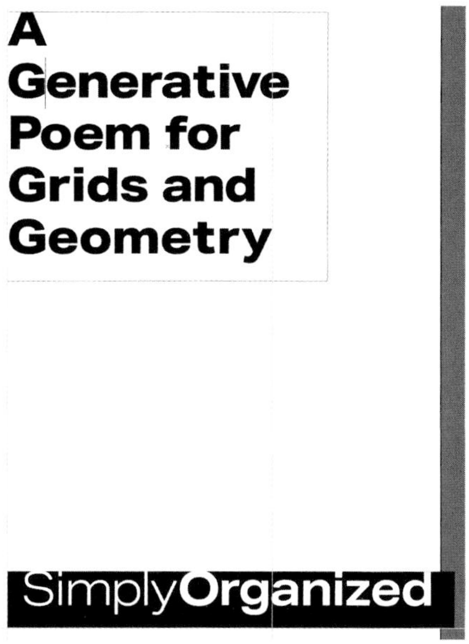

FIGURE 11.26 Adjust the kerning of the text that is accidentally intercepted by the vertical guide.

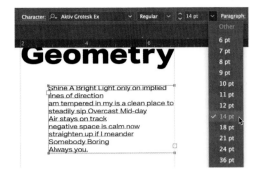

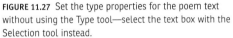

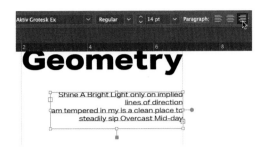

FIGURE 11.27 Set the type properties for the poem text without using the Type tool—select the text box with the Selection tool instead.

FIGURE 11.28 Resize the poem's text box, and right-justify it.

3. Choose File > Place, and select the **poem.docx** file from your **chapter11-start** folder or select a document you created containing your poem. In the Microsoft Word Options dialog box, select Remove Text Formatting. Click the artboard with the loaded pointer to place the text.

4. Choose the Selection tool, and select the text box. Set all of the copy in Aktiv Grotesk Ex Regular at 14 points (**FIGURE 11.27**).

5. Use the Selection tool to resize the text box containing the poem so that the last word that is visible is "Mid-day." Click Align Right in the Paragraph section of the Control panel to right-justify the paragraph and position the text box on the left side of the vertical guide you just placed in Step 1 (**FIGURE 11.28**).

6. Notice the text box has a small box with a red plus sign (+) in its lower-right corner. This indicates there is *overflow* text (text that doesn't fit in the box). While the text box is selected, click the plus sign (+) or overflow text indicator. When you move the pointer away from the text box, its icon should change to the icon for the loaded text pointer (**FIGURE 11.29**). With the loaded pointer, drag to make another text box to the right of the vertical guide (**FIGURE 11.30**). You will measure the space between the guide and the second box in Step 8, again working intuitively and then fine-tuning with the virtual leading spacers.

7. Resize the second text box from the vertical guide on the left to the right edge of the artboard, and left-align the text (click the Align Left button in the Paragraph panel). You should no longer see an overflow text indicator (**FIGURE 11.31**). These two text boxes are now linked. The text from the first box flows into the second text box. If you change the size of the first text box, its copy will automatically flow into the second. The thick blue line between the two text boxes indicates that they are linked.

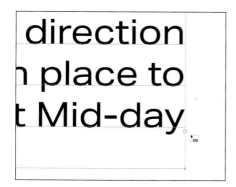

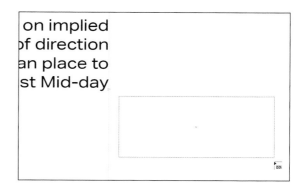

FIGURE 11.29 Overflow text is indicated by the red plus sign in the lower-right corner of the text box.

FIGURE 11.30 The loaded text pointer is used to place text in a new box.

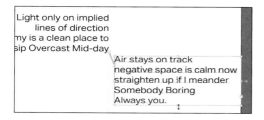

FIGURE 11.31 Resize the second text box from the vertical guide on the left to the right margin of the artboard so all of the copy fits inside the bounding area.

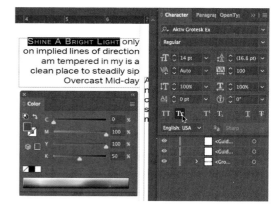

FIGURE 11.32 Call attention to the first few words of the poem by creating contrast in hue and in style.

8. Select the Type tool, then select the words "Shine A Bright Light" in the first text box and change their color to crimson using the CMYK percentage values 0, 100, 100, 50 in the Color panel. Open the Character panel, and click the Small Caps button to transform the case of this part of the copy to small capitals (FIGURE 11.32). This type adjustment substitutes glyphs that simulate uppercase letters with an x-height similar to the lowercase letters in the typeface. Changing the first few words to small caps draws attention to them due to the contrast in form and weight.

9. Make the **leading** layer visible again, and use the magenta boxes to create a geometrical relationship in the gutter space between the guide and the second text box (FIGURE 11.33). Then drag a guide from the top ruler to the baseline of the word "Mid-day." Align the first line of the second textbox so it is on the same baseline (FIGURE 11.34).

FIGURE 11.33 Adjust the distance of the linked text box from the guides using the magenta boxes to measure widths.

FIGURE 11.34 Adjust the position of the linked text box so its first line of copy sits on the same baseline as the last line of type in the first box.

10. Add a guide to the composition at the left edge of the copy that begins with "Air stays on track." You will use it in Exercise 6. I placed mine at 7 inches on the horizonal ruler.

SCREENCAST 11-1 USING THE GRID

Exercise 6 is explained only briefly: you'll complete it mostly on your own. However, I've captured my process in this chapter's screencast to demonstrate how to use measuring blocks to see the relationships between elements on the grid.

All screencasts are available on the companion website, www.digitalart-design.com or on the Vimeo playlist, bit.ly/foundations-demos.

EXERCISE 6 USE THE GRID

To finalize the layout, you will add two new text boxes aligned on guides that provide lines of continuation. So you will need to continue to be aware of spatial relationships in the composition. Font variations will assign contrast and hierarchy in the layout.

1. Reposition the last two lines of the poem, "Somebody Boring Always you" towards the bottom of the composition. You can either use the Type tool to select and cut the text and paste it into a new text box; or you can resize the bounding box of this copy and link a third text box to a lower position in the composition.

2. Set the text in the variation XBold Italic at 10/12 and use the Color panel to change the text from black to the crimson hue with the same values as you used in Exercise 5, Step 7: 0, 100, 100, 50. Use the two vertical guides (at about 6.875 and 7 inches) to horizontally align the first and second lines of copy. I used a few spaces before "Always" to bring its left edge

close to the second guide, then I used kerning to fine-tune the adjustment (**FIGURE 11.35**). You will vertically align the copy in the composition in Step 3.

3. Make a copy of one of the text boxes and change the text to read "Does this poem make sense to you?" Set the question in Light Italic variation 10/14, and change the color to the same crimson hue as in Step 2. Click the Align Right button in the Paragraph panel to right-justify the text and position it along the first vertical guide at 2 inches into the composition from the left margin. My Character panel settings for this step are shown in **FIGURE 11.36**.

4. The vertical alignment of the new text boxes created in Steps 1 and 3 requires some visual thinking. Use the cyan measuring blocks to create contrast while retaining a geometric relationship in the space (**FIGURE 11.36**).

FIGURE 11.35 Move the last two lines of the poem down to the bottom of the composition, and repeat the step-down pattern of the text fields by aligning the separate lines of copy on the two guides.

FIGURE 11.36 Final adjustments made for the two new text boxes are visible; especially notice how the cyan spacers are used to measure the space. They help you to create a relationship between foreground elements in the composition using the geometry of the negative space.

SAVE A PDF WITH TRIM MARKS

Because the size of the poster is 10 by 16 inches and the paper it will be printed on is tabloid size (11 by 17 inches), you'll have to cut the poster from the larger sheet of paper after it's printed. You could measure and mark the page with a pencil, but why add an extra step (and risk human error) when the Save Adobe PDF dialog will print trim marks for you?

1. Choose File > Save (**Command-S/Ctrl-S**) to save the file in native (.ai) format as **chapter11.ai**.

2. Make the **leading** layer invisible by clicking its eyeball icon. Choose File > Save As (**Command-Shift-S/Ctrl-Shift-S**), but this time choose Adobe PDF as the file format (or file type in Windows). Click the Save button.

3. In the Save Adobe PDF dialog box, click Marks And Bleeds in the list at the left. In the Marks And Bleeds area of the dialog box, select Trim Marks (**FIGURE 11.37**). Click the Save PDF button.

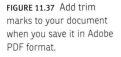

FIGURE 11.37 Add trim marks to your document when you save it in Adobe PDF format.

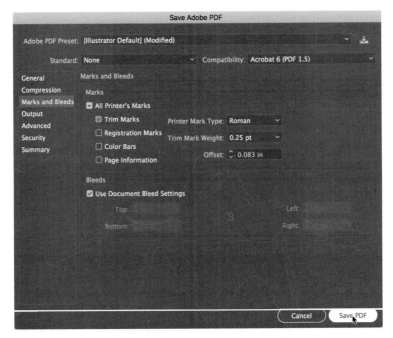

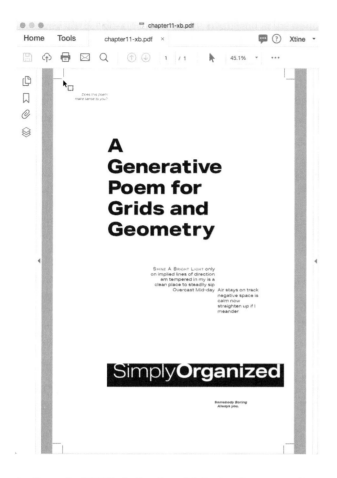

FIGURE 11.38 The final PDF includes trim marks to help you know where to trim the page after you've printed it.

4. Open the PDF file in Preview, Adobe Acrobat, or another application that can open PDF files. Notice the thin black crosshairs at the corners of the document (**FIGURE 11.38**). These trim marks will print on the page. When cutting down the page to its nonstandard size (10 by 16 inches), align your ruler or other straightedge to the trim marks.

 LAB CHALLENGE

Redesign an event poster that you see in your neighborhood using a grid system. Search telephone or lighting poles, coffee shops, school or laundromat bulletin boards, and other public areas for amateur event posters. Comparing the poster before and after your redesign, you'll notice how much more organized and easier to read the content is when it's aligned on a systematic grid.

WATCH OUT! If your PDF shows the cyan and magenta measuring blocks, you forgot to hide the **leading** layer before saving the file. Close the PDF, return to Illustrator, hide the layer, then resave the PDF.

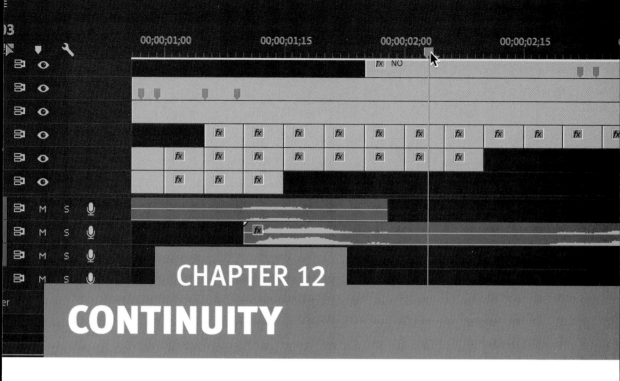

CHAPTER 12
CONTINUITY

THE EXERCISES IN this chapter provide technical and aesthetic lessons in using the Gestalt Laws of Similarity and Continuity to create stylistic consistency when sequencing frames in a multimedia file. Open *The New York Times* to any article, and you'll always know that you're reading *The New York Times*. In the sixth edition of his *Visual Communication: Images with Messages*, Paul Martin Lester defines stylistic consistency as "a design concept in which multiple pages or frames of a piece appear to be unified" [1]. You'll create a multimedia work with moving type and images as you focus on the continuity of the work through time.

THE GESTALT LAWS OF SIMILARITY AND CONTINUITY

REFERENCE [1] Paul Martin Lester, *Visual Communication: Images with Messages*, 6th ed. (Boston: Cengage, 2013), 195.

LINK See a Gestalt playlist I created on YouTube at bit.ly/gestalt-playlist. (Apologies if some videos were removed by the time this book is published.)

You learned about Gestalt laws in the sidebar in Chapter 11, *The Grid*. Study these laws carefully. Understanding them will help you become deft at creating unity, balance, rhythm, and contrast in your designs. These essential, strategic design elements provide a way of developing a focal point or directing the viewer's eye toward or away from selected content. In the exercises in this chapter, you'll refer to the *Law of Similarity* and *Law of Continuity* as you develop a multimedia work including type, image, and sound. (If this sounds familiar, it should—remember that the primary idea of Gestalt is that perception is shaped by organizing small parts into a greater concept.)

To retain consistency when sequencing visual ideas, commit to a small selection of typefaces, colors, and geometric relationships between the positive and negative spaces. Although every part of the project should feel related, individual elements (screens or pages) do not need to look the same. The Gestalt *Law of Similarity* holds that visual items with similar attributes (shape, color, value, texture, size, and so on) should be grouped together or considered to be part of a larger system. Logically, it follows that choosing a set of shapes, colors, values, textures, and sizes to use repeatedly within a designed system would encourage the viewer to recognize the whole as a work that's greater than the sum of its many parts. This is evident in printed works as well as multimedia works developed for the screen.

Nicholas Felton's *Feltron 2006 Annual Report* and *Feltron 2007 Annual Report* utilize different dominant fonts and colors, but the layouts are unified in their use of large typography and an overlay of graphic elements to suggest a timeline and various life activities (FIGURE 12.1). In the 2007 report, a four-column grid is used throughout the document (FIGURE 12.2). Sometimes a chart or graph spans all four columns (FIGURE 12.3). Given the consistency of the color palette, grid layout, and typeface choices, viewers never forget that they are reading a coherent document.

REFERENCE [2] Andrew Demirjian, *I Tremble with Anticipation* (2015), www.andrewdemirjian.com.

Andrew Demirjian's *I Tremble with Anticipation* is a video that remixes stills from dozens of foreign language films to create a poetic narrative set to the artist's immersive 5.1 audio soundtrack (FIGURE 12.4). Demirjian writes, "The work features meticulously selected frames that are orchestrated into verses that juxtapose gesture, light and setting, creating a new dialog across films" [2]. Like Felton's printed work, Demirjian's made-for-screen remix juxtaposes a variety of forms and messages while using consistent design elements that cue

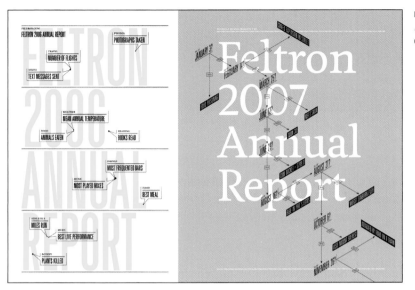

FIGURE 12.1 Nicholas Felton, *Feltron Annual Report* covers in 2006 and 2007.

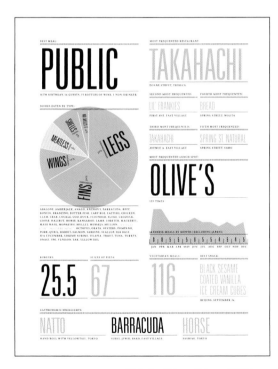

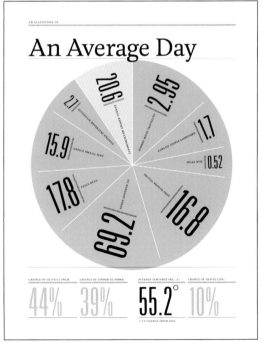

FIGURE 12.2 AND FIGURE 12.3 Nicholas Felton, *Feltron 2007 Annual Report*. This is the third iteration in Felton's continuing exploration of how to graphically encapsulate a year.

FIGURE 12.4 Andrew Demirjian, *I Tremble with Anticipation*, 2015, Video Still.

the viewer into a single viewing experience. Unlike Feltron's printed works, which utilize two-dimensional visual cues, Demirjian relies on an even tempo, linguistic narrative, and cohesive audio soundtrack to create meaningful relationships between the separate film stills he recombines.

The Gestalt *Law of Continuity* accounts for the way that the viewer perceives elements in a continuous relationship, such as those aligned on a grid, as part of a group, or even a time-based relationship. When a viewer notices an implied line, she'll read all the content on the line with the subtle understanding that those items belong together. In the exercises in Chapter 11, you created two implied lines (using guides) to establish the grid for the Lorem Ipsum poster. The *Law of Continuity* helps us see that the blocks of type are unified, even when their sizes, colors, and font variations change. Visit the website for the German design firm, Schoener, and you'll notice how a large, sans serif typeface called *thexx* organizes all of the content in the page. When you hover the pointer over content on the page, the pointer and the content are transformed, adding contrast and variation to the design of the page (**FIGURE 12.5**).

FIGURE 12.5 To see the pointer and page transformations in action, visit Schoener at wirsindschoener.de.

0:00:00:00

The digital artist communicates a coherent message across multiple parameters, such as time—as suggested by the heading of this section, which represents video timecode that is measured in hours, minutes, seconds, and frames. The rate of frames per second is standardized by media industries and technologies. In addition to time, digital artists must communicate their message across multiple pages and interactive screens. In designing any of these systems, the digital artist leverages their knowledge of the Gestalt laws to maintain continuity. In the following exercises you will overlay type that changes over time on top of a composited sequence of video frames. Pay attention to the duration of the changes in the letterforms (which move quickly) as compared to the video (which has a slower tempo).

FOLLOWING AN IMPLIED LINE IN A MULTIMEDIA INSTALLATION

In Jody Zellen's *Trigger*, the type sits on the same baseline despite the juxtaposition of the video throughout the urban space (**FIGURE 12.6**). The contrast between the surfaces of the spaces where the video is projected and the consistency of the baseline of the typography helps the viewer understand the work as a cohesive piece. See www.jodyzellen.com/pace2.html for video documentation of the installation.

FIGURE 12.6 Jody Zellen, *Trigger*, 2005. Pace University Digital Gallery, New York.

TIME AND MEDIUM
Generally, animation and film are recorded at 24 frames per second (FPS). On your mobile device or prosumer video camera, you will likely capture video at 30 FPS. For television broadcasting, video is recorded in the U.S. at 29.97 FPS. Low-bandwidth animation projects often use much lower frame rates. A longer discussion about how time is recorded in the moving image is outside the scope of this chapter. In a book or class about digital video production and editing you should learn about NTSC and PAL formats, various video file types, frame rates, and "codecs," that is, coder-decoders.

REFERENCE [3] www. etymonline.com/word/kern

Every medium is associated with key terminology that was developed to articulate how you interact with it, how you create with it, and how it manifests in culture. For example, in the typography section you learned about kerning and leading, two important terms that allude to the spacing between letters and sentences. The term "kern" derives from a French word that originates from the Latin *cardo* or *cardin*, which means "hinge" [3]. In the early days of printing, metal letters were combined and set in order (called a *sort*), then inked, and pressed to paper to make a print. When letters overlapped, a part of the metal would hang (or hinge) over the edge or extend outward from the letter's body, this was referred to as the kern. "Kerning" would become the term describing the manual adjustment to the space between two letters, such as when a *slug* (a blank piece of metal that would not print) was positioned in spaces where the type needed to be opened or loosened between two letters.

Digital video, like typography, has its own set of terms that are used to describe the process of creating and manipulating it. Most people are familiar with the idea of editing video clips, but there are some lesser-known words that will help you articulate the process of editing digital video in Adobe Premiere Pro. You will learn key terminology and how to navigate the Adobe Premiere Pro workspace in Exercise 1.

READING ON THE SCREEN

You can overlay a display of the title safe area on the Source or Program panel. In Adobe Premiere Pro, click the wrench icon beneath the right edge of the display to open the Program Settings menu and choose Safe Margin. The inner rectangle is the title safe area.

Because the product of the exercises in this chapter will be a digital video intended to be shared onscreen, the typography should best fit the screen environment. Watch out for the type size and how many words appear in short durations of time. The *title safe* area accounts for a standard "safe zone" for text in film or videos, which are viewed at varying ratios depending on the screen. In the following exercises the typography will not be set close to those areas, but in projects you may create later you should be aware of the safe areas. For these exercises, we will assume the reader will be viewing the final file on a personal screen (not sitting at a distance or watching a projected image). The typography will move in time, so it should be larger than the traditional size of body copy in printed text (that is, larger than 11 or 12 points). Also, the typeface will be easiest to read on a screen if it is set in a sans serif font. The serifs that are often used for body copy in printed documents can be difficult to read onscreen, because light is projected through such small graphic details. I used the typeface Futura PT from Adobe Fonts in Exercise 7. If you don't have access to Futura PT, use any sans serif typeface to complete the exercises.

INSPIRATION EVERYWHERE, EVEN RIGHT AT HOME

Exercises in this chapter, the last in the printed book, follow in the spirit of artists who find inspiration in their home lives such as William Wegman—you should see the videos he made early in his career with his Weimaraner dog named Man Ray [4], Sally Mann's photographs of her children [5], or Nan Goldin's candid images of her New Wave friends [6]. Sometimes you work with what is around you, even if what is around you seems as mundane as your dog, your children, or your friends. Great artists can elevate what seems to be the most unnuanced part of everyday life because they show the details that make their stories specifically personal and widely relatable.

I thought about making a video of my Weimaraner, named Nietzsche, but instead decided to go the way of Sally Mann and employed my children. The file you create by following these exercises was inspired by *The Electric Company* and its silhouette words segment. My twin kindergarten boys are learning to read, and they enjoy viewing the online clips from this vintage series—I remember how influential this program was on me when I started elementary school in 1980. I made a few attempts to produce videos of the boys sounding out the word, "know," one of my favorite words. "Know" offers a possibility in its letterforms to "know," "now," and "no." It is as if this word is designed to suggest knowing, temporality, and the impossibility of that knowing, all at once. As you will see in the video files in the **chapter12-start** folder, Parker and Martin are not child actors. The result is an increase in post-production work, as we meld their multiple takes into one multimedia production.

I considered reshooting this on a green screen and transforming their bodies into silhouettes, like the original production, but I decided to leave the home-produced clips as the starting point for these exercises. As digital art and design students or learners, it is more likely that you will have to work with inconsistent files, rather than well-produced videos during the early stages of your career.

REFERENCE [4] William Wegman offers a selection of his early video works on his blog, wegmanworld. typepad.com/wegman_ world/2017/01/6-vintage-videos-by-william-wegman. html. You can also find them on YouTube by searching for his user name, wegmanworld.

REFERENCE [5] A selection of Sally Mann's photographs of her children are collected at The Art Institute of Chicago. See www. artic.edu/artists/44721/ sally-mann.

REFERENCE [6] Works by Nan Goldin are collected by The Guggenheim. See www. guggenheim.org/artwork/ artist/nan-goldin.

WHAT YOU'LL NEED

Download the following source materials to complete the exercises in this chapter:

✔ The **chapter12-workfiles.zip** file, which contains original video source files that you will use to build a project in Adobe Premiere Pro. It also contains a sample of the finished project file in the **chapter12-results** folder.

FIGURE 12.7 The final media file is inspired by *The Electric Company*'s silhouette word blends. You can see these animated segments at http://bit.ly/TEC_SB or by searching YouTube for "Electric Company silhouette letters." Here you can see a single frame of the final video produced in the Premiere workspace.

WHAT YOU'LL MAKE

In the exercises in this chapter, you'll create a multimedia project with images and text that change over time (**FIGURE 12.7**). You should view the final project file in the **chapter12-results** folder now and keep it open as a reference throughout the exercises. When it opens, if you see the Linked Media dialog prompt, point Premiere Pro to the **media** folder inside the **chapter12-start folder** on your hard drive. You'll be working with Adobe Premiere Pro and a typeface from Adobe Fonts obtained through the Adobe Creative Cloud. If you're new to Premiere Pro, you'll find that it's similar to other Adobe applications. It includes a robust set of tools that supports time-based media.

VIDEO TERMINOLOGY AND THE ADOBE PREMIERE PRO WORKSPACE

In this exercise you will learn to navigate the Premiere Pro workspace. I created a new file and imported media in the first Screencast to minimize classroom time. However, all of the media files are included in the **chapter12-start** folder. If you want to start by making a new file you can follow along with Screencast 12-1.

SCREENCAST 12-1 CREATE A NEW PREMIERE PRO PROJECT AND IMPORT MEDIA

In this screencast, I create a new project and explore the Premiere Pro Editing workspace. The final file is developed by exporting frames from a series of unprofessional home videos. As an artist or designer, you always want to work with the best possible media elements, but you also need to learn how to creatively transform less than ideal images, videos, or sound into a cohesive message. I import the media used in the following exercises. You should view this screencast before starting Exercise 1.

All screencasts are available on the companion website, www.digitalart-design.com, or on the Vimeo playlist, http://bit.ly/foundations-demos.

In the Adobe Premiere Pro interface, you will notice there are four main areas. In a description of each area, I will need to use vocabulary words specific to time-based media. Those words are set in italics and defined here. The terms "sequence" and "Timeline" are often used interchangeably, as in "in the sequence" or "on the Timeline." In general, we'll use "timeline" (lowercase) when speaking of a sequence of clips in the abstract, without reference to a specific user interface element.

If your version of Premiere Pro is newer than the one I used when creating the starting file, the Convert Project dialog box will open and prompt you to update the project file for the new version. Go ahead and click OK and give the converted project a unique name.

1. Before you create a new project in Premiere Pro, you should determine where you will save your video files. Drag the **chapter12-workfiles** folder to a location on your hard drive where you plan to keep these files. Do not move the folder or rename the files as you are working through these exercises! Plan to save the project file in the next steps inside the **chapter12-start** folder. Notice that it contains a **media** folder.

2. Double-click **chapter12-start.prproj** from the **chapter-12-start** folder to open the starting file in Premiere Pro.

The Scratch Disk Settings dialog box may also open, asking where you want to store temporary files. Click OK to accept the default settings.

3. The group of panels in the lower-left quadrant contains the Project panel, the Effects panel, and others. The Project panel (click its tab to bring it to the front if it's not visible) lists the media (video, audio, image files) that have been imported into your project. In order to edit video, audio, images, or graphic clips on a timeline you will create one or more *sequences*—they will be listed here, too. Each media format is represented by a distinct icon. I imported media to various *bins* (folders), named **audio**, **still-images**, and **videos** (FIGURE 12.8). You will work on the **composite** sequence in Exercise 3.

If Premiere Pro is not already set to the Editing workspace, choose Window > Workspaces > Editing.

FIGURE 12.8 In the Editing workspace, the Project panel is located in the bottom left of the Application frame. I have selected the movie **martin.mov**, stored in the **videos** bin. Notice the various icons—**martin.mov** has a frame of film and a sound waveform to indicate it is a movie clip, while sequences are represented by a timeline with a playhead. Audio clips (not shown here) are represented by a larger waveform icon.

CAN'T TOUCH THIS (IMPORTED ELEMENTS)

Media imported to the Project panel is not embedded in the Premiere Pro project file. What is actually imported is a pointer to a file that lives in a specific location on your hard drive. If you change the name of the file on your hard drive or if you move it to a new location, Premiere Pro will warn you that your file is "offline." It is not terrible if this happens; you will be asked to relocate the media. However, you should plan for longevity when you are building a Premiere Pro project. Try to put your projects in folders on your hard drive that you think you will be likely to keep for at least the duration of the time you will spend working on the project, and don't rename your files while you are working.

4. When you double-click a sequence icon (not the filename) in the Project panel to see it open in the Timeline panel in the bottom right of the Application Frame **(FIGURE 12.9)**. The *timecode* appears in the top left of this panel as a series of numbers indicating the location of the playhead in the clip. Timecode can be set to display in a variety of ways. Typically, we read the timecode in hours, minutes, seconds, and frames. Sequences, stored in the Project panel, are edited here. Each sequence has its own timeline. While you are editing a sequence, I may refer to its timeline (which is also contained in the Timeline panel).

5. Double-click **martin.mov** in the **videos** bin in the Project panel. The clip opens in the Source panel. Press and hold your mouse over the playhead at the bottom of the Source panel as you drag left to scrub along the timeline, and you will see your clip at various timecodes **(FIGURE 12.10)**. Earlier, in the Source panel, I set *In* and *Out points* (where I chose to start and end the clip, respectively) on this clip to trim it. That meant that when I added the clip to the **martin** sequence (in the **videos** bin) in the Project panel only the desired section of the clip was added.

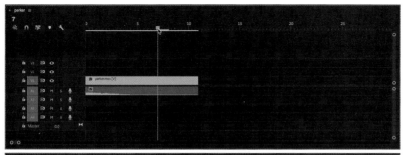

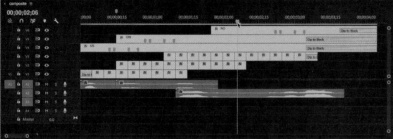

FIGURE 12.9 You can see in this set of images that the **parker** sequence is set to display time in frames, while the **composite** sequence that you will build will become more than four seconds in length (the image shows the sequence as it will look later in the chapter). The composite playback head sits at zero hours, zero minutes, two seconds, and six frames in the second image seen here.

FIGURE 12.10 The Source panel is located in the top left of the Application Frame. Here you can trim clips before adding them to a sequence.

The Source and Program panels are very often referred to as the Source monitor and Program monitor.

6. Double-click the sequence named **martin** from the **videos** bin in the Projects panel. It opens in the Timeline panel. Scrub along the timeline, and you will see the results of trimming the video in the Program panel (**FIGURE 12.11**). From the Timeline, when you double-click a clip it opens in the Source panel. Doing so from the Project panel allows you to suggest edit points for placing the clip in the timeline. However, when you double-click a clip from a sequence in the Timeline panel it is this specific instance of the clip that opens in the Source panel.

FIGURE 12.11 The Program panel displays the results of your edits in the Timeline. It is in the top right area of the Application Frame. I chose Safe Margins from the Settings menu (opened by clicking the wrench icon in the lower right corner of the Program panel) to enable the overlays you see here.

7. In the **martin** sequence in the Timeline panel press **Shift-I** to go to the nearest In point. Because there are no marked In or Out points, this will position the playback head at the start of the timeline, or 0 (zero). Press the **Spacebar** to play the movie. Press the **Spacebar** again to pause playback; if you've reached the end of the movie pressing the **Spacebar** will start playback over from the beginning.

Using the mouse to *scrub* the playhead—move it forward and backward in time—is an intuitive way of moving through a sequence, but you will do this so often that it is worthwhile to learn the keys that advance and rewind the playhead. The same keys scrub the playhead in the Timeline, Source, and Program panels, as well as in other applications.

KEYBOARD SHORTCUTS FOR PLAYBACK

- Press the **Spacebar** to start or pause playback.
- Press **L** once to play forward, press L twice to fast forward, press it three times to move the playhead forward very quickly.
- Press **J** to play backward. Press J twice, then three times to watch the movie rewind very quickly.
- Press **Right Arrow** to move the playhead forward by one frame.
- Press **Left Arrow** to move the playhead backward by one frame.
- Press the **Up Arrow** key to position the playhead at the nearest In point.
- Press the **Down Arrow** key to advance the playhead to the nearest Out point.

8. Double-click each of the other two video clips in the **videos** bin (Projects panel), and play them in the Source window. If you load the sequences instead, practice in the Timeline panel. Practice using the keyboard shortcuts to scrub the playhead along the timeline.

BUILD A COMPOSITE SEQUENCE WITH IMAGES AND SOUND

The final file disrupts the expectations a viewer brings to continuous video. To produce a playful multimedia work that feels more like a graphic sequence than a video, I exported parts of each of three original video clips as a sequence of JPEG images. Those images were imported back into the Project panel to be placed in a sequence in the timeline in this Exercise. View Screencast 12-2 to learn how to prepare the project file provided to you as **chapter12-start.prproj**.

SCREENCAST 12-2 EXPORTING STILL IMAGES FROM A SEQUENCE IN THE TIMELINE PANEL AND IMPORT FILES TO A BIN

The next exercises in this chapter begin at about the halfway point of the production from importing media files to the final edited composition. To keep the total amount of time students might take to complete these exercises to a range consistent with computer laboratory hours, I recorded the steps taken to complete the following actions: setting In and Out points in the Source panel, adding trimmed video clips to the timeline, changing the frame rate in the sequence, and exporting still image frames from the Timeline panel. You will notice that I underwent the same process for transforming video into an imported sequence of JPEG images for the three movie files, **martin.mov**, **parker.mov**, and **no-no-no.mov**. You should view this screencast before beginning Exercise 3.

All screencasts are available on the companion website, www.digitalart-design.com, or on the Vimeo playlist, http://bit.ly/foundations-demos.

You will build the **composite** sequence and add audio recordings to the composite timeline in this Exercise. However, even though I completed some of the work, I left you with the part where things get a little tricky. The boys were not great at following the directions at the time of recording these videos. They do not take turns sounding out the parts of the words. So you have to fabricate the final video by focusing on multiple sets of image sequences with no audio to assist you. You will construct three parts: the two parts of the word "know" (the "nnnn" sound from Martin and the "oooo" sound from Parker), as well as Martin's charming "No, no, no!" for the ending.

Digital artists and designers use iterative processes while they work. You will often find yourself repeating the same steps to achieve similar goals or, as in the case of creating sets of exported still images, in order to build a composite that requires similar steps in a design process. Imagine that each time you repeat a process you gain a new skill. Although this may not feel true, your body will develop kinetic memory. The first time you scrub through video files, you may have to look at the keys while you press **J** to rewind and **L** to fast forward. Later, your fingers will know where the **Up Arrow** key is for toggling back to the start of a clip or a marked In point without having to move your eyes away from the timeline.

1. Close any sequence that may be open by clicking the small "x" to the left of its name in the Timeline panel (**FIGURE 12.12**).

2. Double-click the **composite** sequence from the Project panel. It opens in the Timeline panel.

3. In the **still-images** bin, Shift-click to select all of the Martin JPEG images from **martin00.jpg** to **martin25.jpg**. Drag the selected images to the composite timeline and release them on the first video track (V1) at 0 (**FIGURE 12.13**).

FIGURE 12.12 Click the "x" to close sequences in the Timeline panel.

You can also add a marker to the timeline by choosing Markers > Add Marker.

4. Use the Program monitor to review the sequence as you scrub along it, and watch Martin's mouth. Even though he sounds out the entire word, "Nnnnn—ooo," in the first set of frames that I exported his mouth shape does not show the "n" sound. Find the spot in the timeline where he visibly stops saying "nnnn," just before he says "ooo." With the playhead at this location, press the **M** key to add a marker to the timeline. Notice the small *marker* (flag icon just above the playhead) added to this section of the composite timeline (**FIGURE 12.14**).

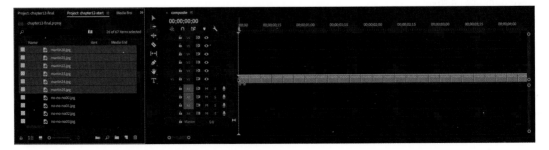

FIGURE 12.13 Add the still images of Martin to the **composite** sequence.

FIGURE 12.14 Markers are helpful when you want to align media to a beat or a particular visual element. The *marker* is the flag icon just above the playhead in the Timeline panel.

If you need to reposition a series of clips or images on the timeline, you can marquee over them as you would in Adobe Illustrator. Start dragging inside the timeline, but not on a specific clip, and continue to drag the pointer over the series of clips you want to select, and then move them.

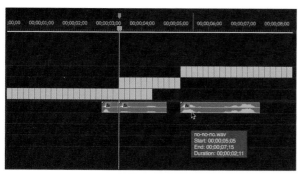

FIGURE 12.15 (ABOVE) Drag frames to the V2 track at the marker location in the Timeline panel.

FIGURE 12.16 (LEFT) The no-no-no images are placed on V3 so you can build a composite with layered images.

5. Shift-click to select all of the Parker JPEG images from the **still-images** bin in the Project panel. Drag them to the Timeline panel, specifically to V2 (a second video track, just above V1) in the Timeline, position the first image file so it lands at the marker you added in Step 4, and drop the files (FIGURE 12.15).

6. Shift-click all of the no-no-no images and place them in the timeline on a third video track, V3, starting after the last parker image clip (FIGURE 12.16).

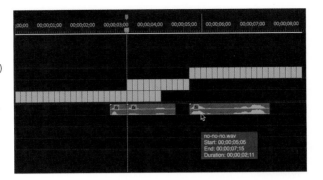

FIGURE 12.17 The three audio tracks are placed on A1, ending (**martin-nnna.wav**) and starting (**parker-ooo-no.wav**) at the marker, and **no-no-no.wav** starting at the first frame in its associated image sequence.

7. Place the audio clips (you'll find them in the **audio** bin in the Project panel) into the **composite** sequence. You will need to make adjustments to the graphics based on the timing of the audio. As a rough edit, place each of the three audio tracks on A1 (the first audio track in the timeline) loosely in position. I put **martin-nnna.wav** so it ends at the marker and the other two audio files at the start of the parker and no-no-no clips (**FIGURE 12.17**). You will make further adjustments to synchronize the audio to the image clips in the next exercise.

 ## EXERCISE 3 ADJUSTING CLIPS IN THE TIMELINE

Because you will be adjusting a series of still images on the timeline you will work through much of this exercise by selecting and deleting or moving image clips. My project appears to have too many Martin images at the start of the **composite** sequence. However, I will use some of those extra clips in Step 3 before deleting unwanted clips. I will start by focusing on Parker's mouth movements and audio, then I will finesse the synchronization of Martin's lips and audio.

1. Parker (the boy on the right) says "ooo, no." Martin should join in on that "no" before he says "No, no, no!" Move the third audio clip so that it overlaps with Parker's "no." Start by dragging **no-no-no.wav** down to track A2, and then position the clip so the first group of waveforms it contains overlap with the final set of waveforms in **parker-ooo-no.wav** (**FIGURE 12.18**).

FIGURE 12.18 The audio clips overlap. Listen to the audio—You can see where the volume increases and decreases by looking at the waveforms. The audio is loudest in places where there are greater values in the y-axis of the waveform graphs. You can see the gaps in information, too, where the silences happen.

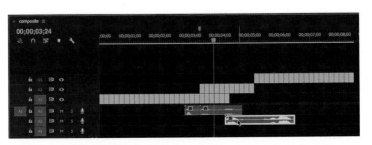

FIGURE 12.19 Change the zoom level of the Timeline panel by sliding these two handles closer together or farther apart from one another.

Drag the zoom scroll bar at the bottom of the Timeline panel to display parts of your sequence that may be off-screen. Each end of the zoom scroll bar has a round handle. Drag one of the handles toward the other to zoom in to the Timeline to see details or more clips in your sequence. Drag a handle away from the other handle to zoom out and get an overview of your sequence (**FIGURE 12.19**).

FIGURE 12.20 Mute some tracks to hear others or to concentrate on the visuals.

2. Watch the sequence without the sound by clicking the M icon (for "mute track") on tracks A1 and A2 or by decreasing the volume on your computer (**FIGURE 12.20**).

3. Find four sequential images on V1 in which one or both of the boys pronounces the full word "no." You will find these within the set of Martin images between timecode 0:0:0:00 and the start of the first audio file. Select those clips (Shift-click or marquee over them) and copy them by pressing **Command-C/Ctrl-C** (**FIGURE 12.21**).

4. To paste the copied clips onto a specific video track, such as the third video track (V3), you need to indicate where you intend to paste by *targeting* the intended track. If the V1 label (at the left end of the timeline) is highlighted, click it to toggle targeting off, then click V3 to toggle targeting on for that track. Position the playhead one frame before the start of the overlapping audio tracks, and choose Edit > Paste or press **Command-V/ Ctrl-V** (**FIGURE 12.22**). Toggle the Mute buttons or turn your volume up to hear the audio as you watch this series of clips.

FIGURE 12.21 Marquee over clips to select them.

FIGURE 12.22 Toggle targeting for audio and video tracks on to indicate where pasting or editing should occur. After you paste clips, the playhead will move to the end of the pasted frames.

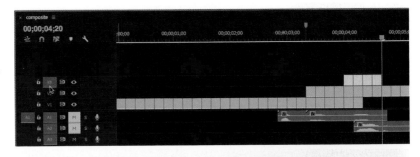

FIGURE 12.23 Start the "No, no, no!" still frames after the last image that was pasted onto V3 previously.

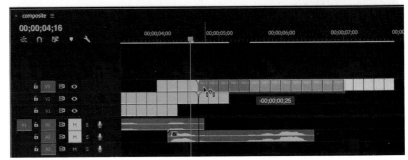

5. You need about fourteen images of Martin waving his finger for the "No, no, no!" audio and portion of the composition. Decide which fourteen image clips you will use; make sure they are consecutive. Be sure to start with an image where his hands are not visible in the frame, and be sure to include images where he makes the gesture with his fingers, and where he puts his hands down again. Delete the images in front of and at the end of the 14 clips you plan to use. Then move the clips on V3 so they begin after the series of martin images you copied in Step 3 and pasted in Step 4 (FIGURE 12.23).

    > I put the start of the new set of images just one frame before the audio started so that the change to the audio and visuals would not happen at the same time. With still images that do not offer fluid transitions, a jump cut, where the dissonance between two non-matching frames is jarring, would be more noticeable if it happened exactly when the audio changes. This is a minor nuance. When you are editing in a timeline you should be attentive to every frame.

6. Finally, delete the clips of Martin from the beginning of the sequence until the first audio clip. Click in the empty space on V1 where those clips left a gap between the start of the timeline and the first audio and image clips (mine is at 2:25). Press the **Delete/Backspace** key. All of the media will move to the left in the sequence to fill the gap (FIGURE 12.24).

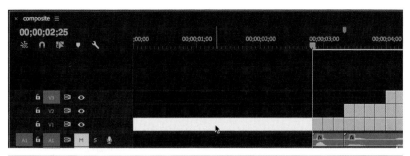

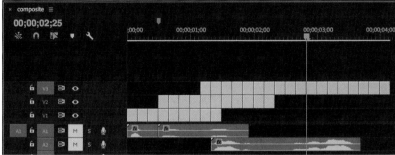

FIGURE 12.24 Delete unwanted clips, then fill the gap in the sequence.

ADDING EFFECTS AND SHARING ATTRIBUTES

Effects are one method to consistently apply design styles to digital video content. In this exercise, you'll add a series of effects to one clip and share those as attributes that can be applied to all of the other clips in the sequence in order to achieve visual continuity.

1. Double-click the first image frame in the **composite** sequence to open it in the Source panel.

> There is a difference between double-clicking media in the Project panel to open it in the Source panel, and double-clicking it in the Timeline panel to open it in the Source panel. When you view a clip in the Source panel from the Project panel, you are viewing the original, imported clip. When you view a clip in the Source panel from the Timeline, you are viewing the version of the clip that sits in a specific sequence in the Timeline panel. So changes you create for this material in the Source panel will be applied to only the version of it that appears in the sequence loaded in the Timeline panel.

2. Click the tab of the Effect Controls panel to bring it to the front of the panel group. Here you can see video effects that you can apply to the media opened from the Timeline panel. Click the arrow next to one of the effects to expand its list of controls (FIGURE 12.25).

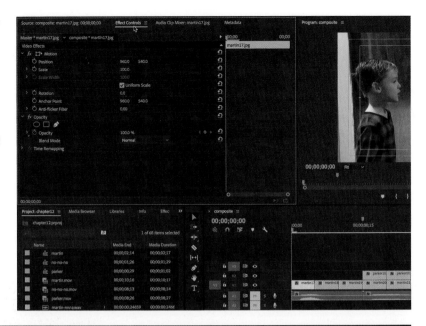

FIGURE 12.25 Motion effects such as Scale and Position, Opacity effects, and others, are accessed from the Effect Controls panel. Because I double-clicked the clip **martin17.jpg** in the **composite** sequence from the Timeline panel, any effects that are applied here will be added to this instance of **martin17.jpg** only.

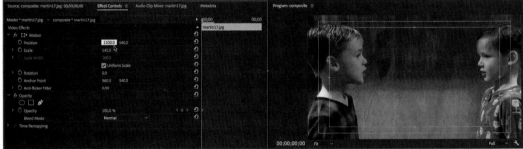

FIGURE 12.26 When the Scale value is greater than 100, the image in the frame seems to "zoom in." Once I increased the scale I also had to modify the position values of the clip.

CHANGING EFFECT VALUES You can enter a number in the value field of property settings for effects such as Scale or Position, or you can drag over the numeric value to the right or left to increase or decrease it while watching the clip's properties change in the Program panel.

3. Increase the Scale value to "zoom in" on the frame. I set mine to 145. After you modify the scale, change the Position values to re-center the image in the Program panel. My x and y values for horizontal and vertical positioning are set at 1100.0 and 540.0, respectively (**FIGURE 12.26**).

4. The panel group that includes the Project panel (in the bottom left of the Application frame) also contains the Effects panel that includes audio and video effects and transitions. You can load these effects into a sequence (such as a fade or transition between clips) or onto a clip (which you would modify in the Source panel). Click the tab of the Effects panel to bring it to the front. If you aren't able to see the tab, click the double-arrows at the top right of the panel and choose Effects from the menu (**FIGURE 12.27**).

5. Expand the Lumetri Presets > Cinematic folder from the list of effects in the Effects panel. Drag the 2 Strip preset to an empty area beneath the Time Remapping option in the Effect Controls panel (FIGURE 12.28).

6. In the Effect Controls panel, expand the Lumetri Color (2 Strip) menu if it is closed, then expand Curves > RGB Curves. Modify the composite curve by clicking the white button. Add contrast and reduce the warm color cast by editing the curve into an S-shape (FIGURE 12.29).

FIGURE 12.27 (ABOVE) The Effects panel includes effects for clips and transitions that may be applied to clips or between clips in the sequence.

FIGURE 12.28 (RIGHT) Drag the 2 Strip Lumetri Cinematic preset from the Effects panel to the Effect Controls panel for the clip you have been editing (in my case, **martin17.jpg**).

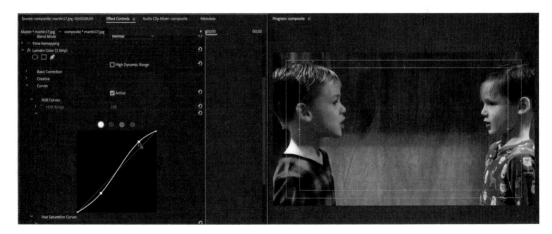

FIGURE 12.29 Modify the overall, or *composite* RGB curve, to create contrast. This will also reduce some of the warm color cast.

7. Click the red button in the RGB Curves interface to modify the red curves. Drag the right end of the red curve down to reduce the amount of red in the midtones—this will correct for some of the red in the warm color cast **(FIGURE 12.30)**.

8. The color cast has mostly been removed. Now decide if you want to continue to work with the green and blue curves to represent colors a viewer would expect from natural light or make more stylistic modifications. I gave the highlights a small amount of green color cast to increase the contrast and saturation of the green cloth behind the boys. I left the blue curve alone **(FIGURE 12.31)**.

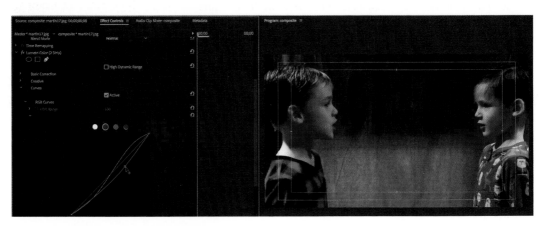

FIGURE 12.30 Modify the red curve by dragging the right half down. This will reduce the amount of red in the midtones and correct the red portion of the warm color cast.

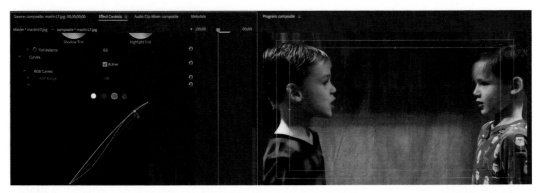

FIGURE 12.31 Modify the green and/or blue curves to add your own stylish color effect. I adjusted the highlight areas in the green curve.

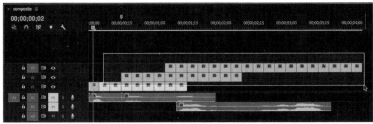

FIGURE 12.32 Share effects from one clip to others by using the Paste Attributes command.

9. Copy the first frame in the **composite** sequence in the Timeline panel—you are copying everything about the clip, including all of the effects you just applied. Marquee over all of the other clips in the sequence on V1, V2, and V3 to select them. Choose Edit > Paste Attributes. In the dialog box, leave all of the options in the Video Attributes section selected and click the OK button (FIGURE 12.32).

10. Play the video and view it in the Program panel.

EXERCISE 5 ADDING TYPE WITH ADOBE FONTS

In *The Electric Company* original segments, the letters that comprise the sound-parts of a word fly out of the mouths of the silhouettes that voice them. You will mimic this in Premiere Pro by adding motion to text clips in the **composite** sequence. You will select a typeface using Adobe Fonts, part of the Creative Cloud that can be accessed in most Adobe applications.

1. Click in the Timeline panel to activate it then add a new video track (V4) by choosing Sequence > Add Tracks. In the Add Tracks dialog box, select 1 new video track after Video 3 (FIGURE 12.33).

2. Add a typeface to use in this video from Adobe Fonts, which is accessible through the Creative Cloud. Choose Graphics > Add Fonts From Adobe Fonts. A web browser will open, and you will need your Adobe ID credentials to enter Adobe Fonts. *The Electric Company* segments used a typeface that looks similar to Futura, so you will try to find a typeface with similar characteristics by filtering the type classes and properties for a sans serif letterform, used as a heading, with a heavy weight and a low x-height. When I filtered for these qualities, I ended up with Futura PT. Activate the typeface by pushing the slider to the right (FIGURE 12.34).

FIGURE 12.33 Choose the placement for your new track in the Add Tracks dialog box.

FIGURE 12.34 Filtering for a typeface similar to Futura on the Adobe Fonts web page.

FIGURE 12.35 The new text graphic is on V4. The type you modify and create in the next steps will overlay all of the image clips.

3. Toggle back to Premiere Pro. Place the playhead in the Timeline panel at the start of the image sequence. Choose Graphics > New Layer > Text, or press **Command-T/Ctrl-T**.

4. A new text layer appears as a clip in the sequence and as a text field in the Program monitor. If you need to, move the clip to V4 in the Timeline panel **(FIGURE 12.35)**. A layer called **Text (New Text Layer)** is also added to the Video Effects area of the Effect Controls panel. You will set the duration of this clip in Exercise 6.

FIGURE 12.36 Modify the text in the Program panel.

5. Triple-click the text field in the Program panel to change the copy from "New Text Layer" to "KN," the letters that make the first sound in the word, "KNOW" (FIGURE 12.36). The text layer in the Effect Controls panel is also renamed to **Text (KN)**.

 WORKING WITH KEYFRAMES

In the Effects panel, you can apply effects, and control how changes to effects happen over time. To make elements, such as position, scale, or opacity, change over time you have to set *keyframes*. Keyframes indicate where a change happens in motion-based media. For instance, clips can fade from transparent to opaque when you set one Opacity keyframe to 0 and another, at a later timecode, to 100.

You will begin Exercise 6 right where you left off after Step 5 of Exercise 5.

1. Double-click the text "KN" so that it is selected, use the Effect Controls panel to change the text's properties. Open the **Text (KN)** layer, then in the Source Text area's Font menu, choose Futura PT Heavy (FIGURE 12.37). Add the following additional modifications:

   - Change the text size to 100, if it is not set to 100 by default.

   - Change the text fill to white, if it is not set to white by default.

   - Change the position of the text (you can do this in the Text (KN) > Transform section of the panel, or you can modify the Motion > Position value for the entire clip) to 205.0, 540.0, or 205 pixels from the left (x-value), 540 pixels from the top (y-value).

2. The text layer will have three properties that change over time: It will get larger (scale), it will move (position), and it will start out invisible before it fades into view (opacity). Click the stopwatch icon to add a keyframe to the Position, Scale, and Opacity values to set starting points for your animations (FIGURE 12.38).

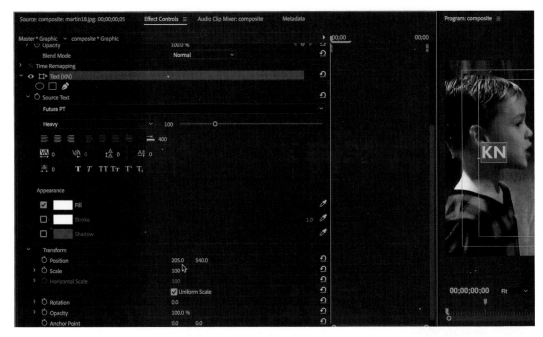

FIGURE 12.37 Change the typeface and text options in the Effect Controls panel.

FIGURE 12.38 Set keyframes for any of the effects that can change over time. Notice how the Position, Scale, and Opacity effects have keyframes added to them: You will see the stopwatch icons are recessed and now include a timer-hand, and their gray outlines have turned blue.

A diamond-shaped icon representing the keyframe appears in the clip's timeline to the right side of the Source panel. It is barely visible here because it was placed at the time "o". In later steps you will more easily see these icons indicating keyframes at specific times.

3. In the Timeline, modify the duration of the type clip for KN. Position the Selection tool over its last frame. When the pointer changes to an icon that looks like a right bracket with an arrow pointing towards the start of the sequence, drag the last frame into position, just before the clips of Parker saying "ooo" (FIGURE 12.39).

4. Move the playhead in the timeline to the end of the type layer using keyboard shortcuts. Press the **Up** or **Down** arrows to move to the last frame of the clip. Because you want to add a keyframe to the end of the clip, you need to position the playhead at the next-to-last frame in the clip. Press the **Left Arrow** key to move back one frame. Use the Effect Controls panel to add keyframes at this new (later) time for the three properties you set first in Step 2:

   - Change the position by increasing the x value. I set mine to 720. Notice the keyframe circle turns blue and a diamond-shaped mark in the timeline area of the Effect Controls panel indicates that a keyframe has been added to the clip (FIGURE 12.40).

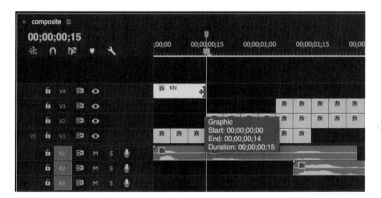

FIGURE 12.39 (LEFT) Adjust the duration of the type clip on V4.

FIGURE 12.40 (BELOW) Change the Position value, and notice a new keyframe is added automatically because once a keyframe is set, a new one is created when a value is changed.

FIGURE 12.41 Add a new keyframe by clicking the Add Keyframe button. If you change the value of a property after the first keyframe has been set, a new keyframe will be added automatically. In this case, you are adding a keyframe before changing a value.

- Increase the scale to 160.

- Leave the opacity at 100 percent. I knew I wanted the text to fade in, but I prefer to work with visible design elements and set the invisible settings last. Because the text fades in, it would have 100% opacity in the position where it lands, and maybe for time after that, too. Click the Add Keyframe icon to the right of the Opacity property. This indicates if a keyframe has been set—you are forcing a keyframe at this time with no change made to the value of the Opacity property (FIGURE 12.41). Then, click the left-facing arrow next to the keyframe icon to move back to the first keyframe . Change the opacity to 0. Now the text begins at 0 opacity and becomes fully opaque at the end of the clip.

EXERCISE 7 ADD NEW TRACKS

You will base the "OW" text on the "KN" typography. To do this, you will copy it and then add a new track, V5, to overlay the text.

1. Copy the KN type clip from the sequence in the Timeline panel. Move the playhead to the end of the KN clip. Before pasting, target the track V4 and toggle targeting off for V3 (if I don't do this, it seems to want to paste in V3, even if V4 is targeted). Paste the clip.

2. Drag the clip upwards, to make a new track, V5, to store this clip (FIGURE 12.42).

3. Change the text field so "KN" becomes "OW" in the clip on V5. The name of the clip will also change.

4. Extend the OW clip by additional frames so it overlays the image sequence of Parker on V2.

FIGURE 12.42 Copy the first type clip, target V4, and paste it. Then move it up to a new track, V5.

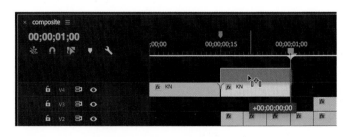

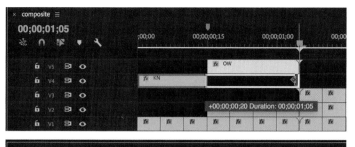

FIGURE 12.43 Modify the duration of the **OW** and **KN** type layers.

5. You will want the type "KN" to remain visible for at least as long as it takes for the OW clip to play. Extend the last frame of the KN clip to the place on the timeline that matches the last frame of OW on V5 **(FIGURE 12.43)**.

Notice if you play this part of the sequence the "KN" letters move into place and stay for the extra half-second (or so) that you added. You did not change any keyframe values, so they remain the same.

SCREENCAST 12-3 MODIFYING KEYFRAMES

Keyframes may be a new concept. In addition to their newness, the interface icons in this part of Premiere Pro are hard to see. In this screencast I demonstrate setting and modifying keyframes.

All screencasts are available on the companion website, www.digitalart-design.com, or on the Vimeo playlist, http://bit.ly/foundations-demos.

YOUR TURN!

Because this chapter appears late in this book, you should be comfortable iterating in your practice. Even if you are selectively completing the exercises throughout the book, this chapter assumes that you will have gained a willingness to experiment and a confidence in troubleshooting while working at the intersection of digital art and design and the Adobe Creative Cloud. This series of steps are suggestions that will lead you towards making the final **composite.mp4** video. You should begin by closely viewing the final movie file, **composite.mp4** (it's in the **chapter12-results** folder). You will attempt to match the typography by setting your own keyframes. If you get lost, open the Premiere Pro project file, **chapter-12-final.prproj** (you'll find it in the **chapter12-results** folder in the download file) to view the timeline I created, and the keyframes I set for this series of steps.

1. Change all of the keyframe values for the "OW" type. It should enter from the right side of the screen (just past Parker's mouth) and land so that the kerning looks even, especially between the "N" and the "O" in "KNOW." Select the OW clip and make sure the Effect Controls panel is still open, then drag the playhead to the first frame in the clip. I changed the starting position to 1635, 540 and the end position to 955, 540.

2. Extend both text layers on V4 and V5 to 00:00:04:05 (four seconds and five frames).

3. Copy and paste the **OW** type layer to V6. Either add the new track first (and target it), or target V5 and drag the clip up to V6 after it is pasted.

4. Change the text from "OW" to "NO". Adjust its first frame so that it is aligned with the first frame of no-no-no01.jpg on V2. Trim the clip so it ends at the same timecode as the clips on V3, V4, and V5 (four seconds and five frames).

5. Select the NO clip from the sequence to use the Effect Controls panel to change its keyframe settings in Steps 6, 7, and 8.

6. Change the scale to 160 (the same as the largest size of the text for "KNOW"), and remove any scale keyframes.

It may be easier to proceed if you remove all additional keyframes so you can enter new ones.

7. Change the Position values so that "NO" is initially at the same horizontal and vertical position as the word "NO" embedded in "KNOW." I increased the opacity value (temporarily) so I could see the word while editing it. Instead of entering values directly, practice sliding the values to the left or right so you can increase or decrease them while viewing the results in the Program panel. Hover your pointer over the position x value, and wait until you see the icon of the finger with left and right arrows next to it. Drag to the left or right to slide the text into position (**FIGURE 12.44**).

I often have to make more than one attempt at this because I make a click (like I am going to enter a value) before starting to drag left or right. If the field opens for an entered value, simply click off of it and try again.

You can add markers to the clip in the sequence while listening to the audio clip to know where to place the keyframes for the NO animation.

8. Animate the word, "NO," around the word "KNOW." Use keyframes to make it float up above the top of, then down below the baseline of "KNOW," then up above the word again. When you find the precise x-value for the word, you can type it in to additional key frames and change the y-values only.

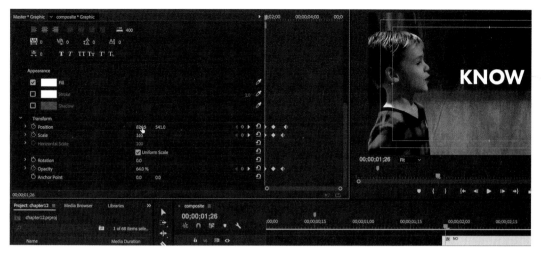

FIGURE 12.44 Modify the position values by dragging on them to the left or right. Align "NO" so it is seamlessly embedded in "KNOW."

EXERCISE
9 **FADE TO BLACK AND EXPORT**

The last steps to take in Premiere Pro are to watch the media very closely, notably for any unwanted gaps between edits. When you believe you are done, decide on how the media will start and finish on the screen. Maybe it cuts in from black, harshly, or maybe you will decide to apply a transition such as a fade. In this exercise, you will fade the project in and out to black, and then export the final **composite** sequence.

1. Fade the project in from black and out to black again by applying a video transition from the Effects panel (it's in the same panel group as the Project panel). Locate Video Transitions > Dissolve > Dip to Black, then drag this effect on top of the first clip on V1 (at 00:00) and at the end of the last four clips on the timeline tracks V3, V4, V5, and V6 (FIGURE 12.45).

FIGURE 12.45 When a transition is in place, you will see a label with the name of the effect on the clip in the Timeline panel.

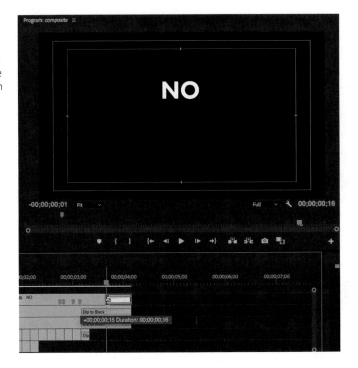

FIGURE 12.46 Delete image clips that would be transparent due to fading out, and apply the Dip To Black transition to the last image on V3. Change the duration of the transition on V6.

2. Play the media in the timeline near where you added the transitions. Make sure there are no surprises, such as gaps between clips or transitions that were not applied.

3. Did you see the image of the kids fade out then in and then out again? Notice that the type layers have long transitional fades on them, but the image clips are much shorter, so the fade is limited to a shorter duration. Delete all of the images that are overlain by the type in transition to black, with the exception of one, and put the Dip To Black transition just on that one image. I also noticed the last "NO" fades out too quickly. Drag the left edge of the Dip To Black transition on the "NO" text (V6) so its duration is about half of the text tracks on V4 and V5 (**FIGURE 12.46**).

Where did the final **composite.mp4** land? If you did not browse to a destination for this export, the file would have been exported to the last place Premiere Pro exported video.

4. While the Timeline panel is still active, choose File > Export > Media. There are many options for video compression and file formats. We will assume this media is meant for social sharing or viewing on a screen. Be sure the format is set to H.264, a common compressor used for online videos. Click the title of the movie in the Output Name field (**composite.mp4**), and browse to the location where you want to save the exported file. In the Basic Audio settings area, leave the Audio Format and Codec on AAC. Click the Export button (**FIGURE 12.47**).

FIGURE 12.47 Export the composite video. Be sure to activate the Timeline panel before attempting to export video. Also be attentive to where you save the file.

 **LAB CHALLENGE**

Create a multimedia project in which you generate a personal expression of visualized data. Choose any time frame (an hour, a day, a year) and create a unified multimedia sequence using Premiere Pro to showcase one aspect of your life. You can track something that seems important or something ordinary. Charts, photographs, and text are all appropriate content elements. Try to achieve similarity and continuity in your time-based design.

REVISION PRACTICES

IN AN ADVANCED COURSE that I teach, the latter half of the semester is used strictly for the revision of projects sketched as quick, weekly drafts during the first eight weeks. I begin the class with a reading and discussion of the *Cult of Done Manifesto* by Bre Pettis and Kio Stark [1]. The manifesto speaks to procrastinators and finishers, though much is lost on the concept of revision. While some of the 13 lines espouse great advice (Line 8 comes to mind: "Laugh at perfection. It's boring and keeps you from being done."), others dismiss revision (or "editing") as a stage of development. Perhaps their point is that revision and editing are the sum total of the process of arriving at the "final" form. Like many manifestos, interpretation allows for different readings of the text and encourages the reader to consider her own process of revision, or at least, of getting things done.

REFERENCE [1] Bre Pettis, *Cult of Done Manifesto,* originally shared on 3/3/09, republished on *Medium,* medium.com/@bre/the-cult-of-done-manifesto-724ca1c2ff13.

REFERENCE [2] Scott Simon, "A Thought That's Worth More Than a Penny (Or a Nickel)," NPR, 1/18/13, www.npr.org/2013/01/19/169723296/a-thought-thats-worth-more-than-a-penny-or-a-nickel.

REFERENCE [3] D. Wayne Johnson, "A Melted Penny for Your Thoughts," *The Wall Street Journal,* 1/14/13, online.wsj.com/article/SB10001424127887323373450457822348411380643 0.html.

What the *Cult of Done Manifesto* doesn't recognize is that for many, getting things done is not always the end goal. Revision is often a process of negotiation with clients or funders who want to meet specific brand and marketing goals. Although aesthetics are important, some decisions are made for political reasons. In Scott Simon's review [2] of D. Wayne Johnson's proposal to eliminate the penny, nickel, and quarter [3] from U.S. currency, Simon makes the argument that the idea "sounds sensible every way but politically." Despite the fact that it costs more than the coins' actual value to make a penny or a nickel, ridding them from popular currency would create a new crisis—one that would pair Lincoln and JFK or Susan B. Anthony and Sacagawea in a face-off for honor.

Although revising U.S. currency makes fiscal sense, Simon suggests that it would create more strife than perhaps the revision is worth. He also observes that the European Union chose details of architectural works to feature on their currency, rather than significant people.

Revision is often considered in reference to a product's identity or brand guidelines. While you may have a brilliant idea for presenting a product, if you fail to abide by the brand guidelines, your presentation will surely be rejected. As a comment on how carefully the presentation of a brand is outlined, designer and artist Christopher Doyle created *Christopher Doyle™ Identity Guidelines 2008* to showcase his personal set of "style guides" (**FIGURE C.1**).

FIGURE C.1 *Christopher Doyle™ Identity Guidelines 2008.* Designed by Christopher Doyle. Photography by Ian Haigh. © 2008 Christopher Doyle & Co.

CLEAR, OPEN COMMUNICATION AND ACCESSIBILITY

It's important to educate clients about how graphic design and visual communication can help create clear and open communication. In *Putting Back the Face into Typeface*, an interview with Erik Spiekermann on Gestalten TV, the typographer illustrates the strength of good design and the power of bad design. He says, "Bad government forms serve to separate us from the government because they make us stupid—because we don't understand—so we do what we're told. If things were designed to be more open or accessible, then we would be able to communicate more with each other" [4]. He advocates for designers to activate the system. "The system itself doesn't really want to communicate because then it becomes messy and dirty...We are supposed to shut up and make our little crosses and fill our forms and be quiet...and that's why I think designers should be in there trying to break things open."

REFERENCE [4] Erik Spiekermann, "Putting Back the Face into Typeface," Gestalten TV, 2011, https://vimeo.com/19429698.

Open communication is important not just for the end user, but also between the artist/designer and the client. The interviews and contributions in the following sections illustrate this importance. You will learn how a miscommunication resulted in a remaking of a product (Pencilbox Studios) and a keen ear for communication resulted in the repackaging of a popular toy (riCardo Crespo). Revisions may also be based on surprise challenges that crop up while executing a concept, as happened to Michael Demers, or you, like The League of Imaginary Scientists, may have to make revisions to meet the demands of curators and funders. Some artists/designers even demonstrate a unique process for revision and editing during the brainstorming phase (Jovenville and Bill Thompson).

PENCILBOX STUDIOS: MISSION HOSPITAL

Having completed assignments for other hospitals and healthcare organizations, Pencilbox Studios included Mission Hospital in its mailing list. So it was of little surprise when first-time client Mission called Pencilbox for a creative meeting.

PRINCIPAL PARTNERS
Kathleen Kaiser, Creative Director, and Bill Thompson, Photographer (www.pencilboxstudios.com).

12-PAGE BROCHURE WITH POCKET FOLDER

During initial meetings, Kathleen Kaiser, Creative Director of Pencilbox, spoke with the Mission Hospital team, including the head of imaging and a marketing specialist who was overseeing the marketing of the new imaging center. A new building with a state-of-the-art imaging wing was in the final stages of development. The hospital was eager to create literature for future patients of the advanced imaging center, while the marketing team was aware of a local challenge. Just miles from Mission Hospital, another hospital in a swanky part of town offered imaging services in a spa-like environment (marble floors, fresh floral arrangements, a limo ride to and from the center, and so on). While Mission's doctors and technicians were as qualified to perform imaging services as the local competition, many referrals went to the "nicer" location. Mission wanted to overcome this stigma and separate itself from its competition with a new, modern identity, specifically for the new location that showcased its new technology. The stakes of the design effort were high: The brochure not only needed to communicate to stressed patients, but it also had to create a public perception that could compete with the imaging spa down the street.

Any time a creative professional works with a large organization, one of the first requests is to review and understand the brand guidelines or specifications. Typically, there are strict rules about logo and color usage, among other design elements. There may be templates that should be used for certain types of visual materials. In this case, existing brand guidelines had been used for other areas of Mission's visual presence. However, the hospital team recognized that creating a new identity to promote the new building and equipment (and to compete with the nearby imaging center) took precedence. The guidelines were reviewed, but Pencilbox and the marketing team reached an understanding that they needn't be closely followed in order to create something unique for the new imaging wing.

As a result, Pencilbox developed a brochure that truly considered its audience. The unique size of the work was determined by the size of the physicians' lab coat pockets so doctors could keep brochures on hand. The colors were warm and relaxing. Topics were color-coded—would you rather have to remember that MRI information is filed under "Magnetic Resonance Imaging" or would you prefer to simply see the purple section? Real doctors and technicians were included in Bill Thompson's photographs, which accurately portrayed the machinery in use throughout the brochure. A custom die-cut pocket created harmony within the layout. Pencilbox team members felt that they were pushing the structure of their design beyond what would be allowed within the constraints of the brand guidelines. They talked about this approach with the client leading up to a final presentation of comps, and were pleased to be given approval to move forward with their strategy.

However, during the final round of proofing, the client delivered a message from someone who had not been directly involved in the process: The brochure would need to be redesigned in order to fit, precisely, the brand specifications.

This came as a surprise to Pencilbox, as they had included the brand guidelines in their communication with the hospital's marketing team. They had been transparent in regard to how much they needed to deviate from the guidelines in order to make a unique visual identity. However, what the marketing team hadn't realized was that the hospital was planning to rebrand the entire institution in the near future. In fact, shortly after this project was completed, Mission changed its marketing team. Kaiser recalls:

> As designers and creative directors, we need to know the bigger picture. Look what happened when we didn't—we didn't know they were facing a rebrand shortly after our project or that they would be hiring a new staff.

BRAND GUIDELINES

Upon reflection, Kaiser offered the insight that a brand guide should consider its audience. Instead of being established to make visual content simply look the same, or to make a template for various departments, the brand guide should consider issues of flexibility and accessibility.

The hospital didn't want to publish something "between" the old brand guidelines and what would become the new identity. If Pencilbox had known this, they might have advised moving forward with a smaller project until the new brand guidelines were established.

The good news for Pencilbox was that the redesign was not too difficult to achieve, because the brand was so specifically designed, and the copy and photography easily fit into the brochure template. The client took responsibility for the miscommunication. In the end, Pencilbox was paid for the work twice over. The redesign matched the overall hospital brand, but lost the unique ideas that Pencilbox had brought to their version of the work. Even copy that Pencilbox authored, such as the front cover copy: "Excellence in Medicine Starts with Knowing and Knowing Starts Here" (which the team leaders appreciated) was changed to "Mission Advanced Imaging Center" to meet the guidelines (FIGURES C.2 and C.3).

FIGURE C.2 In the original eight-page brochure design, the goal of the piece was to be easy to follow and friendly for a reader who would soon be undergoing a diagnostic imaging procedure. The modern design and inclusion of negative space represented the new architecture and advanced, technological equipment. A slightly warmer color palette was chosen based on the hospital's brand colors. Curves and color organization systems were created. © Pencilbox Studios

FIGURE C.3 In the revised design, the custom size was replaced by the traditional size specified by the brand guidelines. The consistent cover and format matches all of the hospital's literature, as does the limited color palette and template die-cut pocket. © Pencilbox Studios

Interestingly, photography was not included as part of the brand standards. Issues such as the colors of the clothing subjects wore or the direction that figures faced in images were unspecified. In Kaiser's and Thompson's working process, the photography was preplanned to fit the needs of the layout and design strategy. The photographs captured the essence of the client's needs. So even though the brand guidelines were not followed in the 12-page brochure, the photography did satisfy the needs of the clients. The imagery showcased the new, technological equipment and the new architecture, two pieces of the design challenge that the client was proud to communicate.

PERCEPTION OF THE PRINCESS:
PHOTOGRAPH, SELF-PROMOTIONAL WORK

As a design photographer and partner in Pencilbox, everything Bill Thompson creates starts with a sketch. His personal compositing project, *Perception of the Princess*, was no different. From that initial sketch, it evolved through a series of image revisions that demonstrate part of Thompson's process. First, he photographs a model he will use as a figure (if required) in the work (FIGURE C.4). Then he gathers and photographs props. The visual message is built around the gestures and positioning of the figure, rather than the other way around (FIGURE C.5).

FIGURE C.4 Human figure and props photographed for the composite image, *Perception of the Princess* by Pencilbox Studios. In this series of images, you can see how the model changes position in collaboration with the photographer. © Pencilbox Studios

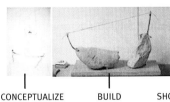

FIGURE C.5 Storyboard planning for *Perception of the Princess*, by Pencilbox Studios. © Pencilbox Studios

| CONCEPTUALIZE AND SKETCH | BUILD MINIATURE SET | SHOOT MINIATURE SET AND FINE-TUNE CONCEPT | OUTLINE AND RETOUCH TALENT SHOT | FINAL ASSEMBLY AND OUTPUT |

SHOOT TALENT AND CHECK FOR ASSEMBLY ISSUES

FIGURE C.6 *Perception of the Princess*, final composite photograph by Pencilbox Studios. © Pencilbox Studios

Based on his sketches, Thompson knew there would be rocks and a tilting structure in the final composite. The woman would represent a princess reigning over her kingdom. With a strong concept in mind, Thompson started by keeping the composition of the photograph tightly related to his original sketch (often referred to as "tight to comp"). The composition loosened as the situation built, and the model was considered a collaborator. In this photo shoot, she would do something, and he would react. When asked to "be tall" or to "look over her kingdom," she stood on her tiptoes. He responded to that, asking her to put her heels together and noticing how her legs resembled a column. This induced the next photograph and repositioning, and so on. Everything Thompson saw in the frame was part of the design composition. In the end, he saw that the one-legged stance would give him more freedom in the final composite image and that the suggestion of dynamic movement made by her asymmetric stance would correspond to the stack of cards.

The final photograph consists of four composited images and includes the acrylic matte medium brushwork technique detailed in the sidebar (FIGURE C.6). Reflecting on Thompson's process, I just can't agree with the third line of the *Cult of Done Manifesto*. "There is no editing stage" might be revised to "every part of the process is an editing stage."

ADDING BRUSHWORK TEXTURE

Many artists and designers use analog techniques in combination with digital strategies. Bill Thompson often uses a coat of acrylic matte medium to create a painterly, atmospheric effect on the resulting digital image. He creates a preliminary composition in Adobe Photoshop and then makes an inkjet print on watercolor paper. He brushes clear matte medium directly on the print. Thompson advises that the amount of matte medium often depends on the amount of ink on the page. The clear coat dries in an evening before he re-photographs the work. It could be scanned, he notes, but it's important to control the lighting when photographing the new work. He again composites the newly digitized piece in Photoshop, paying special attention to areas of the image that will retain their original sharpness and ones left influenced by the matte medium.

RICARDO CRESPO: HOT WHEELS AND STANDING MEETINGS

One of my favorite revision stories is one that riCardo Crespo delivered when he spoke at an AIGA event in Orange County, California. He recounted how after being introduced as "riCardo from Mattel" at parties, he was often asked the same two questions: "Can you get me a deal on toys for my kids?" and "Why is the packaging so difficult to open?" Tired parents posed a good question: Why must toy car packaging be so rigid?

Most designers and creative directors would roll their eyes in agreement and dismiss the design of the plastic packaging as a part of the product for which they weren't directly responsible. Crespo, however, invests himself in all that he does. After reflecting on this constant comment about the toy packaging, he decided to personally revise it to fit the needs of its second-level customers: parents (kids, of course, being the first). This would improve Mattel's reputation as well as his own. Ultimately, he wanted to make the packaging simple enough to open in 30 seconds or less. He achieved this by removing twist ties and plastic parts that held the cars in the plastic packaging. He wanted to be introduced not as "riCardo from Mattel," but as "riCardo who finally made the Hot Wheels packaging easy to open."

Deciding to revise the packaging and actually making the change were two separate initiatives. The first resulted from brainstorming and reflection. The second required activity—a strategy for execution. As Mattel's Worldwide Group Creative Director, Crespo flew to China to work with the factory where the packaging was made. He convinced directors at Mattel to revise the packaging by (what else?) promising that the simplified package, with no twist-ties or additional parts, would be cheaper to produce [5].

STAND UP

Another great story that Crespo recounted was how he changed the format of meetings with his team. Meetings inevitably began with small talk as attendees waited around the table for everyone to trickle into the room. At Mattel, a company housed in a large structure, one meeting might take place 10 minutes away from the next. Crespo was tired of wasting time with chitchat at the start of meetings and then having to run from one side of the Mattel campus to the other. To eliminate chitchat and turn his peers' perception of "meeting" on its head, Crespo called his first standing meetings near plants, water coolers, and other landmarks. Asking someone to meet you in the boardroom at 10:15 (when the day is full of meetings in boardrooms) results in a casual approach

RICARDO CRESPO
has held creative director positions at Mattel and 20th Century Fox. He is currently a chief creative officer at Th13teen Co. in Marina del Rey, California.

REFERENCE [5] Search YouTube for "opening Hot Wheels" and you will find videos that have garnered millions of views, such as, "Let's Open 250 Hot Wheels!" by HotDiecast Garage or "Opening 100 HOT WHEELS Card Surprise Toy Cars - Sports cars, Trucks, Muscle cars, Police, Racecars +" by Peak Time Racing. Both showcase the package design riCardo developed for Mattel.

to timeliness and the typical chitchat. Asking someone to meet you by a plant at 10:15 might actually result in a 10:15 meeting time. Standing, not seated, meeting participants provided the impetus to have an efficient dialogue and stay on task. The revision of the meeting format ultimately affected the amount of time in the day for design and creative thinking.

Crespo's story of standing meetings can be extrapolated to summarize the last section of this text (available online for readers of the printed book). Effective work habits—whether they include using the Actions panel in Photoshop or rethinking your communication strategy with clients or team members—directly impact how much time you have for the creative process. Revision is salient in all aspects of your life. It's not just a way of rethinking your creative output, but a process in which you reflect on the past and make decisions for the future.

MICHAEL DEMERS: THE SKY IS FALLING (A DAY IN THE LIFE...)

MICHAEL DEMERS contributed this story of The Sky Is Falling (A Day in the Life...). His complete portfolio is available at www.michaeldemers. com, and this project is at www.michaeldemers.com/ theskyisfalling_terminal. The full title is *The Sky Is Falling (A Day in the Life...) Elder Scrolls IV: Oblivion; 12:00am to 11:59pm, Heartfire 11, 3E433.* Note that this project may not play correctly in all web browsers, so if it doesn't work for you, try opening the link in another browser.

In 2010, I received a "Terminal: Internet-Based Art" grant from Austin Peay State University for the production of a proposed online artwork that consisted of captured PlayStation 3 game footage from *Elder Scrolls IV: Oblivion.* The work would reflect the seamless passing of game time to contrast with the audience's external experience of real time. One minute of "real" time equaled approximately 30 minutes of game time, and the plan was to capture 24 two-minute videos representing the passing of one game day. These videos would be programmed to play on a web browser with the particular two-minute clip referencing the viewer's local time. (For instance, if a viewer opened the page at 3:40 pm local time, then video 15, containing game footage from 3:00 to 3:59 pm game time, would play in the browser.)

ONLINE DIGITAL VIDEO IN 24 TWO-MINUTE SEGMENTS, KEYED TO THE VIEWER'S TIME OF DAY

References to playable characters, AI characters, and accompanying sound effects would be edited from the video to focus on the notion of a virtual space with the possibility of nonvirtual habitation, defined in part by the passing of game time during the observer's "real" time. The health meter, magic meter, stamina meter, weapon and magic selections, and game compass would remain unedited as a digital referent in the hyper-real environment of the game engine.

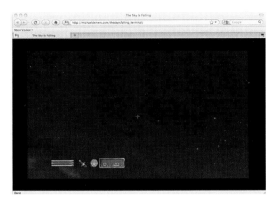

FIGURES C.7 AND C.8 Michael Demers, *The Sky Is Falling (A Day in the Life…) Elder Scrolls IV: Oblivion 12:00am to 11:59pm, Heartfire 11, 3E433*, Terminal: Internet Based Art, Austin Peay State University, 2010.

The reason I chose *Elder Scrolls IV: Oblivion* as my source material was two-fold. First, the idea that game time consistently and uniformly progressed was an interesting one to me. As time was spent in the realm of the game, it passed more slowly in the real world. This was a radical departure from the kinds of games I had played when I was younger, where the idea of diversion from the real world was paramount and any relationship to external reality was suspect. The second reason for this choice related to the first, because *Elder Scrolls IV: Oblivion* presents the player with a robustly detailed environment (apart from the fantasy elements), where the sun rises and sets, clouds cross the sky, and rain falls. Switching from third-person to first-person view and commanding your playable character to look up, you are presented with a nuanced and boundless panorama of the sky and space that changes with each passing minute (**FIGURES C.7** and **C.8**).

THE PLAN AND THE PROBLEM

The actual recording of the game footage was easy: A Hauppauge HD PVR connected between my Mac and my PlayStation 3 copied footage on the television screen. Finding a location from which to command my character to view the sky for 24 hours, however, proved somewhat more complicated. All attempts to find a safe place where my character could stand while looking upward proved hopeless, as some creature or other would inevitably attack. It seemed the only safe option would be to stand on water, where neither the creatures on land nor under the sea could harm me. Doing that required me to locate a particular enchanted item, a ring that allowed walking on water.

Many hours later, with the ability to walk on water firmly under my control, I again set out to watch the sky for the next 24 hours of game time. Although

I was not harassed during this attempt, I found that after about 15 minutes of real time spent looking up, my character's health began to drain. I was dead three minutes later. Knowing that I was not being attacked (as I was unreachable on the surface of the water), and thinking my death to be a system bug, I reset both the game and the Hauppauge HD PVR and tried again. After another 15 minutes, I started dying once more. This continued for another three or four attempts before I found the consistent element: Starting at game-time midnight, 15 minutes of real time brought me to approximately 6:00 a.m., or sunrise. At some point during my adventure to locate the magic ring, I had been afflicted with vampirism. The rising sun was my undoing.

I found a cure for my vampirism (a drawn-out period of collecting ingredients to give to a witch), and hence my demise at dawn, days later. Finally cured, I was able to stand still and gaze at the sky for the 24-hour game day duration. With my footage captured, all that was left for the completion of the project was the video splicing and HTML coding—and some vampire payback.

THE LEAGUE OF IMAGINARY SCIENTISTS: IN LEAGUE WITH AN INSTITUTION

LUCY HG SOLOMON
(Dr. L. Hernandez Gomez of the League of Imaginary Scientists) contributed this revision story. See the League's work at www.imaginaryscience.org.

For artists and collaborators, revision is essential to the working process. Art is arguably a revision of the world itself, certainly, a re-envisioning; and collaborations require endless negotiation and restatements. Revision accounts for creative evolutions, is the product of conceptual decision making, and results in more developed work. When one works with an institution, revision begins with the proposal, and it becomes the focus again with institutional deadlines for press and publicity. Proposals are rarely accepted as initially conceived and written, and publicity must serve the institution first and the art second. There are many institutional considerations—and these typically don't concern artists. Our experience demonstrates this paradoxical element of institutional programming.

We received an invitation—a great opportunity—to have a residency at the Museum of Contemporary Art, Los Angeles (MOCA) from December 2010 to March 2011. Each month was to culminate in a public event showcasing interactive artworks. The League was not new to artist residencies—to the slow and then suddenly fast-paced journey toward an art exhibition or event—often involving collaborators from the sciences.

Due to our frequent collaborations with scientists—waiting on research, discovering that the findings are not in conceptual alignment with the direction of a piece, or that the findings are not the anticipated results at all—the League is accustomed to improvisation and revision. These scientific redirections are meaningful bumps along the road that oftentimes change the course of the road altogether.

Collaborating with the exhibiting institution, however, was a new experience. A team of MOCA Think Tank members supported the residency and was privy to the major creative and budgetary considerations by our group. And with a larger institution came larger considerations—about the location, the rules of engagement with the public, and certainly about the relationship of newer works to the collection of Art (with a capital "A") contained within the museum.

We were transients, and our artwork would be impermanent yet interactive—a point for community involvement. The League of Imaginary Scientists proliferated ideas, most of which were tabled. We wanted, for instance, to perform the greatest museum heist in the history of heists, yet this was not a mission that could be condoned by security. We wanted to have rockets. (Who doesn't?) Budgetary constraints nixed that one. We envisioned a motorcyclist launching off the museum building and over the crowd—not sure why that didn't happen.

In constant communication with MOCA staff, the League of Imaginary Scientists along with MOCA's Think Tank, settled on three events that would emerge from a contraption—one that we would change over the course of the residency. We titled our residency and the project series, *The Evolving Contraption*. The name proved suitable for the residency and, indeed, applies to most collaborative art projects, as they almost always evolve significantly from conception to completion.

The Evolving Contraption began with *Wormholes*, a warped take on airport security and travel (FIGURE C.9). *Wormholes* replicated individual travelers and sent them through a long wormhole security line and eventually placed their replicas into other space-time locations. This project had many permutations and went through a series of sketches—some of the early, discarded ones were considered too ambitious or costly. Ultimately, a long tent served as the conduit to becoming "replicated" and going on the wormhole journey. Small sculptures along the way allowed viewers to peer into other space-time locations, including into a biological engineering lab at MIT in the recent past as well as an artist's studio in the future.

FIGURE C.9 The League of Imaginary Scientists, *Wormholes*, MOCA, Los Angeles, 2011. Participants' replicated selves were sent through a series of tubes into the wormhole. Photo credit: TRYHARDER.

FIGURE C.10 The League of Imaginary Scientists, *The Automatoggler*, MOCA, Los Angeles, 2011. Participants turn the cranks and pull the levers to evolve in The Evolve-You Machine (background); The Universe Works, a finely tuned contraption by which Dr. Stephan Schleidan kept the intricate workings of the universe in order (foreground). Photo credit: Brian Mettee.

The second exhibition, *The Automatoggler*, was to be the greatest invention ever made—a contraption to save humanity from, well, ourselves (**FIGURE C.10**). This project underwent numerous revisions over the course of its month of creation! Unlike many past collaborations by the League, the motto was "Divide and Conquer," as we were determined to create as much as possible so as to visually overwhelm a plaza with strange contraptions. *The Automatoggler* included the Evolve-You Machine (which evolved you to a new you + machine); The Universe Works, a stage for presenting the inner workings of the universe; interactive musical devices that generated images of war and harmony; and an Input-Output Machine that, when people input their arms, would output tattoos, along with real *and* digital toast, and drawings based on doodles inserted by viewers. The evolution of this project veered away from the more streamlined and unified *Wormholes* toward a more ambitious, multifaceted installation.

This ever-evolving (continually revised) project became something entirely different for its third iteration, *The Zephyr Experiment*. Not as singularly themed as *Wormholes* and its journey through space-time, or as multidirectional as *The Automatoggler's* myriad of interactive installations, *The Zephyr Experiment* was a playful exhibit that dabbled with flight in numerous ways (**FIGURE C.11**). Viewers could transform themselves with live puppetry into winged flyers, interact with a floating Dr. Stephan Schleidan, build and then test experimental flying objects through propulsion devices, and partake in the launching of the largest paper airplane ever to be launched at MOCA (by the League). While the rocket launching was intimate (not intergalactic), *The Zephyr Experiment* made for a satisfying culminating event.

The entire three-month residency was a blur of starting and stopping, a constant negotiation with MOCA—mostly to stay on top of publicity. Artists are not always eager to articulate what their projects will be one month before completion, sometimes not even after completion. For this residency, many of the advantages of being the artist—such as the freedom to ignore institutional constraints—were forfeited. The project became an ever-shifting collaboration with a place, a space, and even the people who organized and supported the residency. Revision was a constant.

Continuous, fast revisions like those demanded by these one-month art exhibitions require a slow-down period of reflection upon completion. Extremely fast developments need to be mulled over and digested, as did the League's three-project series at MOCA. Our ruminations on the experience produced insights into the nature of revision and art: Artists need to constantly revise in order to create, yet artists resist revisions imposed by an external entity; revising artworks in a series results in a diversity in style, often leading the artist in a new direction.

Thoughtful revision requires time, which is often a luxury when dealing with institutional deadlines. Fortunately, the fast pace of accelerated creative development can lead to the elements of surprise and delight—two happy results of a whirlwind revisioning!

FIGURE C.11 The League of Imaginary Scientists, *The Zephyr Experiment*, MOCA, Los Angeles, 2011. A MOCA visitor participates in the Learn to Fly station. One participant puppeteers miniature models of wings, while another "flies" through the clouds in an animated atmosphere. This image also appears at the beginning of this chapter. Photo credit: LOIS.

JOVENVILLE: BOARDSTORMING

JOVEN OROZCO
is the Mayor of Jovenville,
www.jovenville.com.

Joven Orozco has been the mayor of Jovenville, his graphic design company located in Newport Beach, California, for more than 17 years. About eight years ago, while working with creatives from other companies such as Disney Consumer Products, Orozco realized that the primary mission of the creative collaboration was to share ideas about solving communication challenges. Because other creatives could understand ideas and visual directions without the aid of a fully developed comp (or composition), the Jovenville team developed a new way to share their brainstorming efforts and named it *boardstorming*.

Instead of meeting with the client to discuss the usual three comps showcasing a simple solution, a middle-of-the-road solution, and a wild version of a solution (neatly, the simple-middle-wild comps), boardstorming allows creatives from Jovenville to showcase 30 to 50 possibilities, including everything on the board from sketch drawings, paper samples, and Internet downloads as visual references or conversation starters (**FIGURES C.12** and **C.13**). The brainstorm process always happens in the design studio—boardstorming simply allows the clients to peak behind the curtain. Orozco notes that with three comps you often find out that you're wrong about a client's needs, brand, or strategic plan. "It's OK to be wrong," he said, "but it's easier to be wrong in an earlier process of discovery. "Boardstorming, he emphasized, helps open a dialogue with the client about what you can't do. Knowing a client's limitations early in the design process is a crucial step in arriving at those final three comps.

REVISING CLIENTS

On another topic that came up in an interview, Orozco shared his strategies for coping with difficult clients. Everyone has hard-to-manage clients at some point. Here are a few tips you can borrow as you enter the professional industry:

- Develop a prequalifying procedure. For instance, Jovenville will not work with clients who spend their own money or who have not worked with an outside firm before. While this limits the clientele and may exclude independent or start-up businesses, Orozco shared that people who spend their own money will pick at the design obsessively and ask for more revisions than were originally contracted. "A seasoned marketer or creative at another company," he said, "will understand deadlines and the process that a Mom-and-Pop wouldn't [know]."

- Diversify your clients. No single client at Jovenville ever defines more than 33% of the business's revenue. If a client becomes unprofitable, the team will finish the contracted work and move on.

- Allow the tough clients to "fire themselves." If a client was unprofitable, for instance due to extensive revisions, then the rate would be increased the next time the client called with a job. Clients will either pay for their former unprofitability after the fact or terminate the relationship.

FIGURE C.12 Jovenville, 2010. Sample boardstorming board. © Jovenville LLC

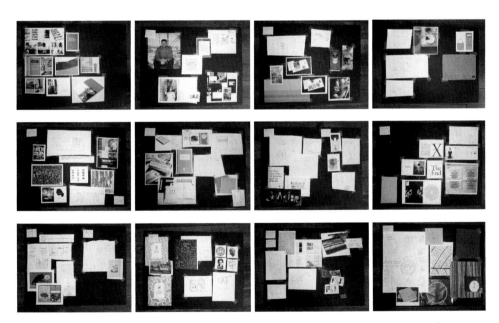

FIGURE C.13 Jovenville, 2010. Boardstorm for the OC Waste & Recycling Annual Report. © Jovenville LLC

After boardstorming with fellow creatives proved helpful, Jovenville took an experimental leap of faith by sharing this revision process with marketing clients. Marketing professionals are usually not trained visual communicators—your job as an artist or designer is in part to educate your viewers, collaborators, commissioners, and clients. When the boardstorm for the *OC Waste & Recycling Annual Report* was sent to the City of Irvine, for instance, Jovenville received a call asking, "What is *this*?" Of course, after meeting and reviewing each concept on the board, the team was better equipped to design the report. As proof of Jovenville's success, the final report was selected as one of *Graphis's* top 100 annual reports of 2010.

Boardstorming is not the end of the revision process (**FIGURE C.14**). Typically, the Jovenville team will review all ideas on the board with a client. Within that meeting, ideas that surpass the limits of the brand or simply don't meet the client's needs are removed. By the end of the meeting, there might be eight rough ideas left. From this, three comps (simple, middle, and wild revisions) are produced before a second round of revisions is created. After this, the final design is approved (**FIGURES C.15** and **C.16**). Boardstorming helps the design team learn about the client so that the initial round of comps is likely to fit the client's needs.

FIGURE C.14 Jovenville, 2010. One of the three creative directions chosen to move forward was to merge visuals suggesting "transparency" (top image) and "organic" (bottom image) in order to suggest the relevance of these themes in the *OC Waste & Recycling Annual Report.* © Jovenville LLC

FIGURE C.15 Round 1 designs, clockwise from the top left: cover design, internal spread (A), financial spread, internal spread (B). © Jovenville LLC

The boardstorming team at Jovenville might include up to three designers and two interns.

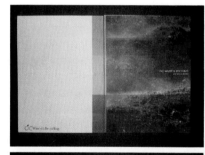

FIGURE C.16 Jovenville, 2010. Round 1 comps became the final design strategy for the *OC Waste & Recycling Annual Report.* © Jovenville LLC

CONCLUSION

The *Cult of Done Manifesto* makes no room for revision, while simultaneously alluding to the idea that all design work is a form of editing. The artists' and designers' stories in this coda suggest otherwise. Revision is a stage of development. However, it can be one that happens during any phase of the design process. While Jovenville's boardstorming demonstrates that revision is essential at the beginning of the design process, Michael Demers's revisions allowed the concept to guide the execution of the process in arriving at the final work of art. Revision is a personal process. As such, there are no rules or methods that will guarantee success. Unlike the binary nature of digital ones and zeros, revision is a human part of the design process. It may be led by intuition or feedback.

With this in mind, there are no exercises or directives that I could write for you in order to better revise one of your former projects. Instead, I'll simply state the obvious: Now that you've completed all of the chapters in this book, you'll notice that the design projects you created when you were in command of the content and skills presented in the first half of the book are not nearly as rich or complex as those you've developed in the latter half. It's probably time to revise!

INDEX

Houde, Stephanie, 197
Hue/Saturation adjustment layer,
    118–122, 183, 184
hues
    adjusting, 120, 122
    complementary, 113, 114, 115
    definition of, 111
    primary, 114, 115
    warm and cool, 117
    See also color
Hughes, Jack, 116
Human Interface Guidelines
    (HIG), 203
Hustwit, Gary, 220

I

Illustrator, 12
    file presets in, 13–14
    layers in, 31–32
    master format in, 41–42
    saving files in, 27, 41
    typography in, 222
Image Size dialog box, 92–93,
    97–100, 171
images
    copying/pasting, 102, 187
    duplicating, 34–35
    linking, 30
    locking, 30–31
    manipulating, 137–142
    placing, 29–30
    reflecting, 58–59
    relinking, 231
    rotating, 186
    scaling, 183, 186
    tracing, 33, 172–176
    type and, 221, 226, 239–242
implied lines, 278, 279
In and Out points, 284
In Re Ansel Adams (Flaxton), 65, 66
InDesign, Adobe, 222, 227
indexical signs, 46
Info panel, 104
inspiration, 281
integration prototypes, 197
inverting
    colors, 125
    layer masks, 188, 191
ISO settings, 74–75

italic type, 218
iterative processes, 288
Itten, Johannes, viii, 43, 44, 112, 117

J

James, Christopher, 94
Johnson, Chris, 95
Johnson, D. Wayne, 310
Jordan, Chris, 10, 11
Jovenville, 324–327
Jungmann, Aleš, 24, 28, 29
juxtaposition
    apps for producing, 168
    in collage creation, 167, 190

K

Kaiser, Kathleen, 311, 312, 313
"Kaleideolism" (2pxBorder), 44–45
Kane, John, 218, 219
kerning
    derivation of word, 280
    process of, 227–228, 229,
        235–236, 239
    rhythm of text controlled by, 255
KERNTYPE game, 236
keyframes, 299–302

L

Lab challenges
    on collage creation, 193
    on color correction, 135
    on grid system, 273
    on hoax creation, 164
    on icon modification, 61
    on letters expressed as
        shapes, 22
    on multimedia project
        creation, 307
    on pencil illustration of
        movement, 42
    on prototype creation, 212
    on time passage theme, 90
    on tonal range expansion, 110
    on type–image relationship, 247
Lasso tool, 156
Lauer, David A., viii
Law of Prägnanz, 250, 252

layer masks
    converting selections to, 181
    fine-tuning, 189
    fundamentals of, 168
    inverting, 188, 191
    layer thumbnails for, 181–182
    situations for adding, 181
    softening cloned edges with,
        162–164
Layer Style dialog box, 123
layers
    blending modes for, 126
    clipping, 192
    copying to open documents,
        184–186
    creating new, 32, 123
    explanation of using, 31–32
    flattening, 232
    grouping in Layers panel, 184
    naming/renaming, 105, 123, 157
    scaling contents of, 183
    stacking order of, 31, 105
Layers panel, 31, 103, 105–106,
    158, 184
LCD screen vs. viewfinder, 72–73
Le, David, 77
leading
    process of adjusting, 227,
        228, 238
    rhythm of text controlled by,
        255, 256
    virtual, 261–266
League of Imaginary Scientists,
    320–323
Lee, Stan, 107
Lehni, Jürg, 224, 225
Lester, Paul Martin, 275
letter spacing, 227, 228, 255
letterforms, 216–220
Levels adjustment layer, 108–109,
    128–129, 130
Library of Congress (LOC), 143, 149,
    171, 216
Lichtenstein, Roy, 5
light
    measuring, 70
    time and, 67
light meters, 70
lightness, 111, 112